100 Hikes in

NORTHWEST OREGON

SECOND EDITION

William L. Sullivan

Navillus Press
Eugene

Middle Lewis River Falls (Hike #28).

©2003, 2002, 2001, 2000 by William L. Sullivan
Maps and photography by the author

Published by the Navillus Press   *www.oregonhiking.com*
1958 Onyx Street
Eugene, Oregon 97403

Printed in USA

Cover: Mt. Hood from the Mazama Trail viewpoint. Inset: Wild rose at Champoeg Park. Spine: Punchbowl Falls. Back cover: Mt. St. Helens from Norway Pass. Frontispiece: Old-growth forest trail.

SAFETY CONSIDERATIONS: Many of the trails in this book pass through Wilderness and remote country where hikers are exposed to unavoidable risks. On any hike, the weather may change suddenly. The fact that a hike is included in this book, or that it may be rated as easy, does not necessarily mean it will be safe or easy for you. Prepare yourself with proper equipment and outdoor skills, and you will be able to enjoy these hikes with confidence.

Every effort has been made to assure the accuracy of the information in this book. The author has hiked all 100 of the featured trails, and the trails' administrative agencies have reviewed the maps and text. Nonetheless, construction, logging, and storm damage may cause changes. Corrections and updates are welcome, and often rewarded. They may be sent in care of the publisher.

Contents

🐎 - Horses OK   🚲 - Bicycles OK
C - Crowded or restricted backpacking area
* May require trailhead parking fee

3

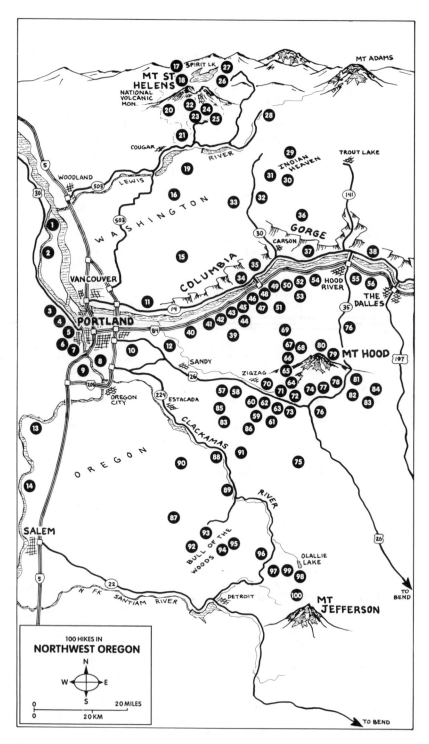

MT ST HELENS
NATIONAL VOLCANIC MON.
SPIRIT LK
MT ADAMS
COUGAR
RIVER
WOODLAND
LEWIS
TROUT LAKE
WASHINGTON
COLUMBIA
INDIAN HEAVEN
GORGE
CARSON
VANCOUVER
HOOD RIVER
THE DALLES
PORTLAND
SANDY
MT HOOD
ZIGZAG
OREGON CITY
ESTACADA
CLACKAMAS
OREGON
SALEM
RIVER
OLALLIE LAKE
N FK SANTIAM RIVER
DETROIT
BULL OF THE WOODS
TO BEND
MT JEFFERSON
TO BEND

100 HIKES IN
NORTHWEST OREGON

N
W   E
S

0   20 MILES
0   20 KM

🐎 - Horses OK   🚲 - Bicycles OK
C - Crowded or restricted backpacking area
* May require trailhead parking fee

🐴 - Horses OK   🚲 - Bicycles OK
C - Crowded or restricted backpacking area
* May require trailhead parking fee

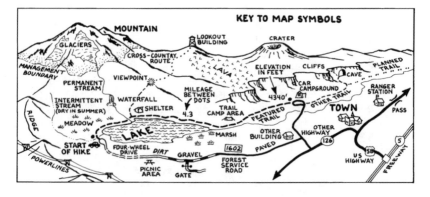

KEY TO MAP SYMBOLS

Introduction

Where else but in Northwest Oregon could hikers have so many great options within a two-hour drive? This guide covers more than just the well-known trails of the Portland area, Columbia Gorge, and Mt. Hood. You'll discover a path to a free Willamette River ferry, a historic cabin overlooking Mt. Jefferson, and a natural rock arch near Hood River. Forty-three of the trips are open even in winter. And because some of the area's newest trails are just north of the Columbia, there's comprehensive coverage of Mt. St. Helens Volcanic National Monument and the Indian Heaven Wilderness, too.

This book features several difficulty levels. Hikers with children will find 49 hikes carefully chosen for them. On the other hand, a quarter of the hikes included are unabashedly difficult. Nearly half of the trails are rated as suitable for backpackers as well as day hikers. At the back of the book you'll find a list of 31 all-accessible trails suitable for strollers and wheelchairs. And if you really want to get away from it all, there's an appendix describing 107 *more* hikes in Northwest Oregon—little-known but interesting trails for adventurous spirits.

HOW TO USE THIS BOOK

It's Easy to Choose a Trip

The featured hikes are divided into 6 regions, from the Clackamas Foothills to Southwest Washington. To choose a trip, simply turn to the area that interests you and look for the following symbols in the upper right-hand corner of each hike's heading. Whether you're hiking with children, backpacking, or looking for a snow-free winter trail, you'll quickly find an outing to match your tastes.

 Children's favorites—walks popular with the 4- to 12-year-old crowd, but fun for hikers of all ages.

 All-year trails, hikable most or all of winter.

 Hikes suitable for backpackers as well as day hikers. Crowds unlikely.

 Crowded or restricted backpacking areas. Expect competition for campsites, especially on summer weekends.

The Information Blocks

Each hike is rated by difficulty. **Easy** hikes are between 2 and 7 miles round-trip and gain less than 1000 feet in elevation. Never very steep nor particularly remote, they make good warm-up trips for experienced hikers or first-time trips for novices.

Trips rated as **Moderate** range from 4 to 11 miles round-trip. The longer hikes in this category are not steep, but shorter trails may gain up to 2000 feet of elevation—or they may require some pathfinding skills. Hikers must be in good condition and will need to take several rest stops.

Difficult trails demand top physical condition, with a strong heart and strong knees. These challenging hikes are 8 to 15 miles round-trip and may gain 4000 feet or more.

Distances are given in round-trip mileage, except for those trails where a car or bicycle shuttle is so convenient that the suggested hike is one-way only, and is listed as such.

Elevation gains tell much about the difficulty of a hike. Those who puff climbing a few flights of stairs may consider even 500 feet of elevation a strenuous climb, and should watch this listing carefully. Note that the figures are for each hike's *cumulative* elevation gain, adding all the uphill portions, even those on the return trip.

The **hiking season** of any trail varies with the weather. In a cold year, a trail described as "Open May through October" may not yet be clear of snow by May 1, and may be socked in by a blizzard before October 31. Similarly, a trail that is "Open all year" may close due to storms.

The **allowed use** of some featured trails specifically includes horses and bicycle riders. Note that many of the hikes do not have a *use* listing at all. These are open to *hikers only*. For a quick overview of paths recommended for equestrians and mountain bikers, refer to the table of contents. Also note that the additional trails listed at the back of the book also include symbols identifying their allowed use. Incidentally, dogs are allowed on all the featured trails unless the text specifically mentions that they are prohibited.

All hikers should carry a topographic **map,** with contour lines to show elevation. Maps listed as "USFS" are available from U.S. Forest Service offices for a few dollars. Those tagged "USGS," published by the U.S. Geological Survey, can be found at many outdoor stores or can be downloaded for free from *www.topozone.com*. The Green Trails and Geo-Graphics maps are available at most outdoors stores and at some bookstores. In addition, it pays to pick up a Mt. Hood National Forest Visitor Map (for the south side of the Columbia) or a Gifford Pinchot National Forest Map (for the north) at a ranger station.

TRAILHEAD PARKING PERMITS

You'll need a **Northwest Forest Pass** to park within ¼ mile of many trailheads described in this book. This permit costs $5 per car per day or $30 per year and can be purchased at ranger stations or outdoor stores. Often you cannot pay at the trailhead itself. The Northwest Forest Pass is valid in all Northwest National Forests, the Columbia Gorge National Scenic Area, and Mount St. Helens Volcanic National Monument.

Permit systems are subject to change, but the featured hikes in this book currently requiring some kind of parking fee are marked with an asterisk in the table of contents. Note that certain state parks, visitor centers, and recreation areas have fees that are not covered by a Northwest Forest Pass. These charges are described in the entries for the affected hikes. For the latest rules, call the trail's administrative agency. Telephone numbers are listed on page 11.

WILDERNESS RESTRICTIONS

Certain restrictions apply to designated Wilderness Areas, and affect many of the hikes featured in this guide:

- Campfires are banned within 100 feet of any water source or maintained trail.

Jefferson Park (Hike #100).

- Groups must be no larger than 12.
- No one may enter areas posted as closed for rehabilitation.
- Bicycles and wheeled vehicles (except wheelchairs) are banned.
- Horses and pack stock cannot be tethered within 200 feet of any water source or shelter.
- Motorized equipment and fireworks are banned.
- Live trees and shrubs must not be cut or damaged.

In addition, some rules apply to all federal lands:

- Collecting arrowheads or other cultural artifacts is a federal crime.
- Permits are required to dig up plants.

SAFETY ON THE TRAIL

Wild Animals

Part of the fun of hiking is watching for wildlife. Lovers of wildness rue the demise of our most impressive species. Grizzly bears are extinct in Oregon. The little black bears that remain are so profoundly shy you probably won't see one in 1000 miles of hiking. In this portion of Oregon, the only reason for backpackers to hang their food from a tree at night is to protect it from ground squirrels. Likewise, our rattlesnakes are genuinely rare and shy—and they never were as venomous as the Southwest's famous rattlers.

Mosquitoes can be a nuisance on hikes in the High Cascades, particularly in the Olallie Lake and Indian Heaven areas. To avoid these insects, remember that they hatch about 10 days after the snow melts from the trails and that they remain in force 3 or 4 weeks. Thus, if a given trail in the High Cascades is listed as "Open mid-June," expect mosquitoes there most of July.

Drinking Water

Day hikers should bring all the water they will need—roughly a quart per person. A microscopic paramecium, *Giardia,* has forever changed the old custom of dipping a drink from every brook. The symptoms of "beaver fever," debilitating nausea and diarrhea, commence a week or 2 after ingesting *Giardia.*

If you're backpacking, bring an approved water filter or purification tablet, or boil your water 5 minutes.

Proper Equipment

Even on the tamest hike a surprise storm or a wrong turn can suddenly make the gear you carry very important. Always bring a pack with the 10 essentials: a warm, water-repellent coat (or parka and extra shirt), drinking water, extra food, a knife, matches in a waterproof container, a fire starter (butane lighter or candle), a first aid kit, a flashlight, a map (topographic, if possible), and a compass.

Before leaving on a hike, tell someone where you are going so they can alert the county sheriff to begin a search if you do not return on time. If you're lost, stay put and keep warm. The number one killer in the woods is *hypothermia*—being cold and wet too long.

COURTESY ON THE TRAIL

As our trails become more heavily used, rules of trail etiquette become stricter. Please:

- Pick no flowers.
- Leave no litter. Eggshells and orange peels can last for decades.
- Do not bring pets into wilderness areas. Dogs can frighten wildlife and disturb other hikers.
- Step off the trail on the downhill side to let horses pass. Speak to them quietly to help keep them from spooking.
- Do not shortcut switchbacks.

For backpackers, low-impact camping was once merely a courtesy, but is on the verge of becoming a requirement, both to protect the landscape and to preserve a sense of solitude for others. The most important rules:

- Camp out of sight of lakes and trails.
- Build no campfire. Cook on a backpacking stove.
- Wash at least 100 feet from any lake or stream.
- Camp on duff, rock, or sand—never on meadow vegetation.
- Pack out garbage—don't burn or bury it.

GROUPS TO HIKE WITH

If you enjoy the camaraderie of hiking with a group, contact one of the organizations that leads trips to the trails in this book. None of the groups requires that you be a member to join scheduled hikes, and when trip fees are charged they're usually just a dollar or two. Hikers generally carpool from a preset meeting place. If you have no car, expect to chip in a few cents per mile.

Chemeketans. Three to 10 hikes a week. Cabin near Mt. Jefferson, meetings at 360½ State St., Salem. Founded 1927. Write P.O. Box 864, Salem, OR 97308.
Lake Oswego Recreation Department. Thursday hikes carpool from Lake Oswego. Call (503) 636-9673.
Mazamas. Three to 10 hikes a week. Cabin at Mt. Hood, office and meetings at 909 NW 19th Ave., Portland, OR 97209. Founded 1894. Call (503) 227-2345.
Portland Park Bureau. Saturday hikes in Forest Park for $2 fee. Wednesday "Tot Walks" in Portland area for $3 fee. Call (503) 823-2223.
Ptarmigan Mountaineering Club. Weekly hikes. Meetings at Vancouver First Presbyterian Church. Founded 1960. Write P.O. Box 1821, Vancouver, WA 98668.
Sierra Club Columbia Group. Weekly hikes except in winter. Meetings at 1413 SE Hawthorne Blvd., Portland, OR 97214. Call (503) 231-0507.
Trails Club of Oregon. Hikes on Saturdays and Sundays. Cabins at Mt. Hood and Columbia Gorge. Founded 1915. Write P.O. Box 1243, Portland, OR 97207.
Tryon Creek Day Trippers. Weekly hikes except in winter. Carpool from Tryon Cr. Park, 11321 SW Terwilliger Blvd., Portland, OR 97219; (503) 636-4398.

FOR MORE INFORMATION

This book is updated each spring. If you'd like to check for news about snow levels, trail maintenance, and new construction, call directly to the trails' administrative agencies. The offices are listed below, along with the hikes in this book for which they manage trails. News updates for trails on National Forest land are also available online at *www.fs.fed.us/r6*.

Hike	Managing Agency
75, 76, 81-84	Barlow Ranger District — (541) 467-2291
58, 87	BLM Salem District — (503) 375-5646
13	Champoeg State Park — (503) 678-1251
11	Clark County Parks — (360) 699-2467
37-39, 42-53	Columbia Gorge Nat'l. Scenic Area — (541) 386-2333
85, 88-100	Clackamas River Ranger District — (503) 630-6861
67-69, 77-80	Hood River Ranger District — (541) 352-6002
29-31	Mt. Adams Ranger District — (509) 395-3400
17, 18, 20-28	Mt. St. Helens Nat'l. Vol. Mon. — (360) 247-3900
12	Multnomah County Parks — (503) 248-5050
56	The Nature Conservancy — (503) 228-9561
40, 41, 44-46, 54, 55	Oregon State Parks (Col. Gorge) — (503) 695-2261
3-8, 10	Portland Parks and Recreation — (503) 823-2223
1, 2	Sauvie Island Wildlife Area — (503) 621-3488
9	Tryon Creek State Park — (503) 636-9886
15, 19, 35	Wash. Dept. of Natural Resources — (800) 527-3305
34	Washington State Parks — (360) 753-5755
14	Willamette Mission State Park — (503) 393-1171
15, 16, 32, 33, 36	Wind River Ranger District — (509) 427-5645
57-66, 70-74, 86	Zigzag Ranger District — (888) 622-4822

Portland
Area

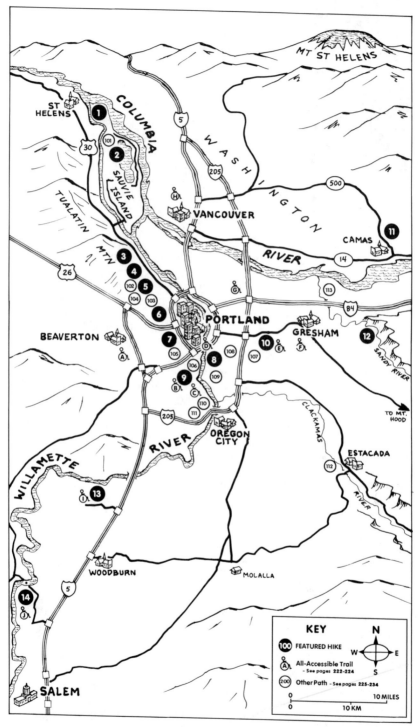

Opposite: The Wildwood Trail in Washington Park (Hike #6).

Warrior Rock

Moderate
7 miles round-trip
No elevation gain
Open except during winter floods
Map: St. Helens (USGS)

At the tip of Oregon's largest island, this woodsy hike along the Columbia River leads to a miniature lighthouse and a secluded, sandy beach. Because the route is within the Sauvie Island Wildlife Area, you can expect to spot great blue herons, geese, or even a bald eagle—particularly in winter. It's also fun to watch ocean-going freighters steam past, and at the end of the island there's a view across to the picturesque old town of St. Helens.

Sauvie Island was once the winter home of the Multnomah Indians, who subsisted mainly on fish and on the potato-like roots of the water-loving wapato (arrowhead plant)—a staple they shared with Lewis and Clark in 1805. In the 1830s a French-Canadian named Laurent Sauve converted much of the island to a dairy farm to supply Fort Vancouver. The southern end of the island was diked against floods in 1941 and now produces an enormous variety of vegetable and berry crops. The northern half of Sauvie Island is managed for wildlife and recreation. Overnight camping and unleashed dogs are prohibited.

To reach the starting point of the hike, drive north of downtown Portland on Highway 30 toward St. Helens. After about 10 miles, turn right across the Sauvie Island Bridge and head north along Sauvie Island Road toward Sam's Grocery. You can stop here to get a Sauvie Island Wildlife Area parking permit (cost: $3.50 a day or $11 a year). Permits are also available at many outdoor stores and at the Oregon Department of Fish and Wildlife in Portland. Equipped with a

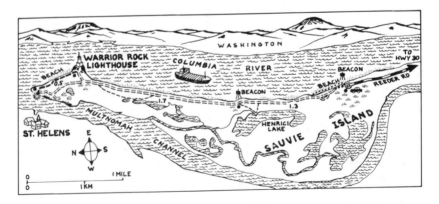

Warrior Rock lighthouse.   Opposite: Stinging nettles.

permit, drive 1.8 miles past the store on Sauvie Island Road, turn right onto Reeder Road, and follow this road for 12.6 miles to its end at a turnaround with a parking area and an outhouse. The final 2.2 miles of Reeder Road are gravel.

Climb over the parking lot fence at the stile and walk cross-country across a cow pasture to the beach. Sharp eyes will already be able to spot the lighthouse 3 miles ahead. The main hiking route to that goal is an old dirt service road that begins at the far end of the pasture and follows the shore. However, it's pleasant to start out walking along the beach itself for half a mile or so. When the sand narrows, climb up to the road and continue.

It's a good idea to wear boots because this road can be muddy after winter floods and for about a month after the Columbia River's usual high water from mountain snowmelt in May. During wet weather, the cows that graze here also trammel the mud. Tall cottonwood trees and August-ripening wild blackberries line the route. Farther on, the forest shifts to ash trees with licorice ferns sprouting from the mossy branches.

After 2.8 miles the road fades in a meadow and forks. Keep right to find the road leading 0.2 mile through the woods to the lighthouse's small rocky headland. A white-sand beach beside the little lighthouse makes an ideal lunch spot. To find the hidden viewpoint of the town of St. Helens, hike to the end of the beach and follow a trail 200 yards across the tip of Sauvie Island.

Other Hiking Options

Hikers who wish to return on a slightly different route can follow a branch of the dirt road back from the viewpoint. Farther toward the car, explorers may also want to try several unmarked side trails veering off to the right. Off limits in winter, these cow paths lead to lakes replete with geese, ducks, and many other birds—but beware of stinging nettles along the way.

Oak Island and Sturgeon Lake.   Opposite: Teasels.

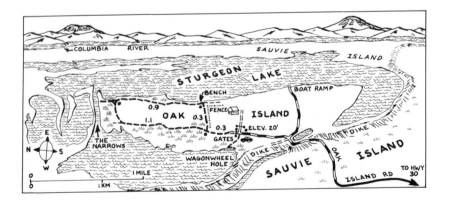

2   Oak Island on Sauvie Island

Easy
2.9-mile loop
No elevation gain
Open April 16 to September 30
Map: Sauvie Island (USGS)

This walk explores an island on an island: an unusually wildlife-rich oak grassland in the middle of Sauvie Island's Sturgeon Lake. Over 250 species of birds visit this portion of the Sauvie Island Wildlife Area, including huge flocks of geese, ducks, and sandhill cranes during the spring and fall migrations. At any time of year it's pleasant to stroll beneath the huge, gnarled white oaks and look across the lake to the pale outlines of Mt. St. Helens and Mt. Adams.

From downtown Portland take Highway 30 toward the town of St. Helens, but after 10 miles turn right across the Sauvie Island Bridge. Head north along Sauvie Island Road past a small grocery store. If you don't have a Sauvie Island Wildlife Area parking permit, stop at the store to get one. Permits are $3.50 a day or $11 a year; they're also available at many outdoor stores and at the Oregon Department of Fish and Wildlife in Portland. Continue driving 1.8 miles past the store on Sauvie Island Road, turn right onto Reeder Road for 1.2 miles, and turn left onto Oak Island Road. After 2.7 miles cross a dike. Ignore a right-hand fork to a boat ramp and continue straight 0.4 mile to a parking area where the road is closed. Overnight camping and unleashed dogs are prohibited.

Start by walking along the abandoned road through oak woods. Wild roses bloom here in early summer. Look for squirrels and listen for pheasants' squawks. After 0.3 mile the road-like path forks at a broad meadow with a view of the Tualatin Mountains. Go straight across the field.

In another 1.1 miles the trail forks again at the beachless, somewhat brushy edge of Sturgeon Lake, with Mt. St. Helens seemingly just across the water. The left-hand fork (blocked by high water in rainy months) leads 200 yards to The Narrows, a neck of Sturgeon Lake edged with picnickably grassy banks. Expect to spot a stilt-legged great blue heron patrolling these shores for frogs and fish.

To continue the loop hike, return to the junction and take the path paralleling the lakeshore. After 0.9 mile watch for a faint fork in a small, grassy opening. Turn right here and head uphill past a bench, a memorial plaque, and a fenceline for 0.3 mile to return to the path leading to your car.

Other Hiking Options

Children will enjoy spotting wildlife on Oak Island, but they might be disappointed by the shortage of good places to get right down by the lake. If so, point them to the little gate at the parking area; a trail here leads 300 yards to Wagonwheel Hole and an accessible, grassy lakeshore ideal for exploring.

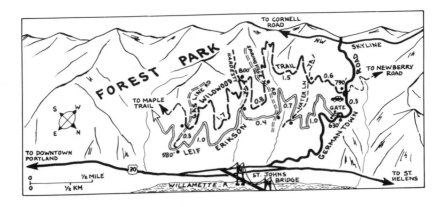

3   Northern Forest Park

Easy (to Springville Rd)
4.6-mile loop
300 feet elevation gain
Open all year
Map: Forest Park (Portland Parks & Rec.)

Moderate (to Gas Line Rd)
8.3-mile loop
400 feet elevation gain

Forest Park is Portland's wilderness secret, with 5000 acres of soothing woodlands draped along a scenic ridge above the Willamette River. The nearly level loop hikes suggested here explore one of the quietest parts of the park. The hikes start on the famous Wildwood Trail, contour along steep hillsides, and return along Leif Erikson Drive, an old road closed to motor vehicles.

From Interstate 5, take Lombard West exit 305 in North Portland, drive west until you cross the St. Johns Bridge, turn right for 0.3 mile, and then turn left onto NW Germantown Road. Drive 1.5 miles up this road to a gravel parking lot on the left with a small sign: "Wildwood Trail, Pedestrians Only." If you're driving here from the west (Washington County), look for the trailhead half a mile past Germantown Road's intersection with Skyline Boulevard.

The Wildwood Trail sets out through a Douglas fir forest full of woodland flowers. April brings yellow violets and white, three-petaled trilliums. May adds stalks of fringecups and paired, white fairy bells. Pink salmonberries, red thimbleberries, and blue Oregon grape ripen as the summer progresses. The dense forest precludes any wide-ranging views, but then you won't see any buildings or automobiles on this hike either. The only clues that you're in a metropolis are occasional clangs and toots from the river docks far below.

Because your return route, Leif Erikson Drive, runs parallel to the Wildwood

Trail but about a quarter mile downhill, you can cut over to it on a number of different cross-trails to make the loop hike as short or long as you wish. Your first option comes after just 0.6 mile, when you cross the Water Line Trail. Turning left here makes a 2.3-mile loop, but then you'd miss the best part of the Wildwood Trail, where it dips into shady canyons to cross creeklets amidst masses of trilliums and maidenhair ferns. So continue on the Wildwood Trail at least to Springville Road, a woodsy path closed to vehicles. To make a 4.6-mile loop, turn left here for 0.4 mile, then turn left onto Leif Erikson Drive for 1.7 miles, and finally walk up Germantown road 600 yards to your car.

If you're still going strong when you reach Springville Road, cross it and continue on the Wildwood Trail. To make a 5.6-mile loop, turn left at the Hardesty Trail junction. If you'd prefer an 8.3-mile loop, wait to turn off the Wildwood Trail until you reach the Gas Line Road, a marked trail running down the end of a ridge. Follow this old, grassy roadbed 200 yards downhill. Just before it gets steep, look for a small path to the left that switchbacks through the woods to Leif Erikson Drive. Then head left on this rustic forest lane to return to Germantown Road.

Other Hiking Options

With a car shuttle you can hike longer sections of the Wildwood Trail one way. From Germantown Road, it's 10 miles to the Saltzman Road trailhead via the Maple Trail (see Hike #4), 18 miles to the Thurman Road Trailhead (see Hike #5), and 24.6 miles to the Vietnam Memorial by the zoo (see Hike #6).

The Wildwood Trail in northern Forest Park.   *Opposite: Maidenhair fern.*

4   Maple Trail

Easy (to Leif Erikson)
4 miles round-trip
350 feet elevation gain
Open all year
Map: Forest Park (Portland Parks & Rec.)

Moderate (to Wildwood Trail)
7.7-mile loop
500 feet elevation gain

In the middle of Portland's vast Forest Park, the surprisingly quiet Maple Trail passes a viewpoint of Cascade peaks and explores grotto-like canyons where mossy bigleaf maples arch above delicate woodland wildflowers. For an easy hike, turn back where the Maple Trail crosses Leif Erikson Drive. For a longer loop hike, continue up to the Wildwood Trail and follow this almost level path as it contours around densely forested ridges back to the start of the Maple Trail.

From the I-405 freeway at the west end of the Fremont Bridge, turn north onto Highway 30 toward St. Helens. After 2.4 miles you'll pass a traffic light for Kittridge Avenue. Continue straight another 0.9 mile. Then turn left at a small, easily overlooked sign for "NW Saltzman Rd." Follow this tiny paved road 0.7 mile through an industrial area and up steeply through the woods to a gate closing the road. Parking space is tight, but don't block the gate.

Start the hike by walking 0.4 mile up the road to a small "Maple Trail" sign on the left. Turn left onto this path, climbing through a forest of bigleaf maples, sword ferns, and western hemlock.

Two kinds of triple-leaved, white wildflowers thrive here: trilliums and vanilla leaf. It's easy to tell the difference in spring when they bloom, because trilliums have a dramatic, three-petaled flower while vanilla leaf puts up a modest, fuzzy stalk. By summer, however, the plants are best distinguished by their three big leaves: teardrop-shaped for trilliums but butterfly-wing-shaped

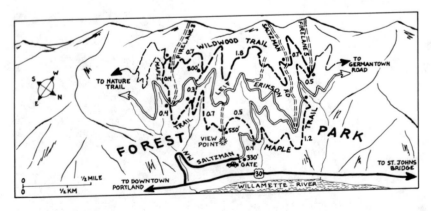

for vanilla leaf. Forest Park's ban on flower picking is particularly important for trilliums, as they require 7 years to bloom again once cut.

After half a mile, the trail crosses under powerlines on an open ridgetop. At this point, sidetrack left 150 yards to a somewhat overgrown viewpoint on the powerline's service road. The vista extends across the Willamette River shipyards and the Fremont Bridge to East Portland, the Columbia River, Mt. Adams, and Mt. Hood.

Returning to the Maple Trail, the path now zigs and zags into mossy canyons with footbridges over little creeks. After 1.1 mile, reach Leif Erikson Drive—an old road closed to motor vehicles. Turn back here if you're tired. If you're interested in a longer loop, however, cross Leif Erikson and continue up the Maple Trail, avoiding the road marked "Firelane 3". After 0.4 mile turn right at a junction, and 150 yards later turn right again onto the Wildwood Trail. Follow this nearly level trail a total of 3.2 miles, crossing a couple of abandoned roads, several small creeks, and a few sets of powerlines. Mile markers on trailside trees measure the distance from the start of the Wildwood Trail in Washington Park. A quarter mile before reaching the "17" marker, you'll come to a ridge end with a sign indicating Firelane 5 uphill to the left. At this junction *take an unmarked trail downhill to the right.* This path leads 0.3 mile down to Leif Erikson Drive.

Head right on Leif Erikson for 300 yards. At the road's first curve, cross a grassy flat on the left to a sign marking the Maple Trail. Follow the Maple Trail 1.2 miles back to Saltzman Road and turn left for 0.4 mile to your car.

Other Hiking Options

The Wildwood Trail continues in either direction from the Maple Trail, so you can hike one-way to a different trailhead by arranging a shuttle. The hike north to the trailhead at Germantown Road is 10 miles (see Hike #3), while it's 8.9 miles south to Thurman Street (see Hike #5) and 15.9 miles south to the Vietnam Memorial by the zoo (see Hike #6).

Ferns along the Maple Trail.   Opposite: View of North Portland.

5 Southern Forest Park

Easy (to Alder Trail)
4.7-mile loop
400 feet elevation gain
Open all year
Use: hikers, bicycles
Map: Forest Park (Portland Parks & Rec.)

Moderate (to Nature Trail)
8.6-mile loop
700 feet elevation gain

This convenient portion of Portland's 5000-acre wilderness park is just a few minutes from skyscrapers, but a world apart. The hiking loops suggested here climb to the Wildwood Trail and return via Leif Erikson Drive, a forest lane closed to motor vehicles. Because the Wildwood Trail and Leif Erikson parallel each other along these forested hillsides, the length of your hiking loop depends on which cross trail you choose between them. The 8.6-mile circuit via the Nature Trail is particularly tempting because it passes scenic Rockingchair Creek and a viewpoint of the mountains. If you're bicycling, you'll have to stick to Leif Erikson Drive and Firelane 1, the only routes open to bikes in this area.

Preservation of Forest Park was originally proposed by the Olmsteads, a visionary New York landscape architect team hired to help Portland prepare for the grandiose Lewis and Clark Exposition of 1905. But most Portlanders of that day had seen more than their fill of forests. The city opened a woodcutting camp in the area to help the unemployed, and developers built the 11-mile Leif Erikson Drive in 1915 as part of a plan to subdivide and conquer the wilds. Fires, landslides, and the Depression finally defeated the realtors' schemes. In 1946 the Mazamas outdoor club began planting trees and building trails in a campaign to revive the Olmsteads' plan. Forest Park was dedicated in 1948—not merely as another manicured garden, but as a refreshing swath of wilderness in the city.

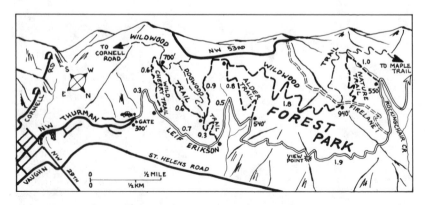

Rockingchair Creek.   Opposite: Trail sign.

To reach this hike's trailhead from downtown, turn off I-405 just before the Fremont Bridge (following Highway 30 toward St. Helens) and immediately take the Vaughn Street exit. Next turn left on 25th Avenue for two blocks, and then turn right on Thurman Street for 1.1 miles. At a switchback to the left, go straight 100 yards to a small parking area and a gate blocking the start of Leif Erikson. If you're driving here from Washington County, take Cornell Road to 25th Avenue, turn left 8 blocks, and turn left on Thurman for 1.1 miles.

Start by walking along Leif Erikson 0.3 mile before turning uphill onto the well-marked Wild Cherry Trail on the left. Here the sound of the city below— like the roar of a distant river—finally begins to fade. Douglas firs and maples form a canopy above bold clumps of sword ferns, spiny-leaved Oregon grape, and spring wildflowers: trillium, fairy bells, and candyflower.

Turn right at the junction with the Wildwood Trail. If you only have time for an hour's walk, it's possible to follow the Wildwood Trail just 0.6 mile, turn right onto the Dogwood Trail, descend a ridge to Leif Erikson, and walk back to your car for a 2.8-mile loop. If you're in for a longer hike, however, continue north along the Wildwood Trail. After briefly approaching NW 53rd Drive, you'll reach the Alder Trail junction and face another choice. Either you can descend on the Alder Trail and return to your car via Leif Erikson for a 4.7-mile loop, or you can hike further on the Wildwood Trail.

Let's assume you've got plenty of energy and march on. The Wildwood Trail contours along the hillside, zigging in to little canyons and zagging out to little ridges. After 1.8 mile, turn right on Firelane 1 for 150 yards and then fork left onto the Nature Trail. After half a mile, the Nature Trail turns right at a trail junction and descends along Rockingchair Creek. At trail's end turn right onto Leif Erikson Drive—a 3.4-mile promenade with occasional views across the Willamette River to the shipyards, the University of Portland campus, Mt. St. Helens, Mt. Adams, and Mt. Hood.

6   Washington Park

Easy (to Hoyt Arboretum)
3.6-mile loop
500 feet elevation gain
Open all year
Map: Forest Park (Portland Parks & Rec.)

Moderate (to Pittock Mansion)
6-mile loop
800 feet elevation gain

   The walk through Washington Park is a reminder of what's so wonderful about Portland. What other city would have a forest path leading from a world-class zoo, past a Japanese garden, to a mansion with a mountain view?

   This first portion of the famous, 30.2-mile Wildwood Trail begins beside the Vietnam Veteran Memorial. To get there, take the MAX light-rail train to the underground Washington Park station and ride the elevator up. If you're driving, head west from Portland on Highway 26 toward Beaverton, take the zoo exit, and park at the far end of the zoo's huge parking lot beside the MAX station, opposite the Forest Discovery Center (formerly the World Forestry Center).

   Then you can walk up the road from the MAX station 100 yards to a sign marking the start of the Wildwood Trail on the left. But along the way you'll pass the steps for the entrance to the Vietnam Veteran Memorial—and it's actually more dramatic to start your hike here, going under the memorial's

The Wildwood Trail in the Hoyt Arboretum.   *Above: The Pittock Mansion.*

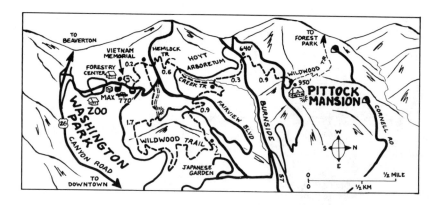

bridge and following its spiral path up to the Wildwood Trail. From there on, expect trail junctions every few hundred yards. Just keep an eye out for the Wildwood Trail signs. Within 0.4 mile you'll cross a paved road and pass a huge green water tank to a viewpoint of Mt. St. Helens and Mt. Rainier. Even if the weather hides these distant peaks, you'll still be able to spot a potential goal of your hike: the Pittock Mansion, atop a forested ridge.

After 1.7 miles on the Wildwood Trail you'll get a glimpse down through the forest to the Oriental bridges and manicured greenery of the Japanese Garden. Shortly afterward, a side trail switchbacks down to the right. If you have time, it's tempting to detour here to visit this acclaimed, 6.5-acre garden, complete with Japanese pavilion and a Portland panorama. Otherwise continue on the Wildwood Trail, which now climbs, crossing several paved roads and a ridge-crest before descending into the Hoyt Arboretum.

Arboretum means "tree museum," and in fact this entire valley is filled with native and exotic trees. You'll switchback down through ponderosa pines reminiscent of Central Oregon and then traverse an impressive grove of coastal redwoods and giant sequoias. Finally you'll reach a footbridge over a creek. If you're tired or if you're hiking with children, turn left onto the Creek Trail here to complete the shorter, 3.6-mile loop. In this case, follow the Creek Trail across a paved road, turn left onto the Hemlock Trail, and take that path over the ridge (crossing Fairview Boulevard) back to the Vietnam Veteran Memorial.

If, however, you've got enough energy for a 7-mile hike, continue on the Wildwood Trail through the Hoyt Arboretum. Soon the path crosses Burnside Street—a busy, fairly frightening highway you'll have to cross at a run. Then the trail climbs 0.9 mile through a Douglas fir forest, crosses a paved road, and reaches the Pittock Mansion parking lot. Walk through the portico on the left side of the mansion to the spacious front lawn where there's a magnificent view of downtown Portland and the mountains.

The 16,000-square-foot palace was built in 1909-14 by banker, real estate magnate, and *Oregonian* editor Henry L. Pittock. For its day, the mansion was astonishingly modern, with an elevator, intercom, and central vacuum cleaning. Tours are available daily between noon and 4pm (adults $4.50, children $2).

To complete your hike, return on the Wildwood Trail to the Hoyt Arboretum footbridge, turn right onto the Creek Trail until it hits the Hemlock Trail, and then follow this path left, over the ridge to the Vietnam Veteran Memorial.

7   Council Crest

Easy
3.8-mile loop
700 feet elevation gain
Open all year
Map: Portland street map

Just a few blocks from downtown Portland, the path through Marquam Nature Park climbs a remarkably unspoiled forest canyon to Council Crest, a historic viewpoint of 5 Cascade peaks. The highest point in the City of Portland, Council Crest was named in 1898 by a gathering of church council picnickers. In 1906 the hilltop was converted to an amusement park, complete with roller coaster, observation tower, and landlocked riverboat. An electric streetcar brought excursionists up from the city in style. The carnival was gone by 1942 when a huge water tank was built here. But picnickers still love this grassy crest.

The easiest way to find the trailhead is to walk here; it's only a half-hour stroll from City Hall. Walk south on SW 6th Avenue until it turns into Terwilliger Boulevard. A long block later, keep right onto Sam Jackson Drive for 0.2 mile to a hairpin curve. Here turn right on gravel Marquam Road to a large, pyramidal shelter at the trailhead. It's also easy to arrive by Tri-Met, since the #8 Jackson Park bus stops at the corner of Terwilliger Boulevard and Sam Jackson Drive.

Car access is a bit more confusing due to the concrete spaghetti of off-ramps at the intersection of I-5 and I-405. Take an exit for the Ross Island Bridge and follow blue "H" hospital signs toward the University of Oregon Health Sciences Center. This will get you heading south on Terwilliger Boulevard. Then go straight onto Sam Jackson Drive, following a Shriners' Hospital sign. At the first hairpin curve turn right onto graveled Marquam Road and the parking area.

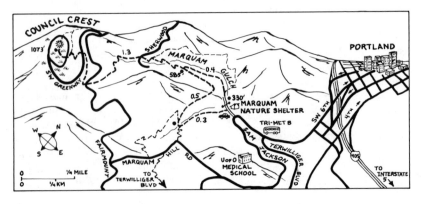

Trail in Marquam Nature Park.　　*Opposite: Rhododendron at viewpoint.*

Marquam Nature Park's steep canyon was originally saved from development because of the unstable geology that makes Portland's west hills such a tricky place to build. Although Ice Age glaciers never reached Portland, their outwash plains repeatedly filled the flatlands with dusty silt. During arid interglacial periods, huge dust storms blew this silt onto the hills, leaving a layer of slippery topsoil up to 30 feet thick. Prolonged rains can launch landslides, especially where this layer is disturbed by houses or roads. Despite the danger, a trio of dentists proposed building 200 apartments in this canyon in 1968. Instead of merely protesting, a scrappy group of volunteers raised over $1 million in a citywide campaign and bought the land for the public.

To start the hike, follow the broad gravel trail up the canyon to the right. Keep straight on this well-graded path, steadily climbing amid ferns and maples. In spring, expect two kinds of white wildflowers with sprays of tiny blossoms: large smilacina (alias false Solomon's seal) and star-flowered smilacina. In summer, look for the delicate fronds of black-stalked maidenhair ferns along the trail. In autumn, the leaves of vine maple paint the woods scarlet.

By following signs to Council Crest and always keeping uphill, you'll cross 4 paved roads in 1.6 miles to reach an unmarked trail junction at the edge of a park lawn. Go left across the lawn to the brick observation patio on the summit, where plaques identify sights from Mt. Rainier to Mt. Jefferson. Even in less-than-perfect weather, views still extend from Beaverton to the Fremont Bridge.

After you've taken in the view, it's quickest to return as you came. But you can also try either of two slightly longer loops. First retrace your steps downhill across the 4 paved roads to a trail junction. If you veer left here you'll tour the north side of Marquam Gulch on a new loop path. If you turn right and keep right at the next junction you'll tour a side canyon en route back to the trailhead.

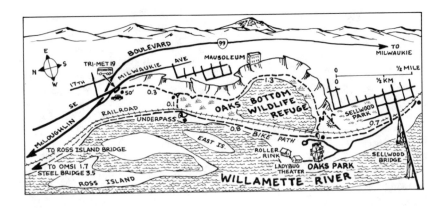

8   Oaks Bottom

Easy
2.8-mile loop
100 feet elevation gain
Open all year
Use: hikers, bicycles
Map: Lake Oswego (USGS)

In the midst of the city but shielded by a 100-foot cliff, the animals in this riverside wildlife refuge don't seem to realize they're in a metropolis. As you hike the trail around these wetlands you're almost certain to see ducks, beaver-gnawed trees, and great blue herons calmly fishing for frogs. But wildlife watching isn't the only reason this trip is a hit with families. At the far end of the loop you can visit Oaks Park, an old-timey carnival midway complete with kiddy rides and refreshment stands.

To find the trailhead, drive south from the Ross Island Bridge on McLoughlin Boulevard (US Highway 99E). After 1 mile take the Milwaukie Avenue exit and immediately pull into a paved parking area on the right, at a sign for the Oaks Bottom Wildlife Refuge. You can get here easily by bus, too, since the #19 Woodstock bus stops by the trailhead.

The broad, graveled trail starts beside a sign reminding visitors that camping, fishing, hunting, and motorized vehicles are banned in the wildlife refuge and that dogs must be leashed. After 0.3 mile the trail forks. Veer left on a smaller path through shady bigleaf maples and soon cross a footbridge with your first view across the refuge's extensive swamplands. Waterfowl thrive in this Everglades-like sea of reeds and willows.

After another half mile pass beneath the 7-story fortress of the Portland

Memorial Funeral Home and reach a couple of small gravelly beaches—the trail's only access to the refuge's large central lake. Look here for freshly-gnawed beaver wood in the swampy forest ringing the shore.

At the end of the lake keep right to an underpass beneath a set of railroad tracks by the main entrance of Oaks Park. This entire railroad track was moved a few feet east in 1999 to make room for a bike path that extends 5 miles along the Willamette River's bank, from the Sellwood Bridge through Oaks Bottom and OMSI to the Steel Bridge. Paving of the path is set for 2001. If it isn't open yet, settle for a tour of the amusement park before heading back the way you came. If the new path is finished, continue your loop by following the railroad to the right.

Oaks Park opened in 1905 just 2 days before tourists descended on Portland for the city's grand Lewis and Clark Exposition. The following year Portland had a second amusement park at Council Crest (see Hike #7), also located at the end of a trolley line to entice excursionists. The Great Depression and the decline of trolleys killed the Council Crest carnival and nearly bankrupted Oaks Park. In 1985 the owner donated the park to a non-profit group dedicated to restoring the amusement park to its former splendor. Today admission is free and tickets to the 28 rides cost about $1 apiece. From mid-June to early October the park is open Tuesday through Sunday, noon to 10pm. From spring vacation to June it's only open weekends.

If you're continuing on the loop along the railroad you'll gain some nice views across the Willamette River to East Island and Ross Island. Stick nests in the tall cottonwood trees of these islands are home to the great blue heron, Portland's symbol. The railroad embankment itself has Scotch broom that blooms yellow in spring and blackberries that ripen in late summer. After a mile, duck through another underpass beneath the railroad. From there a wide path across a field returns to the trail to the parking area.

Oaks Park from Sellwood Park.   *Opposite: Trailhead for Oaks Bottom Wildlife Refuge.*

9   Tryon Creek Park

Easy
2-mile loop
200 feet elevation gain
Open all year
Use: hikers, horses, bicycles
Map: Tryon Cr Trail Guide (State Parks)

Quiet paths and scenic footbridges highlight this densely forested canyon, a pocket wilderness tucked between Portland and Lake Oswego. The woods here are particularly beckoning in spring when the trilliums bloom, but any season is fine for a morning stroll or an afternoon outing with the kids.

Take Terwilliger exit 297 of Interstate 5 and drive south on Terwilliger Boulevard through numerous twists and intersections, following "Tryon Creek State Park" signs. After 2.2 miles, turn right onto the entrance road and park at the end of the loop. Dogs are allowed only on 6-foot or shorter leashes.

Start with a visit to Nature Center, an interpretive center with exhibits and a staff naturalist to help identify plants and explain forest ecology. Pick up a map brochure here, too. The trail route described below is open only to hikers, but the park brochure describes similar loops designed for horses and bicycles.

Now walk back out the front door of the Nature Center and turn right at the signboard. In 100 feet the paved Trillium Trail veers off to the left. Detour briefly to visit this pair of short, all-accessible nature loops if you like, or else simply continue straight, following the Old Main Trail and then the Red Fox Trail 0.3 mile to Red Fox Bridge. Along the way, look for big white trilliums, yellow wood violets, stalks of white fringecups, and stands of stinging nettles. Also notice the little licorice ferns sprouting from the mossy branches of bigleaf maple trees.

After crossing the Red Fox Bridge it's worth detouring 0.3 mile downstream

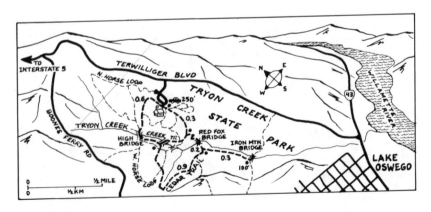

Path in Tryon Creek State Park.   Opposite: Trillium.

along the South Creek Trail to the Iron Mountain Bridge, just to see Tryon Creek grow wider and lazier in this lower end of the park. Then return to a trail junction near the Red Fox Bridge and turn left.

If the weather's dry enough that the paths aren't slick, follow the Cedar Trail on a tour of a side canyon. The forest floor here is carpeted with waterleaf—a wildflower with large, dramatically lobed leaves. After 0.7 mile the Cedar Trail twice crosses a confusing horse trail, but simply head for Tryon Creek and follow it upstream to reach High Bridge. (In wet weather this portion of the Cedar Trail is so slippery it's safer to shortcut on the Middle Creek Trail from Red Fox Bridge to High Bridge.) Then cross High Bridge, turn right, and follow "Nature Center" pointers back to your car.

A non-profit group, the Friends of Tryon Creek State Park, sponsors a number of activities at the park, including school class tours, a "Sunday at Two" lecture series, a photography club, a library of nature-oriented books, and organized hikes in the Portland area. In addition, the Trillium Festival on the first weekend in April brings wildflower exhibits, house plant sales, and a photo contest to the park. Call (503) 636-4398 for more information about these programs or about the Friends of Tryon Creek.

Powell Butte

Easy
3.1-mile loop
300 feet elevation gain
Open all year
Use: hikers, horses, bicycles
Map: Brochure at trailhead

Perfect for a spring picnic or a quick winter walk, this convenient loop explores Powell Butte's broad summit meadow—with views across East Portland to 3 snowpeaks—and then winds through a quiet woodland glen. The route described here is for hikers only, but maps at the trailhead describe alternate, similar tours for bicyclists and equestrians.

Like Mt. Tabor and some 72 other hills between Portland and Sandy, Powell Butte is a volcanic cone less than 10 million years old. The butte earned its name when 3 pioneers by the name of J. Powell, all of them unrelated, took up homesteads near its base in 1852-53. The small orchard of walnut, apple, and pear trees on the butte's top was planted in the late 1800s. Today the delightfully wild 570-acre Powell Butte Nature Park coexists peacefully with a 50-million-gallon reservoir buried beneath the summit meadow. The unseen tank is the hub of Portland's water supply, receiving 152,000 gallons a minute from the Bull Run Watershed.

To reach the park, take exit 19 of Interstate 205, follow SE Powell Boulevard eastward 3.5 miles, turn right at 162nd Avenue, and drive up to the main parking area (at the restrooms). Alternatively, you can ride Tri-Met's #9 bus to the corner of Powell and 162nd.

Start up the paved Mountain View Trail through a meadow of buttercups and clover. Birds sing from hawthorn shrubs. The view of Mt. Hood is quite good,

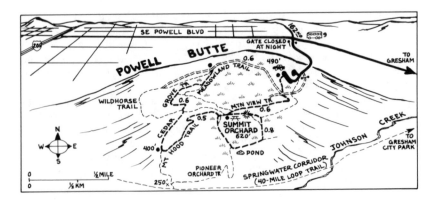

Mt. Hood from Powell Butte's summit.   *Opposite: Fringecup.*

with flat-topped Mt. St. Helens to the north and Mt. Adams' white tip emerging above the foothills as you climb.

Pavement ends and the trail splits when you reach the butte's broad summit in 0.6 mile. Here there are picnic tables in an old walnut orchard with ripe blackberries in August. If you're hiking with children, you might take a shortcut by going straight at this trail junction to the signed Mt. Hood Trail. (If this sign is missing, walk directly *away* from Mt. Hood past a white survey monument post and take the first path to the right.) For a longer tour, turn left onto the Orchard Loop Trail to add a 0.8-mile summit loop. To follow the loop, keep right at all junctions until you return to the summit crest. Then, just before a white survey post, veer left onto the Mt. Hood Trail.

The Mt. Hood Trail dives into a lush forest of Douglas fir, bigleaf maple, and droopy red cedar, with white wildflowers in spring: candyflower, fringecup, and smilacina. Beware of trailside nettles and expect a bit of mud in wet weather. After half a mile turn right on the Cedar Grove Trail and follow signs for this path 0.6 mile until it returns to the meadow. Finally turn left on the Meadowland Trail and follow it 0.6 mile back to the parking area.

Other Options

For a bike trip nearby, tie into the Springwater Trail Corridor. This paved path follows a former railroad line west from Powell Butte 6.1 miles to Tideman Johnson Park, and east 5.5 miles to Hogan Road. A good place to start is at Gresham's Main City Community Park. From there, bike 4.2 miles west to the signed Powell Butte junction, and keep right on the Pioneer Orchard Trail to the summit.

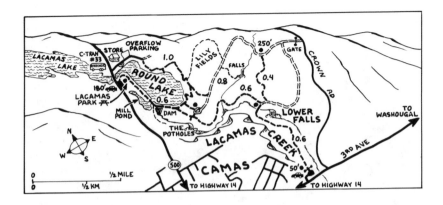

11   Lacamas Park

Easy
3.4-mile loop
200 feet elevation gain
Open all year
Use: hikers, bicycles
Map: Camas (USGS)

Who would have guessed that Camas—the Washington mill town on the Columbia River—is hiding a miniature wilderness with a scenic lake, waterfalls, and a forest canyon? In fact this convenient park is just the right kind of quiet, woodsy place for a winter stroll or an easy hike with the kids.

Take Interstate 5 or 205 north across the Columbia, immediately turn right onto Highway 14, and drive east to Camas exit 12. Follow the exit road 1.4 miles to town, continue straight on 6th Avenue for 6 blocks, turn left on Garfield Street, and follow "Hwy 500 West" signs for 1.1 zigzagging miles to the Lacamas Park parking lot on your right. On summer weekends the lot may be full, but you can drive 100 yards up the highway and turn right on Leonard Road to an overflow parking area. The C-Tran #33 Camas bus also stops at Leonard Road. Camping and unleashed pets are prohibited in the park.

Start at the inlet of Round Lake in a picnic area with barbecues, restrooms, and a playground. Take the lakeshore path to the right 0.3 mile through a Douglas fir forest, cross a footbridge beside a humming fish-screening device, and then cross a 50-foot-tall concrete dam built early in the 20th century to provide power and water for the Camas papermill.

Beyond the dam is a confusion of paths. Stick to the lakeshore for 300 yards to a large signboard with a park map. At this point it's possible to opt for a very short, 1.6-mile loop by simply keeping left around the lake. For the longer loop, however, turn right for 100 yards to the turnaround of a gravel road. Here turn right again on an unmarked path 50 feet to a wire fence at an overlook of The Potholes. There you'll find a pair of circular green pools separated by a 20-foot waterfall and weirdly pockmarked bedrock. The pockmarks were created when floodwaters swirled small rocks in depressions in the soft rock.

At The Potholes, turn left along the fence and follow Lacamas Creek 0.6 mile downstream to a 150-foot metal footbridge above Lower Falls. The creek bank here, polished into chutes and pools, makes a nice lunch stop.

To continue the loop don't cross the footbridge, but instead walk left up an old gravel road for 100 yards and take an unmarked path uphill to the left. After 0.4 mile turn left on another old gravel road to return 0.8 mile to Round Lake. Along the way, optional, marked side paths lead to a patch of April-blooming blue camas lilies (on the right) and a very small waterfall (on the left).

Back at the lake, follow the shore path 0.7 mile to the right and continue briefly on a paved road around to your car.

Other Hiking Options

If you're not hiking with kids you might prefer a slightly longer loop beginning at the much quieter 3rd Avenue trailhead. To find it from Highway 14, take exit 12 for 1.4 miles into Camas, turn right on Adams Street for 3 blocks, turn left on 3rd Avenue for 0.8 mile to the American Legion Hall at East First Street, and turn left to a locked gate. Lower Falls is 0.6 mile up a wide graveled path through the woods.

The Potholes. Opposite: Footbridge and small waterfall at Lower Falls.

12   Oxbow Park

Easy
3.5-mile loop
100 feet elevation gain
Open all year
Use: hikers, horses, bicycles
Map: Brochure at park entrance

Just 7 miles east of Gresham the whitewater Sandy River winds through a gorge where patches of old-growth forest still remain. The trails in popular Oxbow Park are never far from the swift, 200-foot-wide river, with its brushy islands and log jams. Hikers can picnic on pebble beaches, look for great blue herons, discover beaver sign, and watch drift boats negotiate the riffles. The park charges a $3-per-car fee, allows no pets, and closes at legal sunset except for the campground.

From Interstate 205, take exit 19 and head east on Division Street, which crosses Burnside Street in Gresham and eventually becomes the Oxbow Parkway. After 13 miles reach a 4-way junction, turn left following a park sign, and descend 1.6 miles to an entrance toll booth. Then continue 2.2 miles along the river past numerous pullouts, picnic areas, and hiking signs. After passing Group Area D, park at an unmarked boat ramp parking area on the left.

Walk down to the boat ramp and a small sandy beach with fishermen and chilly bathers. Then turn right along the river trail through a mossy forest of red cedars, Douglas firs, sword ferns, and cottonwoods. A lack of signs makes the park's trail network a little confusing. Turn left after 0.2 mile, avoiding log steps up to the right. In another 0.2 mile, where the path crosses a trail in a gully, go straight. Then keep left along a pebble beach at the tip of the river's 180-degree oxbow bend, where deep green eddies swirl against rock banks.

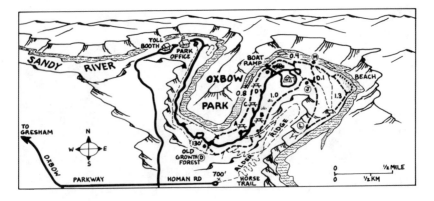

The Sandy River at Oxbow Park.　　*Opposite: Whitewater raft.*

Continue upriver half a mile, always keeping left along the riverbank, to a trail junction in the forest at a post marked "L." The river trail peters out beyond this junction, so turn right for 0.2 mile to join a wide graveled path at a post marked "J." From this junction it's possible to shorten the hike by turning briefly right and then turning left on a gully-bottom trail back to the river. But if you're not yet tired, turn left at "J" and keep left at all junctions for 0.6 mile. When you reach an old gated road, turn right for 150 yards. Here the loop trail leaves the road, climbing to the left up steep steps overhung with maidenhair fern and bleeding hearts.

After climbing the steps, keep right at trail junctions to traverse a lush old-growth forest and reach the paved park road in 0.4 mile. The trail continues from a pullout on the far side of the road and leads to the riverbank. Follow the river trail to the right, passing several picnic lawns, to return to your car.

Other Hiking Options
For a longer hike, add a 1.6-mile loop atop Alder Ridge, a plateau with treetop osprey nests and a clifftop river overlook. Start the loop by walking up the old gated road across from Group Picnic Area A.

Horseback riders should start tours of Oxbow Park from the equestrian trailhead at the end of Homan Road. The $3 park fee is waived here, which would make this upper trailhead attractive for hikers too, except that then the day's hike ends with an uphill climb.

13   Champoeg Park

Easy (around townsite)
3.2-mile loop
No elevation gain
Open all year
Use: hikers, bicycles
Map: Champoeg Park (State Parks)

Moderate (to Butteville)
8-mile loop
No elevation gain

In 1843, when the Oregon Country didn't officially belong to any one nation, pioneers met at Champoeg, the earliest white settlement on the Willamette River, to discuss setting up a provisional government. At first it seemed the 100 white men at that meeting might reject the idea of government altogether. British traders and French-Canadian trappers feared the new American settlers would take control. When a line was drawn in the sand and sides were taken, the vote stood deadlocked, 50 to 50. Then a pair of French-Canadians threw in their lot with the Americans and Oregon has belonged to the US ever since.

Floods in 1861 and 1890 erased the old town of Champoeg. Today this scenic stretch of riverbank is a state heritage area with museums, monuments, picnic

The Willamette River at Champoeg State Park.   Above: Pioneer Cabin Museum.

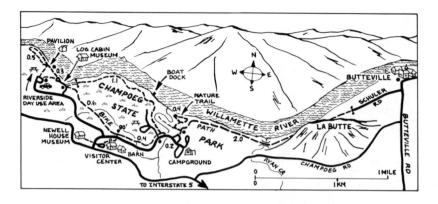

areas, and trails. A 3.2-mile hiking loop visits the most important sites, but it's tempting to extend the loop to 8 miles by hiking the paved bike path to the quaint old town of Butteville. For bicyclists, this paved path is the only option.

Drive Interstate 5 south of Portland 20 miles to Donald exit 278 and turn west, following signs 5.7 miles to Champoeg Heritage Area's entrance. Stop at the visitor's center to see the historical displays there. Additional exhibits are in the 1862 Donald Manson barn beside the visitor center. You might also cross the entrance road to see the restored Robert Newell House Museum (open summer weekends 1pm-5pm). Because it was on high ground, the 1852 Newell House was the only Champoeg home to survive the 1861 flood.

After inspecting the exhibits, get back in your car and drive on into the park, keeping left to the Riverside Day Use Area. Park at the end of the Riverside loop.

Begin your hike by following the "Pavilion" trail sign to a monument and shelter built near the site of the famous 1843 meeting. Then walk through the pavilion to the Willamette—a broad, lazy river reflecting clouds, a few geese, and perhaps a great blue heron. Turn left here to explore a paved but scenic 0.4-mile loop path through a stand of 4-foot-thick cottonwoods. In spring look for wildflowers: fringecup, star-flowered smilacina, and wild rose.

When this little loop returns to the pavilion, continue east along the riverbank. The trail ends at a paved road in front of a 1931 log cabin museum where an exhibit of pioneer artifacts is open Wednesday through Sunday, noon to 5pm.

Next continue 200 yards up the road to a curve where a paved bike path begins. Veer left here, following a "Champoeg Townsite Trail" sign, to find a bark dust river path. After 0.6 mile the river path circles a group camping area with a boat dock. Then the path skirts the Oak Grove Day Use Area lawns and ends at a wide, paved bike path beside a road. To complete the 3.2-mile hiking loop, turn right on the bike path and follow it across the fields back to the log cabin museum and your car.

If, however, you'd like to walk the bike path toward Butteville, turn left when you reach the bike path, cross Champoeg Creek on the road bridge, and head left again. After 100 yards, be sure to detour left onto the lovely, 0.4-mile nature loop to the mouth of Champoeg Creek. A short spur trail of this graveled path passes an 1845 grave and deadends at the site of a pioneer gristmill. Then continue on the wide, paved bike path 1.5 miles along the river's edge to Schuler Road. Rustic Butteville is a half-mile roadside walk beyond.

14 Willamette Mission Park

Easy
2.7 mile-loop
No elevation gain
Open all year
Use: hikers, horses, bicycles
Map: Mission Bottom (USGS)

This riverside loop through Willamette Mission State Park not only visits the world's largest cottonwood tree and the site of a historic 1834 settlement, it also includes a free ferry ride across the Willamette River and back.

To find the park, drive Interstate 5 north of Salem 9 miles to Brooks exit 263. Then head west on Brooklake Road for 1.7 miles, turn right onto Wheatland Road for 2.4 miles, and turn left at the Willamette Mission State Park sign. Follow the entrance road 1.8 miles, keeping left at all junctions, and park at the Filbert Grove Day Use Area—a picnic area set in an old hazelnut orchard. Some years the trees still produce a bumper crop of nuts that you can gather for free in autumn.

Equestrians and bicyclists have their own, separate loop trails through this park. A detailed map of the routes is at the equestrian trailhead, on the left just before the Filbert Grove parking area.

The hiking trail starts beside the restrooms at the far end of the Filbert Grove parking loop. Walk 0.2 mile to the riverbank and turn right on a paved bike path between the bank's cottonwood trees and a grassy field. Follow this promenade a mile to the Wheatland Ferry landing.

This is the oldest ferry landing in Oregon, dating to 1844 when mules winched a log barge across the river with ropes. The present steel vessel uses an overhead cable and electric engines. Pedestrians ride free, but car drivers pay 50 cents.

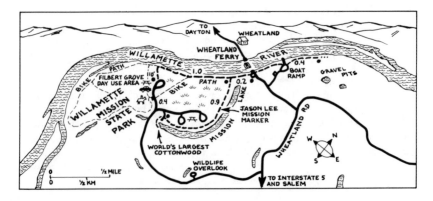

The Wheatland Ferry.   Opposite: Mission monument.

The ferry runs from 6am to 9:45pm every day except Christmas and Thanksgiving—and about 30 or 40 days in winter when it closes for high water or repairs (call 503-588-7979 for schedule information).

The gravelly shore beside the landing is perfect for skipping rocks and watching the river. Children delight in finding tadpoles, frogs, and crawdads here. Look in the wet sand for the palm-sized tracks of great blue herons and the little hand-shaped tracks of raccoons. It's also fun to explore the riverbank beyond the landing; a path continues 0.4 mile before petering out.

To return to the loop, hike 300 yards back from the landing on the bike path and turn left onto a broad trail. This path leads through the woods to the shore of marshy Mission Lake. Before a flood changed the course of the Willamette River in 1861, this oxbow lake was the main channel. A trailside monument describes the mission built on the old riverbank by Methodist minister Jason Lee in 1834. In 1840, weary of the river's floods and the swampy environment, Lee moved operations to Chemeketa (now Salem), where he founded the Oregon Institute, which later became Willamette University. At the same time Lee gave up on teaching Indians and turned his attention to the children of white settlers instead.

After passing the monument, the trail enters a developed picnic area in an old walnut orchard. Keep left at all junctions for half a mile to the trail's end at a road. A sign here points out the world's largest black cottonwood—155 feet tall and over 26 feet in circumference. Walk along the road to return to your car, turning left at the first stop sign and right at the next.

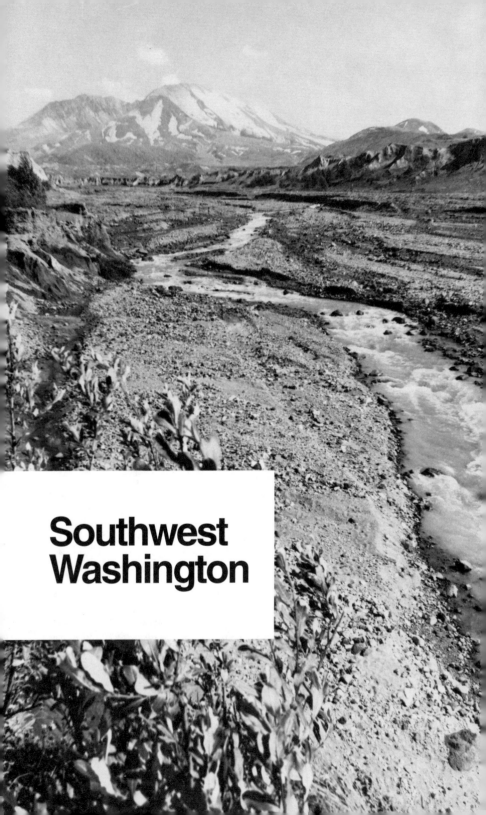

Southwest
Washington

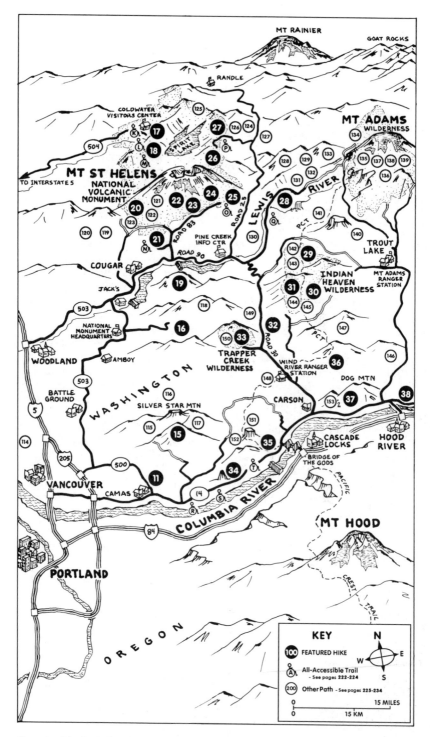

Opposite: Mt. St. Helens from the Hummocks Trail (Hike #17).

15   Silver Star Mountain

Difficult
9.7-mile loop
2400 feet elevation gain
Open May to mid-November
Use: hikers, horses, bicycles
Maps: Larch Mtn, Bobs Mtn
      (Washington, USGS)

From Portland, Silver Star Mountain appears as a humble brown ridge. From the mountain's wildflower-spangled meadows, however, the view is proud indeed, encompassing 4 snowpeaks and a long, silver ribbon of Columbia River.

In 1902 the mountain was overswept by the Yacolt Burn, largest forest fire in Washington history. Today, beargrass meadows thrive on the ridges where trees failed to reseed. Many of the trails in the area are abandoned, rock-strewn roads shared with horses and sometimes even motorcycles. If you walk straight to the summit and back the hike's only 6.6 miles, but for 3.1 extra miles you get a loop past a hidden waterfall and a side trip to a mysterious collection of Indian pits.

Take the freeway north over the Columbia River and immediately turn right toward Camas on Highway 14. When you reach milepost 16, turn left at the Washougal exit and go straight for 6.9 miles on what becomes Washougal River Road. Turn left at a sign for Bear Prairie, climb 3.2 miles to an "Entering Skamania County" sign, and turn left onto Skamania Mines Road for 2.7 miles. Then turn left on gravel 1200 Road and keep left on this rough, rocky road for 5.7 miles to Grouse Creek Vista, a pass with a trail sign on the right: "Tarbell Campground 10-1/2 Miles."

This trailhead can also be reached by car from the north. To try this route, take Highway 503 north from Vancouver. Beyond Battle Ground 6.5 miles, turn right on Rock Creek Road (which becomes Lucia Falls Road) for 8.8 miles, turn right

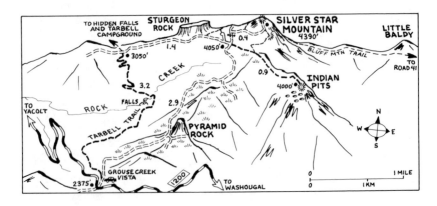

Indian pit.   Opposite: Silver Star Mountain.

on County Road 12 for 1.9 miles, turn right onto paved Dole Valley Road (which becomes gravel Road L1000) for 5.1 miles, and then veer left onto Road L1200 for 4.5 miles to Grouse Creek Vista's pass.

Hike past the trail sign up a blocked, abandoned road. After 200 yards ignore the Tarbell Trail angling off to the left—it's the return route of the loop. Continue up the rocky road a mile to meadows and views. At first the fields are thick with huckleberry bushes, fireweed, and pearly everlasting. As you climb past Pyramid Rock the flowers shift to beargrass, blue lupine, and red paintbrush.

Keep left for 2.9 miles until you reach a 4-way junction. The road straight ahead leads to the summit, but it's worth it to turn right on the signed trail to the Indian pits. This path goes up and down along a fabulous alpine ridgecrest for 0.9 mile and ends at a rockslide with a sweeping view. The ancient stone walls and 6-foot pits here are thought to be vision quest sites where young Indian men fasted until they saw a guiding spirit. Do not remove anything.

As you walk back from the pits watch for a trail on the right that scrambles up to Silver Star Mountain's twin summits, one of which still has foundations of a lookout tower. Soak in the view, and then hike 0.4 mile down the road back to the 4-way junction.

If you have time for a longer, woodsier return path, turn downhill to the right from the 4-way junction. This steep, rocky road soon forks, but keep left for 1.4 miles, passing beneath the columnar basalt cliffs of Sturgeon Rock. Then turn left onto the well-marked Tarbell Trail. This path switchbacks gently down to a footbridge over Rock Creek, To see the hidden waterfall downstream, look back as you hike on. The trail contours through second-growth woods to your car.

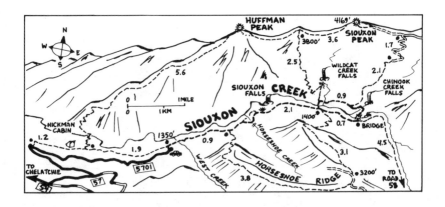

16   Siouxon Creek

Moderate
7.6-mile loop
700 feet elevation gain
Open all year
Use: hikers, horses, bicycles
Map: Lookout Mtn (Green Trails)

Ancient forest frames Siouxon Creek's green pools and waterfalls. The trail here follows the creek 3.7 miles to a footbridge in a mossy grotto ideal for a picnic. If you don't mind a bridgeless creek crossing you can return on a loop past two tall waterfalls in side canyons.

The drive to Siouxon Creek is entirely paved. Take Interstate 205 north across the Columbia River to Orchards exit 30. Go right on Highway 500, which becomes Highway 503 through Battle Ground and makes three sharp corners in Amboy. A total of 26.2 miles from the freeway—just past the Mt. St. Helens National Monument Headquarters—turn right on NE Healy Road for 9.2 miles to a fork. Watch your odometer, because road signs may be missing. At the fork, veer uphill to the left on Road 57 for 1.2 miles to a pass. Then turn left onto Road 5701 for 3.8 miles to a path on the left, 100 feet before road's end.

Hike down the path and turn right on the Siouxon Creek Trail. This trail descends 0.2 mile to a footbridge over West Creek, passes 3 campsites, and then follows Siouxon Creek amid big Douglas firs and red cedars. After 1.4 miles the path bridges Horseshoe Creek between a pair of charming little waterfalls. Side trails to the left end at brushy viewpoints. Continue on the main trail 0.3 mile to Siouxon Falls, a 40-foot, S-shaped slide that sloshes into a huge green pool.

At the 3-mile mark the path to Wildcat Falls joins from the left—the return route of the loop. For now, go straight another 0.7 mile and turn left across a footbridge over a deep-pooled gorge with mossy rock ledges suitable for use as lunch tables. After resting here, continue 1/4 mile to a creek crossing below lacy, 50-foot Chinook Falls.

To complete the little loop, continue past Chinook Falls to the trail's first switchback and go straight onto an unmarked trail. This narrower tread leads 0.7 mile to the Wildcat Trail. If you have the energy, turn right for a steep 0.3-mile climb to a viewpoint of Wildcat Falls' 100-foot ribbon. Otherwise turn left to a ford of Siouxon Creek and the trail back to the car. In summer it's possible to make this creek crossing dry footed, but plan on a cold, difficult wade during winter high water. And incidentally—the name Siouxon rhymes with Tucson.

Other Hiking Options

Backpackers or rugged day hikers can choose among 3 more difficult loops. For a sweeping view from Siouxon Peak's former lookout site, take the Chinook Trail up from Chinook Falls to a jeep track, keep left to the peak, and return via the Wildcat Trail—a 16.6-mile trip gaining 3700 feet. For a 10.8-mile loop that gains 2600 feet, take the well-marked Horseshoe Ridge Trail up a steep, viewless crest, across a logging road, and back to Siouxon Creek. Finally, a 13-mile loop up Wildcat Creek passes within a cross-country scramble of Huffman Peak's scenic summit and follows a long, wooded ridge west to a lower portion of the Siouxon Creek Trail, gaining 3900 feet in all.

Bridge over Siouxon Creek.   Opposite: Tiger lily.

17   Coldwater Lake

Easy (to lakeshore)
2.4 miles round-trip
700 feet elevation gain
Open March through November
Map: Mt. St. Helens Nat'l. Mon. (USFS)

Moderate (to bridge)
9.2 miles round-trip
900 feet elevation gain

Easy (Hummocks Trail)
2.5-mile loop
250 feet elevation gain

Most of Mt. St. Helens' summit slumped to the north and slid down the Toutle River valley during the mountain's 1980 eruption. The slide dammed 4-mile-long Coldwater Lake and left an eerie collection of 200-foot-tall hummocks strewn across the valley floor. Today throngs of tourists view the results of this volcanic mayhem from a visitor center atop Coldwater Ridge. But surprisingly few take the local trails for a closer look. One path drops from the visitor center to the new lake and ambles along its shore to a dramatic bridge over a gorge. Nearby, an easy loop trail tours the weirdly scenic Hummocks.

Start by driving Interstate 5 to Castle Rock exit 49. Then take Highway 504 for 43 miles to the Coldwater Ridge Visitor Center. National Forest parking permits are not required here, but if you bring one you'll get one free admission to the visitor center, where visitors over the age of 15 otherwise are charged an entrance fee of about $3. Remember that pets are not allowed on the trails.

The path down to Coldwater Lake begins a hundred yards left of the visitor center, by the far end of the parking lot at an "Elk Bench Trail" sign. Expect views on this route, but not much shade. Stumps show that most of the area was clearcut before the 1980 eruption. The volcano's blast snapped the remaining trees. Today, wildflowers seem to dominate. Watch for white ox-eye daisies,

Mt. St. Helens from the Hummocks.   Above: Coldwater Lake.

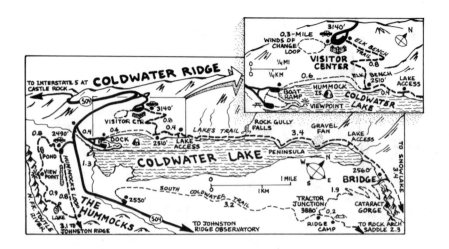

purple foxglove, blue lupine, and yellow lotus. Also expect to see a sparrow-sized bird, the junco, that flashes a white V in its tail feathers as it flies.

After a steep descent, the path crosses Elk Bench, a meadow popular with blacktail deer and golden-mantled ground squirrels. At the 0.8-mile mark you'll reach the lake trail. Turn left on it for 0.4 mile to a lakeshore access point. If you're hiking with children, this is a good place to let them clamber on the driftwood logs of the beachless shore before heading back.

If you're going strong, continue on the trail to the far end of the lake. Along the way you'll pass a small waterfall in rock gully, a panoramic peninsula, and the gravel fans of rockslides from the denuded slopes above. After 3.4 miles, turn right at a trail junction for the Coldwater Trail. In just 100 yards this path crosses a spectacular, 50-foot bridge over Coldwater Creek. Below, a cataract rages through a gorge of pink stone. This makes a good turnaround point.

To try the loop hike through the Hummocks, drive onward from the Coldwater Ridge Visitor Center toward Johnston Ridge for 2.2 miles and turn right to the well-marked parking area. Parking permits are required. The trail start at the right-hand side of the parking lot and descends through a colorful badlands of hundred-foot rockpiles left by the eruption's landslide. In many places, substantial alder groves have already sprung up. Ponds dot the uneven terrain. After 0.8 mile the trail skirts a cliff with a dramatic view across the North Fork Toutle River's stripped-out floodplain to Mt. St. Helens. Continue 0.9 mile to a junction with the Boundary Trail and turn left to complete the Hummocks loop.

Other Hiking Options

If you can arrange a shuttle, consider tackling the spectacular, 14.4-mile trail from the Coldwater Ridge Visitor Center to the Johnston Ridge Observatory (Hike #18). Start by hiking to the Coldwater Trail's bridge as described above, but continue up to Tractor Junction, where a relic of rusting logging equipment remains. Turn left for 2.5 miles to Arch Saddle. Then turn right on the Boundary Trail, which ducks through a rock arch and passes knockout views of Mt. St. Helens on its way to Johnston Ridge. If you're backpacking, pick up a permit in advance for the route's only campsite: Ridge Camp, a barren bowl with a snowmelt creek that often runs dry. Maximum group size for campers is four.

18   Johnston Ridge

Easy (to great viewpoint)
3.8 miles round-trip
400 feet elevation gain
Open early June through October
Map: Mt. St. Helens Nat'l. Mon. (USFS)

Moderate (to Harrys Ridge)
8 miles round-trip
1000 feet elevation gain

Difficult (to Coldwater Peak)
12.8 miles round-trip
2000 feet elevation gain
Open July through October

When Mt. St. Helens unexpectedly aimed its 1980 eruption toward this ridge, David Johnston, the Forest Service observer stationed here, had time to radio just 5 words: "Vancouver! Vancouver! This is it!" Today the most popular drive in the national monument leads to an observation building atop Johnston's ridge. The view of the ruined volcano is both chilling and inspiring. But the panorama actually gets better the farther you hike from the visitor center: 1.9 miles to a bluff, 4 miles to Harrys Ridge, or 6.4 miles to Coldwater Peak.

Drive Interstate 5 to Castle Rock exit 49 and take Highway 504 for 52 miles to its end at the Johnston Ridge Observatory. Parking permits are not required, but if you want to tour the building, expect to pay about $3 for each visitor over the age of 15. The observatory is open 10am-6pm daily from April 26 to September 26. Remember that pets are banned on the trails here. And be sure to bring plenty of water, because the route has none.

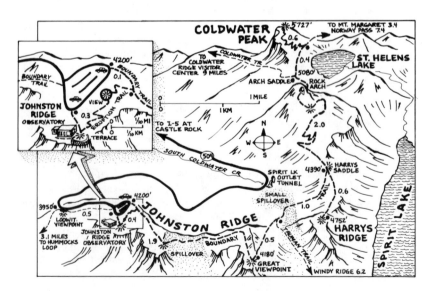

Coldwater Peak and St. Helens Lake.   Opposite: Mt. St. Helens from Harrys Ridge.

After touring the observatory, head uphill from the terrace on the paved Eruption Trail, which loops across a viewpoint knoll. After 0.3 mile, just before the paved path returns to the parking lot, turn right onto the unpaved Boundary Trail. (If you'd rather skip the visitor center's crowds and shorten the hike, start at a "Boundary Trail" signboard at the far end of the parking lot instead.)

The Boundary Trail ambles east along Johnston Ridge amid splintered logs. Blue lupine and purple penstemon brighten the stark slopes in summer. After half a mile the path dips to the Spillover, a barren saddle where a landslide from the volcano's 1980 eruption sloshed over the top of Johnston Ridge. The massive slide swept away soil and logs, but left behind lava boulders. At the 1.9-mile mark, the Boundary Trail switchbacks around the end of a ridge with the best view so far. If you're hiking with children, make this your turnaround point.

For a longer tour, continue 1.5 miles on the Boundary Trail to Harrys Saddle, where the vista opens up across Spirit Lake to distant Mt. Adams. Here you face another choice. For the moderate hike, turn right on a path that climbs 0.6 mile up Harrys Ridge, with its close-up panorama of Mt. St. Helens and Spirit Lake. This ridge was named for Harry Truman, the curmudgeon who died with 40 cats in his Spirit Lake Lodge during the 1980 eruption. Ruined scientific equipment from before the blast remains on the summit.

If you're up to a difficult hike, skip Harrys Ridge and continue straight across Harrys Saddle on the Boundary Trail, heading for the loftier viewpoint atop Coldwater Peak. After climbing 1.7 miles, the path ducks across a ridgecrest through a natural rock arch. Visible far below is blue St. Helens Lake, in a craggy mountain bowl lined with standing dead snags. Continue 0.3 mile down to a trail junction at Arch Saddle, keep right on the Boundary Trail for 0.4 mile, and turn sharply left at a sign for the Coldwater Peak Trail.

Patches of snow linger until mid-summer on this steep, switchbacking path, but it's also a place to find vibrant alpine wildflowers: beargrass plumes and pasque flower anemones. Coldwater Peak's summit, once the site of a fire lookout, now has a small collection of antennas and solar panels. The dizzying view extends from Mt. Rainier to the Pacific.

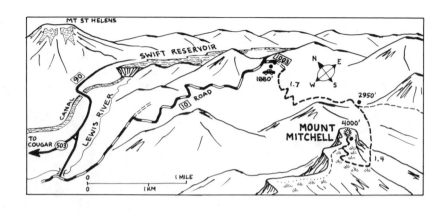

Crags near the summit of Mt. Mitchell.   Opposite: Bluebells.

19　Mount Mitchell

Moderate
6.2 miles round-trip
2100 feet elevation gain
Open April through November
Use: hikers, horses, bicycles
Map: Mt. Mitchell (Wash. USGS)

The best viewpoint of Mt. St. Helens' truncated south flank isn't in the National Monument at all—it's from this little-known peak above Swift Reservoir. The unmarked but easy-to-follow Mount Mitchell Trail leads through a high meadow of beargrass and blue gentian to an old lookout site amidst scenic crags.

To find Mt. Mitchell from Portland, drive 25 miles north on Interstate 5 to Woodland exit 21 and turn right for 31.5 miles, following signs for Cougar. Beyond the town of Cougar 3.2 miles—immediately before Highway 503-Spur becomes Forest Road 90—turn right onto an unmarked paved road for 0.3 mile, cross a bridge, and turn left on an unmarked gravel road. At a junction after 1.6 miles, turn sharply right onto a gravel road marked "10". Large pieces of gravel on the 10 Road makes it slow and bumpy. After another 2.4 miles (and just before the 10 Road starts heading downhill), veer right onto Road 1003. Park on the right after 200 yards, where this dirt track becomes undrivably rough.

After parking, walk along the jeep track into a mossy second-growth forest of alder, cedar, sword fern, and Oregon grape. After 0.2 mile the track turns right and narrows to a rocky trail that switchbacks steeply up through the woods. At the 1-mile mark the path straightens out on a pleasanter, less steep traverse around the mountain's slopes. At 1.7 miles ignore a side trail to the left; it leads across private land.

The main path's final mile ambles through ever grander beargrass meadows before climbing past the summit crags to the old lookout site, marked today only by foundations, glass, and a toppled outhouse. In addition to brilliant blue gentians, look for cushions of white phlox, delicate bluebells, purple penstemons, and spiny gooseberry plants. The view across Swift Reservoir shows Mt. St. Helens' relatively intact southern face. But the old lava flows and recent lahars (mudflows) snaking down from the long gray rim prove this topless volcano is no heavy sleeper.

For an adventurous side trip on the way back, hike a few hundred yards down the trail to the second switchback and go straight on a faint path that heads through the woods. to a broad, meadowed ridge, where you can easily bushwhack 0.8 mile west to another clifftop viewpoint.

20   Sheep Canyon

Difficult
11-mile loop
1900 feet elevation gain
Open late June through October
Map: Mt. St. Helens Nat'l. Mon. (USFS)

On the western edge of Mt. St. Helens' 1980 blast zone, this loop has a little of everything: intact old-growth forests, desolated canyons, wildflower-strewn timberline meadows, and a truly astonishing view of the mountain from the South Fork Toutle River's moonscape gorge. The river is still struggling to cut a chasm into a half-mile-wide mudflow unleashed by the flash melting of the Toutle and Tallus Glaciers.

Floods washed out the access road to the original Sheep Canyon Trailhead in 2002. Since then visitors have had to park 2 miles farther away at the Blue Lake Trailhead, leaving the Sheep Canyon area quieter and perhaps more attractive than ever. Because road repair funds are short, the change may become permanent.

Take Interstate 5 to Woodland exit 21 (north of Portland 25 miles) and turn right for 27.7 miles, following signs for Cougar. Half a mile before the town of Cougar turn left onto Road 8100 at a sign for Merrill Lake. Follow this paved road 11.5 miles and then continue straight on gravel Road 8123 for 1.7 miles to the Blue Lake Trailhead. Parking permits are required.

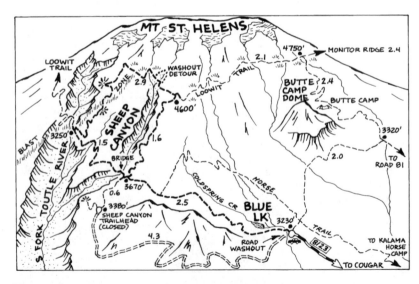

Start out on the trail to the left that crosses Coldspring Creek. This path climbs along a ridge above Blue Lake through a forest of big hemlocks and firs. Look for the hand-sized triple leaves of vanilla leaf, a humble white wildflower that gives off a sweet smell as it wilts.

After 2.5 miles, turn right on the Sheep Canyon Trail , climbing through old-growth woods alongside this flood canyon 1.6 miles to meet the Loowit Trail at timberline. Turn left on this round-the-mountain path, contouring through delightful alpine meadows of bluebells, red paintbrush, blue lupine, and huckle-berries. Along the way you may have to detour uphill to the right to circumvent a trail washout at the head of Sheep Canyon.

After 1.4 miles the Loowit Trail suddenly enters the volcano's blast zone and turns downhill on a ridge that marks the edge of the 1980 eruption's blast, with standing dead trees on one side. In another 1.5 miles you'll reach a trail junction at the rim of the South Fork Toutle River's mudflow canyon. The loop route turns left here, but first detour a few hundred yards to the right for a view up the river's tiered canyon to Mt. St. Helens. The raging, bouldery river is milky with pulverized rock from the grinding glaciers above.

Then turn around to continue on the loop route 1.5 miles to a footbridge across Sheep Canyon. Turn briefly left on the far side of the bridge, and then turn right to find the 2.5-mile path back to your car at the Blue Lake Trailhead.

South Fork Toutle River.   Opposite: Sheep Canyon footbridge.

21   Ape Cave

Easy (Lower cave)
2 miles round-trip
200 feet elevation gain
Open all year
Map: Mt. St. Helens Nat'l. Mon. (USFS)

Moderate (Upper cave)
2.7-mile loop
400 feet elevation gain

Longest lava tube in the western hemisphere, Ape Cave features a 0.8-mile lower section that's easy to hike and a rugged, 1.4-mile upper section that's fun for adventurers. The lower section, with a smooth, sandy floor, leads to The Meatball, a lava boulder wedged halfway to the cave's 30-foot ceiling. The rugged upper section of the cave offers a skylight and two frozen lava "waterfalls," but a jumble of rocks on the cave floor make walking difficult.

Bring *at least* one lantern or flashlight for each person and be sure to dress warmly. Even on hot summer days the drafty cave remains a constant, chilly 42 degrees Fahrenheit. Pets, smoking, food, and beverages are banned in the cave. At the cave entrance, expect to pay about $3 for each visitor over the age of 15. If you have a National Forest parking pass, bring it for one person's free admission. There are no fees if you visit between December 1 and April 15, but the entrance road is gated closed then, adding a mile to your hike each way.

Ape Cave formed 1900 years ago when Mt. St. Helens erupted a runny kind of basalt lava known as pahoehoe. As the flow's crust hardened, the liquid lava underneath drained out along the course of a buried stream gully, leaving a 11,334-foot-long tube. In places the tube was so tall it pinched into two separate levels, one above the other. Watch along the walls for stripes, the "high-water marks" left by flowing lava. Also look for solidified puddles of the lava river on the cave floor, often with ripple patterns like cake batter poured in a pan.

As the lava ebbed, superheated gases blasted through the tube, remelting the walls' surface and leaving tiny, fragile stalactites known as "lava drips." Since then, earthquakes have shaken loose portions of the upper cave's ceiling. An eruption of Mt. St. Helens 450 years ago loosed a mudflow that spilled into the cave's main entrance and paved the lower cave with sand. Remarkably, the 1980 eruption had almost no effect here.

Discovered in 1946, Ape Cave was named for the Mt. St. Helens Apes, a group of Boy Scout cavers who took their tongue-in-cheek name from an alleged 1924 sighting of Sasquatch on the mountain's east flank at an otherwise unrelated valley, Ape Canyon (Hike #24).

To find the cave, drive Interstate 5 north of Portland 25 miles and turn right at Woodland exit 21, following signs for Cougar. After 35 miles (beyond the town of Cougar 6.7 miles), turn left onto paved Road 83. After another 1.7 miles, turn left on Road 8303 for 0.9 mile to a parking lot at "Ape's Headquarters," a staffed information cabin.

Mt. St. Helens from the cave's upper entrance.   Opposite: Ape Cave's main entrance.

Take a short path to the cave's main entrance, go down the stone stairs, and a few hundred feet later descend a metal stairway to the cave's main floor. No signs point the way here, but the route behind you (under the stairway) leads to the rugged upper cave while the route ahead of you goes to the easier lower cave. Explore the popular, 0.8-mile lower cave first. Then, if you'd like to get away from the crowds, return to the stairway and try the rougher upper cave.

The upper cave begins with a 40-foot-tall room, but the route then arduously clambers over the first of 10 major rockfalls. At the 0.8-mile and 0.9-mile marks you'll have to climb up 8-foot lava falls using whatever handholds and footholds you can find. The skylight opening after 1.1 mile is too high to use as an exit, but continue 0.3 mile and you'll reach a metal ladder to the upper entrance, just before the cave ends. The above-ground trail back to the main entrance crosses a sparsely forested lava bed and mudflow.

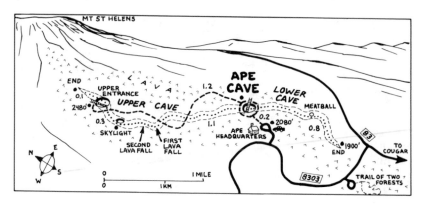

22   Mount St Helens Rim

Moderate (to Dryer Creek Meadows)
8 miles round-trip
1100 feet elevation gain
Open late June through October
Map: Mt. St. Helens NW (Green Trails)

Very Difficult (to summit)
9.4 miles round-trip
4500 feet elevation gain
Open mid-July to mid-October

From Mt. St. Helens' summit rim, the new crater gapes like the broken edge of a shattered planet. Rock avalanches rumble in slow motion down 2000-foot cliffs to the steaming lava dome. On the horizon, the snowpeaks of Washington and Oregon float above the clouds.

Now that the volcano has calmed, the Forest Service issues permits for 100 people a day to hike to the rim either by way of Butte Camp (Hike #122) or up the shorter Monitor Ridge route described here. The climb requires no technical climbing skills—only stamina and strong knees. Hikers start out on a well-graded forest path to timberline, then follow poles marking the way up a ridge of lava boulders, and finally trudge up a dune-like slope of ash. Don't take pets.

If you're unsure about attempting the climb—or if you can't get a permit—consider taking the round-the-mountain Loowit Trail to the wildflowers at Dryer Creek Meadows instead. This alternative skips the steep climbing, yet still visits Monitor Ridge's interesting lava fields and offers views to Mt. Hood.

Dryer Creek Meadows.   Above: Mt. Adams from Mt. St. Helens' rim.

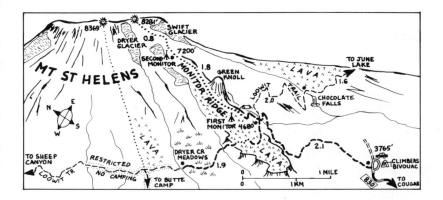

Climbing permits cost $15 per person and are required for travel above the 4800-foot level between April 1 and October 31. Sixty permits for each day are available for reservation. For forms, call (360) 247-5800 or write the Climb Coordinator at the National Monument Headquarters at 42218 NE Yale Bridge Road, Amboy, WA 98601. Applications are not accepted before February 1.

Even with a reservation you must pay for your permit at Jack's Restaurant in Cougar by 5:30pm on the day before your climb. It's easier, but riskier, to show up at Jack's between 5:30pm and 6pm for a permit lottery. At 6pm, names are drawn for 40 permits (plus unclaimed reservations) valid for the following day. In addition, all climbers must sign in at a register outside Jack's both before and after their climb. Remember to pack plenty of water for the long, dry climb.

To find the trailhead, drive Interstate 5 north of Portland 25 miles and turn right at Woodland exit 21, following signs for Cougar. After 35 miles (beyond the town of Cougar 6.7 miles), turn left on paved Road 83 for 3.1 miles. Then, following "Climbers Bivouac" pointers, turn left on Road 8100 for 1.7 miles and turn right on gravel Road 830 for 2.7 miles to a turnaround. Climbers determined to get an early morning start can either pitch their tents in the 1976 clearcut here or backpack to a small, crowded, often waterless dale at timberline.

Start on the Ptarmigan Trail and climb steadily 2.1 miles to a junction with the Loowit Trail amid the pink heather and snow-bent firs of timberline. If you're headed for Dryer Creek Meadows, turn left, follow the sometimes-faint Loowit Trail 0.9 mile across a rugged lava ridge, and continue another level mile through lovely August lupine fields to the mudflow gorge of the Dryer Glacier's outwash creek—a suitable turnaround point.

If you're climbing the mountain, cross the Loowit Trail to the signed climbers' route. The tread soon ends atop a rugged lava flow near one of the two tripod monitors that gave this ridge its name. The tripods' mirrors reflected laser beams to gauge the swelling of the mountain and thus predict eruptions.

Continue on a braided path marked by posts and then scramble up a ridge of boulders to the second monitor tripod. Shortly beyond this point the boulders end and the route ascends an ash slope between the Swift Glacier and a snowfield. Winds here often whip up gritty clouds of dust. When you reach the rim, don't venture too close to the unstable edge. Hiking is barred along the cliff to the right, but you can explore left as far as the Dryer Glacier headwall, which blocks safe access to what is technically the mountain's highest point.

23   June Lake

Easy (to June Lake)
2.6 miles round-trip
410 feet elevation gain
Open June to mid-November
Use: hikers, bicycles
Map: Mt. St. Helens NW (Green Trails)

Moderate (to Chocolate Falls)
5.4-mile loop
1000 feet elevation gain
Open late June through October

The forests on this southern side of Mt. St. Helens weren't hurt by the 1980 eruption, but if you stroll through the woods to June Lake's 40-foot waterfall you'll see other proof that you're on a volcano. A volcanic mudflow created the lake itself about a century ago, and the waterfall drops off the edge of an ancient lava field. If you continue up to Chocolate Falls, you'll scramble across fresh-looking lava to a stripped-out gorge where an ash-choked waterfall sometimes runs as dark as chocolate milk.

Start by driving Interstate 5 north of Portland 25 miles to Woodland exit 21. Turn right, following signs for Cougar. After 35 miles (beyond the town of Cougar 6.7 miles), turn left onto paved Road 83 for 7.2 miles. At a "June Lake" sign, turn left for 200 yards to the trailhead turnaround. Bicycles are permitted, but are impractical on the lava beyond June Lake.

The first mile of the trail climbs gradually through a second-growth fir forest where huckleberry bushes hang heavy with blue fruit in late August. Expect to hear two common birds along the route. The tiny winter wren pours out a full 10 seconds of cheerfully twittering musical madness from the vine maple underbrush. The robin-sized varied thrush pipes a single tone, like a slowly squeaking wagon wheel up in the firs.

After 1.3 miles you'll cross the old mudflow—now a pleasant, sandy plain—

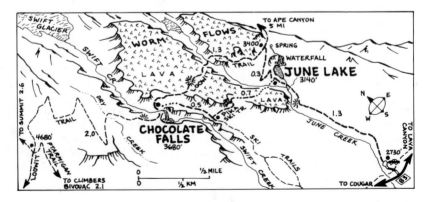

June Lake's waterfall.   Opposite: Swift Creek above Chocolate Falls.

to Lake June. A lacy waterfall splashes at the far side of the shallow pool amidst old-growth hemlocks.

The lake makes a lovely goal, but if you'd like a more challenging destination, walk to a "June Lake" sign 100 feet left of the shore and look for a path angling up into the woods ahead. This trail switchbacks up 0.3 mile to a junction just above the sudden spring that feeds June Lake's entire waterfall. Turn left on the Loowit Trail, a path that soon climbs across the Worm Flows—lava fields so rugged that hikers are left to hop from boulder to boulder, following rock cairns and trail posts. Views extend across the lava to Mt. St. Helens' snowy rim.

After crossing 3 lava fields in 1.3 miles, the Loowit Trail dips to Chocolate Falls, a dramatic pair of 40-foot plumes in a canyon scoured by floods from the 1980 eruption. Even when the falls are too full to run brown, the water is milky with rock silt from the Swift Glacier.

The simplest return route to June Lake is the way you came, but hardy route-finders can loop back to the lake on rugged trails designed for Nordic skiers in winter. To try this loop, head downstream from Chocolate Falls, walking cross-country along a bench on the left side of the creek. After 300 yards, cross a gully to the left, following the blue arrows of diamond-shaped ski markers. Here you'll find a path that soon becomes an ancient road. After half a mile, turn left at a sign for the Pika Ski Trail. This route is a brushy and rough, and crosses a rugged lava flow, but if you steadfastly follow the blue diamond markers you'll reach June Lake in 0.7 mile.

Other Hiking Options

For a longer hike, continue as far as you like on the 29.5-mile Loowit Trail, which circles Mt. St. Helens at timberline. To the west of Chocolate Falls the route climbs 2 miles through woods to a climbers' campsite at the Ptarmigan Trail junction (see Hike #22). To the east of June Lake the Loowit Trail is sometimes faint, crossing lava fields and mudflow gullies for 5 miles to Ape Canyon (Hike #24).

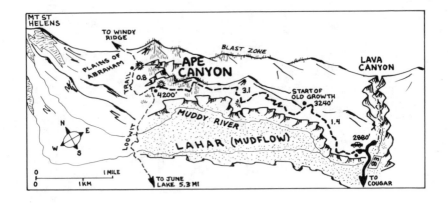

24 Ape Canyon

Difficult
10.6 miles round-trip
1300 feet elevation gain
Open July through October
Use: hikers, bicycles
Map: Mt. St. Helens Nat'l. Mon. (USFS)

This path climbs along an old-growth forest ridge beside an awesome, mile-wide mudflow with views up to Mt. St. Helens' decapitated rim. At the top of the trail you'll get a view down Ape Canyon's eerie, 300-foot-tall rock slot at the edge of the 1980 blast zone. If you continue another 0.8 mile you'll reach the other-worldly desolation of the Plains of Abraham.

Ape Canyon won its name in 1924 when an ape-like creature threw rocks at two miners in a cabin here. In 1982 an old-timer confessed that he and another boy had staged the entire incident. But in the meantime the Sasquatch tale inspired a local Boy Scout group to name Ape Cave (see Hike #21), a lava tube 8 miles away on the mountain's south flank. Today, visitors are often confused that the canyon and cave are otherwise unrelated and are located so far apart.

Drive Interstate 5 to Woodland exit 21 (north of Portland 25 miles), and turn right, following signs for Cougar. After 35 miles (beyond the town of Cougar 6.7 miles), turn left on Road 83 for 11.2 paved miles to the Ape Canyon Trailhead on the left, just a few hundred yards before the road ends at Lava Canyon.

The Ape Canyon Trail starts out along a cliff overlooking the Muddy River's vast lahar—a flow of mud, rock, and ash unleashed when the volcano's 1980 eruption melted much of the Shoestring Glacier. The forest beside the moon-scape lahar was unscathed by the blast. However, the first 1.4 miles of the trail's route are still recovering from a 1968 clearcut. Deer and elk frequently browse the vine maples and alder here. Look for red paintbrush, dwarf blue lupine, and purple asters, too. Then the path dives into an impressive old-growth stand of 6-foot-thick hemlocks and Douglas firs hung with gray-green old-man's-beard lichen. White June wildflowers here include delicate inside-out flower and vanilla leaf.

At the 4-mile mark the trail enters the blast zone of trees killed by superheated air. Ahead, the lahar's mudflow plain snakes up toward the gray volcano, serrated by gullies. To the right, Ape Canyon's still-green valley gradually narrows to a slot-like chasm framing a view of snowy Mt. Adams.

The path joins the round-the-mountain Loowit Trail in a pumice plain with an "Ape Canyon" sign. Unless you're bushed, it's worth turning right here to hike the Loowit Trail 0.8 mile to the Plains of Abraham, a rock-strewn desert backed by the mountain like a wall. Overhead hang the Shoestring, Ape, and Nelson Glaciers, slowly dwindling for lack of a summit.

Old-growth forest along the Ape Canyon Trail.   Opposite: Alpine lupine leaves.

25   Lava Canyon

Easy (to suspension bridge)
1.3-mile loop
300 feet elevation gain
Open mid-April to mid-November
Map: Mt. St. Helens Nat'l. Mon. (USFS)

Moderate (to third bridge)
5.3 miles round-trip
1400 feet elevation gain

This spectacular trail follows a mudflow-scoured chasm past waterfalls and ancient lava cliffs. An easy loop circles the upper gorge, crossing the canyon twice on scenic footbridges. More adventurous hikers can continue downstream on a narrower tread that descends a dizzying 40-foot ladder before leveling out in the vast mudflow flats of raging Smith Creek. Pets are not allowed. Entrance fees are no longer charged at Lava Canyon, but you will need a standard National Forest parking permit for you car.

The recently exposed rock formations in Lava Canyon are remnants of a Mt. St. Helens lava flow that coursed down the Muddy River's valley 3500 years ago. The basalt lava fractured into a honeycomb of pillar-like columns as it cooled. When the river then cut down through the flow it carved waterfall chutes and left free-standing lava towers such as The Ship. Later stream debris buried the formations until the 1980 eruption, when the melting Shoestring Glacier loosed a gigantic lahar (mudflow) that washed Lava Canyon clean.

To find the trailhead, drive Interstate 5 north of Portland 25 miles to Woodland exit 21 and turn right, following signs for Cougar. After 35 miles (beyond the town of Cougar 6.7 miles), turn left onto paved Road 83 for 11.3 miles to a turnaround at road's end.

The path is wide and paved for its first 0.4 mile, with viewpoint decks and interpretive signs. Then turn right to cross a metal footbridge. Below the span

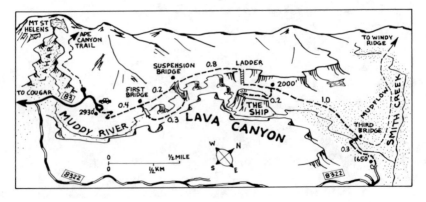

The suspension footbridge.   Opposite: Waterfalls in Lava Canyon.

are a series of frothing waterfalls and churning river cauldrons. Hang tight to small children from here on. The path downstream follows a basalt cliff for 0.3 mile and then recrosses the gorge on a high, scary-looking suspension bridge.

For the short loop, turn left after crossing the suspension bridge and return to the car. For a more rugged hike (not suitable for children), turn right and continue downstream past a string of colossal waterfalls. The steep trail crosses cliffy slopes with no railings, and the tread can be slippery in wet weather, so be sure to wear boots with good soles. Climb down a 40-foot metal ladder and a few hundred yards later turn right on a side trail that scrambles 0.2 mile to a viewpoint atop The Ship, a 100-foot-tall lava block in mid-canyon. Then return to the main trail and continue downstream.

The trail's final section crosses a 1980 mudflow plain that's slowly regrowing with dwarf lupine wildflowers and scattered fir trees. An elk herd commonly ranges here. Make your turnaround point the third bridge of the hike, where the path crosses the Muddy River in this mudflow plain. Return as you came.

Other Hiking Options

If you can arrange a short car shuttle, you can hike the Lava Canyon Trail one way, all downhill. To leave a car at the lower trailhead, turn off Road 83 just 0.7 mile before the Lava Canyon Trailhead and follow gravel Road 8322 downhill for 4.8 miles to its end at the Smith Creek Trailhead.

26 Mt. St. Helens Crater

Moderate (to Loowit Falls)
8.8 miles round-trip
800 feet elevation gain
Open late June through October
Map: Mt. St. Helens NW (Green Trails)

Difficult (to Plains of Abraham)
11.7-mile loop
1400 feet elevation gain

Now that Mt. St. Helens has quieted, a trail has been opened to the ragged mouth of the crater, where steaming, 200-foot Loowit Falls tumbles through a badlands chasm. Pioneer wildflowers struggle from the ash at oasis-like springs. Log-jammed Spirit Lake stretches to the north.

Because this route crosses a restricted zone under scientific study, hikers must stay within 10 feet of the trail. Pets and camping are banned. If you'd like to return on a slightly longer loop, however, you can hike beyond the restricted zone to the breathtakingly desolate Plains of Abraham and a view-packed ridge ablaze with wildflowers. No trails access the lava dome inside the volcano's crater because of rockfall and eruption danger. Per-person fees are no longer charged at the Windy Ridge trailhead, but you will need a standard National Forest parking permit for your car.

To find the trailhead, drive Interstate 5 to Woodland exit 21 (north of Portland 25 miles), turn right toward Cougar, and continue a total of 88 paved miles, following signs for Windy Ridge. Along the way, you'll drive Highway 503 through the town of Cougar, continue straight on what becomes Road 90 to the Pine Creek Information Station, go straight on Road 25 for 25 miles, and turn

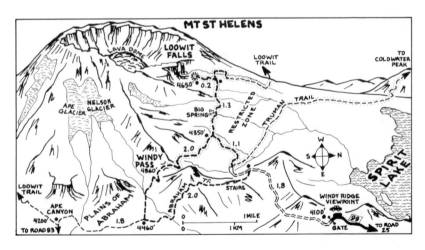

Loowit Falls.   Opposite: Spirit Lake from the trail.

left on Road 99. Follow this paved road for 16 miles to its end.

Park at the Windy Ridge Viewpoint and walk up the gated gravel road ahead. Since the 1980 blast, only scattered trees have taken root on this ridge, but wildflowers have flourished. Look for tall red fireweed, pearly everlasting, purple daisy-shaped asters, and clumps of big purple penstemons. National Monument rules forbid disturbing plants or rocks, so don't take samples of the pumice littering the road.

After 1.8 miles the Abraham Trail joins on the left—the return route of an optional loop. Continue to road's end and take the Windy Trail. This path follows big cairns across a barren pumice plain and climbs a mile to the round-the-mountain Loowit Trail. Turn right across a creek gully, contour 1.3 miles to the crater's mouth, and take a 0.2-mile side path up to the Loowit Falls viewpoint. While this ridgecrest is dramatic, it's a bit bleak for lunch. So go back down to the Loowit Trail and turn left a few hundred yards to a cozier canyon where the path crosses the crater's cascading outlet creek. The lava dome, out of sight in the crater above, heats this creek to a steamy 96 degrees Fahrenheit.

If you'd like to make a loop on your return trip, hike back along the Loowit Trail and continue straight, climbing over Windy Pass to the eerily barren Plains of Abraham. The mountain rises like a wall from this rock-strewn desert. Camping is permitted, but the only water is a weird creek of what looks like chocolate milk oozing from the decapitated Nelson Glacier. Turn left at a well-marked junction, recross the sludgy creek, and traverse a glorious ridge packed with July wildflowers and views of Mt. Adams before descending two sets of steps to join the road back to the car.

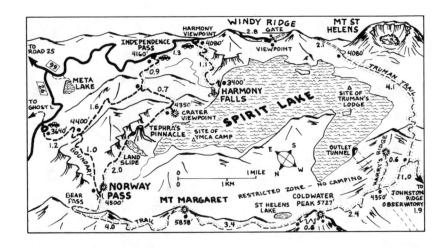

27   Spirit Lake

Easy (to Harmony Falls)
2.2 miles round-trip
700 feet elevation loss
Open late June through October
Map: Mt. St. Helens Nat'l. Mon. (USFS)

Easy (to Crater Viewpoint)
3.2 miles round-trip
650 feet elevation gain

Moderate (to Norway Pass)
7.1-mile loop
980 feet elevation gain

When Mt. St. Helens' summit slid into Spirit Lake in 1980 it not only buried Harry Truman's famous lodge under 200 feet of rubble, but it also launched a gigantic wave that sloshed 800 feet up the lake's far shore, obliterating three youth camps and denuding the slopes. Today wildflowers and small trees are gradually returning to this landscape, but hikers can still see the pale high-water mark left by the wave and the vast jumble of driftwood it washed into the lake.

The best views of Spirit Lake are from two dramatic trails: the short, heavily-used Harmony Falls Trail that descends to the actual lake shore, and the nearby Independence Pass Trail that climbs past Crater Viewpoint to Norway Pass. The paths are short enough that some hikers do both in a day. Both offer picturesque views across the lake to the crater's smoldering lava dome. Pets are not allowed.

To start, drive Interstate 5 to Woodland exit 21 (north of Portland 25 miles). Turn right toward Cougar and follow signs for Windy Ridge a total of 85 paved miles. Along the way, you'll follow Highway 503 through the town of Cougar, continue straight on what becomes Road 90 to the Pine Creek Information Station, go straight on Road 25 for 25 miles, and turn left on Road 99 for 13.3

miles to the Harmony Viewpoint (2.7 miles before road's end at Windy Ridge). Per-person fees are no longer charged at this trailhead, but you will need a standard National Forest parking permit for your car.

The 1.1-mile Harmony Trail descends from the viewpoint amid blast-killed snags, young alders, and hopeful firs. Red fireweed dominates these slopes, but also look for pearly everlasting, blue huckleberries, salmonberries, and inside-out flower. The path dips below a cliff and then traverses a dusty plain with flotsam logs left from the gigantic wave. Finally descend along Harmony Creek's stairstep falls to the shore, 200 feet above Spirit Lake's old level. Off-trail hiking, camping, and venturing out on the driftwood logs are banned.

To hike the next trail, drive 1.3 miles back on Road 99 to the Independence Pass Viewpoint. This path climbs a ridge ablaze with fireweed. Look for Mt. Adams to the east and Mt. Hood to the north. After 0.9 mile, keep left. In another 0.7 mile a short side trail to the left descends to Crater Viewpoint, a knoll almost 800 feet above Spirit Lake's log-jammed shore.

You could turn back at Crater Viewpoint, but the next 2 miles of trail are spectacular, passing Tephra's Pinnacle (a 100-foot spire of welded ash) on the way to a picture-postcard view of Mt. St. Helens from Norway Pass. To return on a loop, turn right at Norway Pass. Follow the Boundary Trail a mile, and then keep right on a 1.6-mile connector path that climbs across a rocky ridge amid blast-killed snags en route back to your car.

Mt. St. Helens from near Norway Pass.   *Opposite: Driftwood logs in Spirit Lake.*

Upper Lewis River Falls.   Opposite: Lower Lewis River Falls.

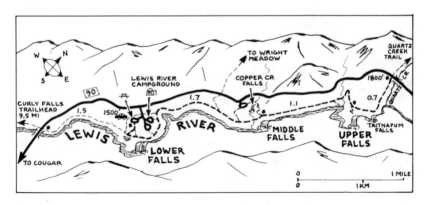

28   Lewis River Falls

Easy
7 miles round-trip
500 feet elevation gain
Open all year
Use: hikers, horses, bicycles
Map: Lone Butte (Green Trails)

The Lewis River thunders over three colossal falls along this riverbank path. Because a paved road parallels the route, it's easy to plan a car (or bicycle) shuttle and hike the 3.5-mile trail one way—but the path's pretty enough you probably won't mind hiking it twice.

Drive Interstate 5 north of Portland 25 miles, turn right at Woodland exit 21, and follow signs for Mt. St. Helens for 46.7 miles. Along the way, you'll follow Highway 503, go through the town of Cougar, and continue straight on what becomes Road 90. Just beyond the Pine Creek Information Station, turn right toward Carson on what is still Road 90 and follow this paved road for 14.2 miles to the Lower Falls Recreation Area on your right. Keep right to the picnic area loop and park by the restrooms.

A graveled trail sets off through Douglas fir woods with lots of pointy-leaved Oregon grape, dark-berried salal, and vine maple. After 100 yards take a right-hand fork of the trail that leads to an overlook of Lower Falls, where the Lewis River takes a magnificent Niagara-like plunge into a huge green pool.

Several trails from the nearby campground confuse things a bit here, but if you simply follow the riverbank upstream and ignore all left-hand forks you can't go wrong. After half a mile the graveled path turns to duff. In another mile you'll cross a footbridge above Copper Creek's 200-foot, double-humped waterslide into the Lewis River. You can visit another of Copper Creek's waterfalls by taking a half-mile loop to the left on well-marked side trails—but save this detour for the return trip.

Continue along the Lewis River past Middle Falls, a 100-foot-long, milky-looking slide. The river trail soon ducks below a huge, overhanging cliff and enters a grove of massive old-growth Douglas firs and red cedars up to 10 feet thick. About 0.8 mile past Middle Falls you'll pass a trailside campsite with a bouldery beach and a glimpse ahead to Upper Falls. This is the only beach on the hike where kids can safely play by the river.

Next the trail bridges Alec Creek and climbs above Upper Falls, where a side trail leads to the 80-foot cascade's lip. The final 0.7 mile of the Lewis River Trail passes humble Taitnapum Falls and follows Quartz Creek to a bridge on Road 90, just 2.7 miles by road from your car.

29   Cultus Lake

Moderate (to Cultus Lake)
4.4 miles round-trip
1100 feet elevation gain
Open July to mid-Octobe
Use: hikers, horses
Map: Indian Heaven Wilderness (USFS)

Moderate (to Lake Wapiki overlook)
6.8 miles round-trip
1600 feet elevation gain

The Indian Heaven country features alpine meadows, sparkling lakes, and world-famous huckleberry fields—but because this Wilderness lacks a major Cascade mountain it seldom draws crowds. The trail to Cultus Lake makes up for this by sneaking views of not-so-distant Mt. Adams. And if you hike an extra 1.2 miles through the heather you'll get even better views from craggy Lemei Rock, an ancient volcano that cups Lake Wapiki within its crater.

Until the 1920s Indians came to this high country each August to pick berries, hunt, and race horses. Natural and set wildfires maintained the berry fields and meadows. Even today the non-Wilderness huckleberry fields northeast of Highway 24 are reserved for Indians. Then as now, mosquitoes are a problem in July.

Drive Interstate 84 to Cascade Locks exit 44, pay a 75-cent toll to cross the Bridge of the Gods, turn right on Highway 14 for 5.9 miles, and turn left through Carson on Highway 30 for 14.5 miles. Next, following a sign for Mt. St. Helens, turn right on paved Wind River Road 30 for 15.8 miles. Then turn right onto gravel Lone Butte Road (Road 30) for 7.9 miles, and finally turn right on gravel Road 24 for 4.2 miles to the Cultus Creek Campground. Park at the far end of the campground loop by a sign for the Indian Heaven Trail.

The trail climbs steeply through Douglas fir woods for a mile to a view of several peaks—from left to right, Sawtooth Mountain, Mt. Rainier, the Goat Rocks, and Mt. Adams. Then the path continues uphill to a small meadow below Bird Mountain's cliffs before leveling off for a mile. You'll reach a trail junction at your first glimpse of Cultus Lake. Explore to the left if you wish— the path deadends in 0.3 mile at Deep Lake. Otherwise keep right around beautiful, alpine Cultus Lake to a junction with the Lemei Trail. In Chinook jargon, the old trade language of Northwest tribes, *Lemei* means "old woman" and *Cultus,* oddly enough, means "worthless."

For a longer hike, take the Lemei Trail up through a mile of gorgeous heather meadows, switchback up to the base of Lemei Rock's summit crags, and continue a few hundred yards to the red cinder rim of the old crater overlooking lovely Lake Wapiki, Mt. Adams, and Mt. Hood. If you're eager for a swim, it's 1.1 miles further down to the meadows and sandy beach at Lake Wapiki, but remember to save energy for the return climb.

Other Hiking Options

Two moderate loop trips also begin with the hike to Cultus Lake. For a 9.2-mile

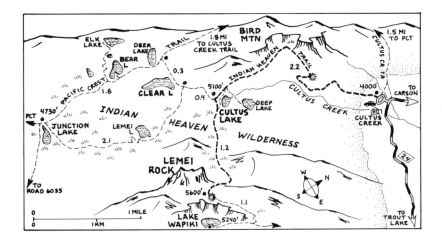

meadow tour of 6 lakes, continue straight on the Indian Heaven Trail to the Pacific Crest Trail, turn left to Junction Lake (also accessible via Hike #30), and turn left on the Lemei Lake Trail. For a woodsy 6.2-mile loop around Bird Mountain, take the Indian Heaven Trail to the PCT, turn right for 1.8 level miles, and turn right on the Cultus Creek Trail over a low pass for the steep descent to your car.

Lemei Rock from its base.   Opposite: Lemei Rock from Cultus Lake.

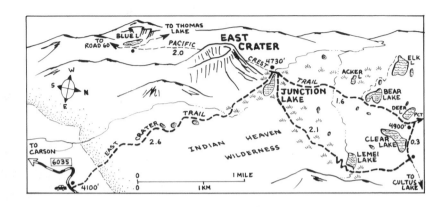

TO THOMAS LAKE
TO ROAD 60
BLUE L
PACIFIC 2.0
EAST CRATER
CREST 4730'
ELK
ACKER L
TRAIL
JUNCTION LAKE
BEAR LAKE
DEER
PCT
1.6
4900'
0.3
TO CARSON
6035
EAST CRATER TRAIL 2.6
INDIAN HEAVEN WILDERNESS
2.1
CLEAR LAKE
LEMEI LAKE
TO CULTUS LAKE
4100'
W N S E
0   1 MILE
0   1 KM

Junction Lake. Opposite: Clear Lake.

30   Junction Lake

Easy (to Junction Lake)
5.2 miles round-trip
700 feet elevation gain
Open mid-June to mid-October
Use: hikers, horses
Map: Indian Heaven Wildns. (USFS)

Moderate (to Lemei Lake)
9.2-mile loop
900 feet elevation gain

The East Crater Trail provides the easiest route to the famous alpine meadows of the Indian Heaven Wilderness. And once you reach huckleberry-rimmed Junction Lake, it's tempting to make an additional 4-mile loop on the Pacific Crest Trail past four other large lakes and vast fields of heather.

Drive Interstate 84 to Cascade Locks exit 44, pay 75 cents to cross the Bridge of the Gods, turn right on Highway 14 for 5.9 miles, and turn left through Carson on Highway 30 for 5.7 miles. Following signs for Panther Creek Campground, turn briefly right and then jog left on what becomes Road 65. Follow this curvy paved road for 11 miles, turn right on gravel Road 60 for 8.6 miles, and then follow an "East Crater Trail" pointer left onto Road 6030 (which becomes Road 6035) for 4.1 miles to a trailhead sign on the left.

The path's first 1.4 miles climb gradually through unremarkable mountain hemlock woods— a long stretch for hikers with small children. But then you pass three tadpole-filled ponds and the meadowed openings become larger and larger, leading over a low pass to Junction Lake. The heather blooms here in July—a month when mosquitoes are a real problem. In August the huckleberries ripen, while the crisp nights of September turn the huckleberry leaves gold and red. If you're backpacking, be sure to camp in the woods and not in the fragile meadows.

To continue on the loop, go to the Pacific Crest Trail junction at the far end of the lake, turn right across the outlet creek's bridge, and promptly turn right on the Lemei Lake Trail. This path ambles through heather and past grassy-banked Lemei Lake. After 2.1 miles turn left on the Indian Heaven Trail, which leads between a huge rockslide and Clear Lake. Then turn left on the PCT to complete the loop. Short side trails to the right of the PCT lead down to forest-rimmed Deer and Bear Lakes, as well as to unseen Elk Lake.

Other Hiking Options

To explore more of this high country, either take a side trip from Clear Lake north 0.4 mile to Cultus Lake (see Hike #29), or take the PCT south from Junction Lake 2 miles to Blue Lake (see Hike #31). Adventurers who are careful to use compass can also bushwhack due south a mile from Junction Lake up the steep, forested flank of East Crater to a viewpoint on the volcano's east rim. In the middle of the crater is an eerie, hidden meadow with a rarely visited pond.

31   Thomas Lake

Easy (to Thomas Lake)
1.4 miles round-trip
300 feet elevation gain
Open mid-June to mid-October
Use: hikers, horses
Map: Indian Heaven Wilderness (USFS)

Moderate (to Blue Lake)
6.8 miles round-trip
900 feet elevation gain

Children and lake-lovers of all ages enjoy exploring the five lakes clustered in the forest within the first mile of the Thomas Lake Trail. For a longer hike, cross Indian Heaven's glorious heather-and-huckleberry meadows to sapphire Blue Lake, backed by the cliffs of Gifford Peak.

To find the trailhead, take Interstate 84 to Cascade Locks exit 44, pay 75 cents to cross the Bridge of the Gods, turn right on Highway 14 for 5.9 miles, and turn left through Carson on Highway 30 for 5.7 miles. Following signs for Panther Creek Campground, turn briefly right and then jog left on what becomes Road 65. After 12.9 paved miles, fork to the right on a gravel continuation of Road 65 for 6.7 miles to the signed Thomas Lake Trail parking area on the right.

The trail begins in a partially logged area with a view of Mt. St. Helens, but soon climbs into uncut woods of lichen-draped mountain hemlock and Pacific silver fir. Blue huckleberries ripen here in August. Mosquitoes can be thick in July.

After 0.7 mile the path squeezes between three lakes. Just beyond a little footbridge, explorers might want to try a side trail to the right that leads past several heavily used campsites and continues faintly 0.5 mile around Thomas Lake. Otherwise continue on the main trail 100 yards to a major, unmarked fork.

The left-hand fork deadends in 0.2 mile at Eunice Lake. If you've set a more distant goal, keep right and climb up a steep, rough switchback to a wooded

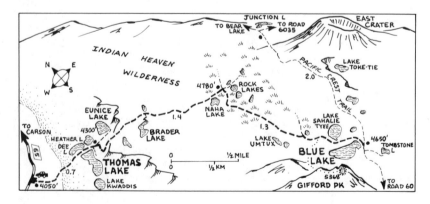

plateau. After another half mile you'll pass a pond on the left. Immediately opposite this pond, on the right-hand side of the trail, a faint side path leads 100 yards over a small ridge to hidden, rarely-visited Brader Lake.

Beyond this point the main trail has a few more steep, rocky pitches before leveling off amid heavenly alpine meadows. Turn right at a 4-way junction, ramble 0.8 miles to a T-shaped junction at a pond, and turn right for a final half mile through the woods to the Pacific Crest Trail at the end of Blue Lake.

Other Hiking Options

The lake-dotted high meadows invite exploration. For a loop along an abandoned trail, turn left at the T-shaped junction 0.5 mile before Blue Lake, pass a "Trail Not Maintained" sign, and take the easily followed path 1.7 miles through the meadows to Junction Lake (also accessible via Hike #30). Then turn right on the PCT for 2 woodsy miles to Blue Lake.

Adventurers with compass in hand can also bushwhack to a rare viewpoint atop Gifford Peak. From Blue Lake, hike back past Sahalie Tyee Lake to the Thomas Lake Trail's highest point in the forest and strike off to the left up a wooded ridge, gaining 700 feet in 0.8 mile.

Thomas Lake.   Opposite: Blue huckleberries.

32　Falls Creek Falls

Easy (lower trail)
3.4 miles round-trip
650 feet elevation gain
Open April 1 to November 30
Use: hikers, bicycles
Map: Wind River, WA (Green Trails)

Moderate (to top of falls)
6.3-mile loop
1150 feet elevation gain
Use: hikers, horses, bicycles

The Lower Falls Creek Trail crosses a suspension footbridge over a mossy gorge on its way to a colossal, 200-foot waterfall. For a loop, return via a longer, upper path along the forested canyon's rim.

Start by driving Interstate 84 to Cascade Locks exit 44. Pay a 75-cent toll to cross the Bridge of the Gods, turn right on Highway 14 for 5.9 miles, and then turn left through Carson on Highway 30 for 14.5 miles. Next, following a sign for Mt. St. Helens, turn right on paved Wind River Road 30 for 0.8 mile. Then turn right onto gravel Road 3062 for 2 miles and fork to the right onto Road 057 for half a mile to road's end, where there's a turnaround for the Lower Falls Creek Trail.

The path begins in a second-growth forest where ancient stumps still show the springboard notches left by timber fallers with crosscut saws. Soon the path enters old-growth woods with Douglas firs five feet in diameter. Also look for larch (or *tamarack*), a tree that usually grows east of the Cascades. This conifer packs 17 to 21 needles in each cluster, but loses them in fall, so it looks dead all winter.

After 0.4 mile the path crosses Falls Creek on a 30-foot suspension footbridge. Frilly stalks of maidenhair fern waft from the gorge cliffs below. Continue 1.3 miles upstream, climbing to trail's end at a viewpoint beside Falls Creek Falls. The 3-tiered cascade starts with a hidden 50-foot falls, spreads across a 70-foot

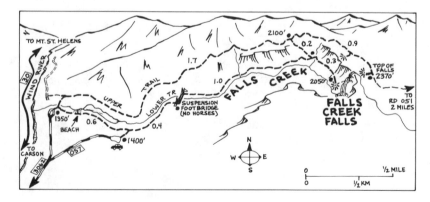

Falls Creek Falls. Opposite: The suspension footbridge.

fan, and finally thunders 80 feet into a rock punchbowl.

If you'd like to return on a loop, walk back from the falls 0.3 mile, watching for an unmarked scramble trail on the right. It starts a few hundred yards beyond a bouldery side creek. This unofficial but obvious path climbs steeply up a ridge 0.2 mile to the Upper Falls Creek Trail. To visit a viewpoint near the top of the falls, turn right on this upper trail 0.9 mile and take a spur 100 yards to the right. Although you can't see much of the falls from this clifftop perch, the view of the valley below is nice. A very rough scramble trail does continue down to the actual falls, but it's too steep to risk. Instead declare victory here and head back down the Upper Falls Creek Trail.

After descending 2.6 miles through the woods, turn left at an unmarked trail junction just before an abandoned road, cross the creek on a wide footbridge, and turn left again along a creekside trail. Soon you'll pass a small gravel beach, a good place for kids to play in the water on a hot day. When the path rejoins the Lower Falls Creek Trail, turn right 150 yards to your car.

Other Options

Because the suspension footbridge on the lower trail is closed to horses, equestrians start at the end of Road 3062 and take the Upper Falls Creek Trail instead. After passing the top of the falls, this path levels off for 2 viewless miles to its end at gravel Road 051.

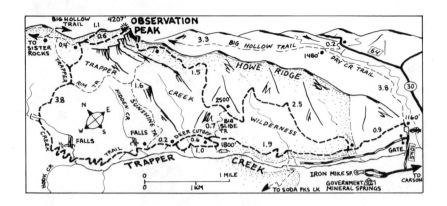

33   Trapper Creek

Moderate (to Deer Cutoff loop)
7.2 miles round-trip
1000 feet elevation gain
Open all year
Map: Trapper Creek Wilderness (USFS)

Difficult (to Observation Peak)
14.6-mile loop
3200 feet elevation gain
Open June to mid-November

Just 15 miles north of the Columbia Gorge, the densely forested Trapper Creek Wilderness features a well-marked network of hiking paths. For a moderate trip, explore the valley's jungly old-growth groves on rugged trails built by Portland Mazama club volunteers. For a challenging loop with plenty of elevation gain, continue on smoother Forest Service trails to Observation Peak, a former lookout site with views from Mt. Rainier to Mt. Jefferson.

Health-conscious tourists were first attracted to the Trapper Creek area by a bubbly, metallic-tasting bubbly soda spring. Entrepreneurs built a 3-story spa hotel by the spring in the early 1900s. The lodge burned in 1934 but the spring remains in a picnic area, the Government Mineral Springs Day Use Area.

Drive Interstate 84 to Cascade Locks exit 44, pay a 75-cent toll to cross the Bridge of the Gods, turn right on Highway 14 for 5.9 miles, and turn left through Carson on Highway 30 for 14.5 miles to a junction. Go straight on Mineral Springs Road for 0.4 mile and then turn right onto gravel Road 5401 for 0.4 mile to the trailhead parking lot.

Hike a few feet up the path and turn left on the Trapper Creek Trail, which contours 0.9 mile through second-growth Douglas fir woods to a 4-way trail junction. To the right is the return route of the loop to Observation Peak, but for now keep straight. Follow the narrowing Trapper Creek Trail another 1.9 miles and then go straight on the Deer Cutoff Trail 0.6 mile to a junction.

For the moderate hike, turn left here and descend a steep, rooty path to a mossy grove of huge, 7-foot-thick Douglas firs in the canyon bottom. Here you'll gain your first views of rushing Trapper Creek, though access to the brushy bank amidst this jungle still requires some scrambling. The 1-mile path passes a small campsite and climbs steeply back to the route to your car.

For the longer loop, continue straight from the Deer Cutoff Trail onto the upper continuation of the Trapper Creek Trail. The path is narrow and rooty for 1.4 miles. Then the path crosses Trapper Creek on a single-log footbridge and switchbacks steeply up a 1000-foot ridge, passing a viewpoint of 100-foot Trapper Creek Falls. Follow the path across a forested plateau, recross Trapper Creek, and 0.8 mile later ignore a junction for the Rim Trail on the right. In another 0.1 mile, however, turn right at a fork for the Observation Cutoff Trail. Ceramic insulators and wire along this route show it follows the old telephone line for the peak's long-gone fire lookout tower.

When you reach a larger trail at a saddle, turn right a few feet to another T-shaped junction. To the right is the 0.6-mile path to the summit viewpoint amid clusters of big blue gentians and delicate bluebells. To the left is the loop's return path— an amazingly well-graded 6-mile route down Howe Ridge.

Other Hiking Options

The Big Hollow Trail provides an easier route to Observation Peak, gaining 2700 feet in just 4.5 miles. Drive as to the Trapper Creek Trailhead, but stick to Highway 30 for an additional 2.2 miles (following signs for Mt. St. Helens) and veer left on Dry Creek Road 64 for 2.3 miles to the trailhead on the left. The trail crosses Big Hollow Creek (use stepping stones or a nearby log) and climbs 3.8 miles up a ridge to a saddle junction. Here you can either turn left for 1 mile to Observation Peak or turn right for 0.5 mile and bushwhack left 0.5 mile up through huckleberry meadows to a similar view atop Sisters Rocks.

Mt. St. Helens from Observation Peak.   *Opposite: Trapper Creek.*

34 Beacon Rock Park

Easy (to Beacon Rock)
1.8 miles round-trip
600 feet elevation gain
Open all year
Map: Bridal Veil (Green Trails)

Easy (to Rodney Falls)
2.2 miles round-trip
600 feet elevation gain

Difficult (to Hamilton Mountain)
7.6-mile loop
2000 feet elevation gain

Beacon Rock State Park boasts two of the Columbia Gorge's most famous and popular trails: a switchbacking path up Beacon Rock's 848-foot-tall block of basalt, and a longer trail that passes beautiful Rodney Falls before climbing steeply to cliff-edge viewpoints on Hamilton Mountain.

Lewis and Clark named Beacon Rock in 1805 while paddling past its cliffs. In 1915 a man named Henry Biddle bought the rock and arduously constructed a well-graded trail to the top, incorporating 47 switchbacks and dozens of railed catwalk bridges. When the Army Corps of Engineers suggested the monolith be blown up for use as a jetty at the mouth of the Columbia, Biddle's family tried to make the area a state park. At first Washington refused the gift. But that decision quickly changed when *Oregon* offered to accept.

To find the park, take Interstate 205 north across the Columbia River and turn right on Highway 14 for 28.6 miles. Expect a special $5 parking fee. If you're driving here from the east, take Interstate 84 to Cascade Locks exit 44, pay 75 cents to cross the Bridge of the Gods, and turn left on Highway 14 for 6.9 miles.

To climb Beacon Rock, park in one of the roadside pullouts on either side of Beacon Rock and walk 50 yards along the highway to the signed trailhead, halfway between the parking areas. Although nearly all of the 0.9-mile route has railings, parents may want to hold small children's hands to make sure they

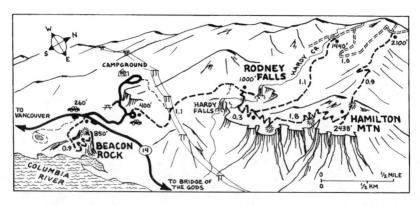

View from Hamilton Mountain's cliffs.   Opposite: Beacon Rock from Nesmith Point.

stay on the path. From the top, the view stretches from Crown Point to Bonneville Dam. Kids love to point out Burlington Northern's toy trains chugging by, far below. Tiny powerboats cut white V's in the Columbia's green shallows.

If you'd rather take the Hamilton Mountain Trail, turn off Highway 14 opposite Beacon Rock, drive 0.3 mile up a paved road toward the campground, and then veer to the right into a trailhead parking lot.

The path climbs through a second-growth Douglas fir forest with red thimbleberries, blue Oregon grape, and bracken fern. Soon you pass under a powerline, where a trail from the campground joins on the left. At the 1-mile mark a side trail to the right descends to a poor viewpoint of Hardy Falls. Continue on the main trail a few hundred yards and go left on a side trail that ends at a railed cliff beside Rodney Falls, a fascinating, 50-foot cascade trapped in an enormous rock-walled bowl. Return to the main trail and switchback down to a footbridge below the falls — a good turnaround point for hikers with children.

If you're continuing, switchback uphill, keep left at an unmarked fork (the right-hand path descends to the creek above Hardy Falls), and climb 0.2 mile to a fork marking the start of the loop. Keep right on a steep, switchbacking trail up a cliff-edged ridge with dizzying views across the Columbia Gorge. After 1.8 miles you'll finally reach a T-shaped junction at the summit ridgecrest. The path to the right promptly deadends at Hamilton Mountain's summit, where the view is partly obscured by brush.

To continue the loop, turn around and follow the ridgecrest trail past better viewpoints of Mt. Hood, Mt. Adams, and Table Rock. After 0.9 mile, turn left down an abandoned road. Keep left on the road for 1.0 mile to a meadow at a creek crossing. Here veer left onto a level path through a cool alder forest. After 1.1 mile, this path joins the main trail. Turn right to return to your car.

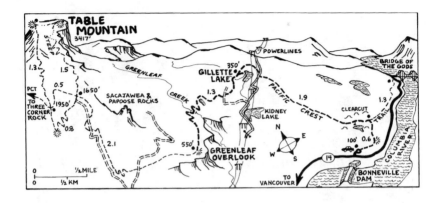

35   Gillette Lake

Easy (to Gillette Lake)
5 miles round-trip
300 feet elevation gain
Open all year
Use: hikers, horses
Map: Bonneville Dam (Green Trails)

Moderate (to Greenleaf Overlook)
7.6 miles round-trip
600 feet elevation gain

This convenient stretch of the famous Pacific Crest Trail heads north from Bonneville Dam through a nearly level forest (and a half-mile-long clearcut from 2001) to the grassy bank of Gillette Lake. For a slightly longer hike, continue past two pretty creeks to a view of the Columbia Gorge at Greenleaf Overlook. Truly hardy hikers can go on to climb landmark Table Mountain — a grueling 15.1-mile round-trip.

The hike's route crosses an enormous landslide that sheared off Table Mountain 700 years ago and dammed the entire Columbia River for days or possibly even months, giving rise to Indian legends of a "Bridge of the Gods" that could be crossed dry-shod. Forest has regrown on the 14-square-mile slide, but the river still swerves toward Oregon here. Watch for other landslide souvenirs along the trail: house-sized boulders, hummocky terrain, and lakes.

Drive Interstate 84 to Cascade Locks exit 44, pay 75 cents to cross the modern-day Bridge of the Gods, and turn left on Highway 14 for 2 miles to the Bonneville Trailhead on the right. Walk briefly up a gated gravel road to a sign announcing the Tamanous Trail to the PCT. Equestrians share this route, so be sure to step off the trail on the downhill side if you meet horses.

The path climbs through a Douglas fir forest with yellow-blooming Oregon grape in spring, red thimbleberries in summer, and scarlet vine maple leaves in fall. Traverse a low, meadowed ridge with a fine view across the Columbia to

Ruckel Ridge (Hike #48) and the canyon of Eagle Creek (Hike #47).

Turn left on the PCT after 0.6 mile amid a clearcut that removed half a mile of trailside forest on private property in 2001. At the 1.7-mile mark the trail briefly skirts a 1990 clearcut. Then the path meets a gravel road, continues on the far side 50 feet to the right, and descends under a powerline. Look on the horizon for Sacajawea and Papoose Rocks, natural rock statues to the left of massive Table Mountain. Then a short spur to the left leads to green Gillette Lake—a pleasant picnic spot. Beware of patches of poison oak brush nearby. Also be sure not to litter, build fires, or wander far afield, because the Pacific Crest Trail here is on a narrow easement across private property.

For a better view, hike another 1.3 miles along the PCT to Greenleaf Overlook, a mossy rim at the edge of the ancient landslide. From here you can survey the broken wall of Columbia Gorge cliffs on the Oregon shore.

Other Hiking Options

For a genuine challenge, continue past Greenleaf Overlook for 2.6 miles on the PCT and turn right on a very steep 1.3-mile path to Table Mountain, a pinched plateau with stunning viewpoints on either edge. Be warned that the climb calls for 3500 of elevation gain—most of it in the grueling final mile. And although it's possible to make a loop of this steep pitch, the eastern path to the top requires some scrambling that's dangerous, particularly in wet weather.

Viewpoint near the start of the trail.   Opposite: Gillette Lake.

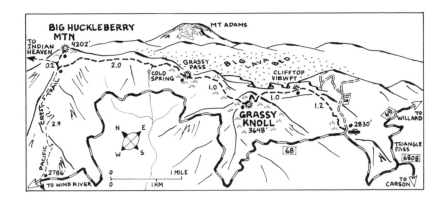

BIG HUCKLEBERRY MTN

MT ADAMS

TO INDIAN HEAVEN

4202'

0.2

2.0

COLD SPRING

GRASSY PASS

BIG LAVA BED

CLIFFTOP VIEWPT

1.0

1.0

GRASSY KNOLL 3648'

1.2

2.9

N E W S

2830'

68

TO WILLARD

TRIANGLE PASS

680g

2786'

0 1 MILE
0 1 KM

PACIFIC CREST TRAIL

68

TO WIND RIVER

TO CARSON

Mt. Adams from clifftop viewpoint.   *Opposite: Mt. Hood from Grassy Knoll.*

36   Grassy Knoll

Moderate (to Grassy Knoll)
4.4 miles round-trip
1200 feet elevation gain
Open April to December
Use: hikers, horses, bicycles
Maps: Big Huckleberry Mtn., Willard
    (Washington, USGS)

Difficult (to Big Huckleberry Mountain)
10.8 miles round-trip
2850 feet elevation gain
Open late May to early November

With wildflower meadows and views of Mt. Adams and Mt. Hood, this ridgecrest path provides an uncrowded alternative to the steep, heavily used Dog Mountain Trail nearby (Hike #37). For a short hike, follow the rolling ridge to a former lookout site at Grassy Knoll. For a longer walk, continue to a taller lookout site atop Big Huckleberry Mountain.

To find the trailhead, drive Interstate 84 to Cascade Locks exit 44, pay 75 cents to cross the Bridge of the Gods, turn right on Highway 14 for 5.9 miles, turn left through Carson on Highway 30 for 4.2 miles, and then turn right on Bear Creek Road. Follow this road—which becomes Road 6808—for 3.6 paved miles and an additional 7.2 miles of curvy, one-lane gravel to Triangle Pass. Then turn left onto Road 68 for 2.1 miles to where Road 511 joins from the right. Look for the Grassy Knoll Trail sign 50 feet up this side road.

After starting in a small meadow, the path climbs through Douglas fir woods where star-flowered smilacina and vanilla leaf bloom white in May. Although some trees are 5 feet in diameter, winds from the Columbia Gorge keep them short.

After a few steep pitches the trail passes a gravel pit and a clearcut, and then levels off along a lovely clifftop rim with views of Mt. Adams across the Big Lava Bed's forested plain. About 300,000 years ago, basalt from the edge of the Indian Heaven high country leveled this 20-square-mile valley, surged down the Little White Salmon River, and briefly dammed the Columbia.

Continue up and down through increasing meadows for a mile to Grassy Knoll, where sunflower-like balsamroot blooms in May. Foundation piers mark the lookout site. Mt. Hood rises above Nick Eaton Ridge and conical Wind Mountain. Unless you're really tired, it's worth it to continue another mile along the rolling ridgecrest through meadows of beargrass, lupine, and blue huckleberries to the first-rate view from Grassy Pass.

Beyond this open saddle the trail traverses 2 miles through the woods to the Pacific Crest Trail. Turn right here—and keep right at junctions in the next few yards—to find the short path up to a panoramic view in a berry patch at Big Huckleberry Mountain's summit.

37   Dog Mountain

Moderate (to lower viewpoint)
3 miles round-trip
1500 feet elevation gain
Open all year
Map: Trails of the Col. Gorge (USFS)

Difficult (to summit)
6.9-mile loop
2820 feet elevation gain

The most spectacular wildflower meadows of the Columbia Gorge drape the alp-like slopes of Dog Mountain. In May and June these hills are alive with yellow balsamroot, red paintbrush, and blue lupine. Even flowerless seasons provide breathtaking views of the Columbia Gorge. Such beauty has made the steep climb popular, but with three trails to the top, you can choose your route.

From Portland, drive Interstate 84 to Cascade Locks exit 44, take the Bridge of the Gods across the river (paying a 75-cent toll on the way), and turn right on Washington Highway 14 for 12 miles. Between mileposts 53 and 54, at a large sign for the Dog Mountain Trailhead, park in a huge pullout on the left.

Which of the trails up Dog Mountain should you take? For the best views, head uphill on the steep, scenic route. Then you can return on a gentler, longer loop that's easy on the knees. So start out from the far, right-hand end of the parking lot on the Dog Mountain Trail. This path begins along an ancient road but after 100 yards turns sharply left and begins a relentless, switchbacking climb. Beware of lush, three-leaved poison oak along these lower slopes. Also notice early summer wildflowers: baby blue eyes, lupine, yellow desert parsley, and purple cluster lilies on onion-like stalks.

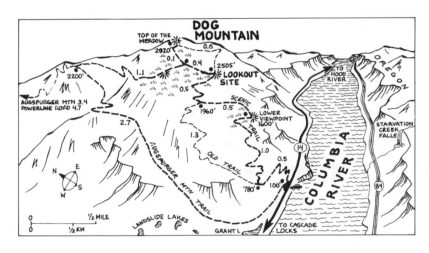

The Columbia Gorge from the summit meadow.   Opposite: Balsamroot.

After half a mile the trail forks. Ignore the left-hand path—the precipitous, viewless Old Trail. Instead turn right, through a Douglas fir forest brightened in spring by big 3-petaled trilliums and tiny 6- or 7-petaled starflowers. This path climbs almost a mile before suddenly emerging at a viewpoint on a windswept, grassy knoll. In early summer, sunflower-like balsamroot and red paintbrush spangle this pleasant picnic spot—a satisfactory turnaround point for a moderate hike. The view extends across the chasm of the Columbia Gorge to Starvation Creek Falls and sometimes-snowy Mt. Defiance.

The grander meadows on Dog Mountain's summit are nearly twice as high as this lower viewpoint. If your legs are up to the challenge, continue half a mile to another junction with the Old Trail. Head uphill here at a gruelingly steep grade for half a mile to an old fire lookout site in a steep wildflower meadow. Take a sharp left turn here and keep heading uphill for another half mile to your destination: the top of the meadow, afloat in panoramic vistas from Hood River to Mt. Hood and Cascade Locks. Notice the flavorful assortment of wildflowers at this lookout: wild strawberry, chocolate lily, and wild onion.

Turn back after soaking in the view from the top of the meadow. (If you keep going, the trail ahead merely dives into viewless woods.) So turn around, hike back down through the meadow 200 yards, and turn right at a sign for Augspurger Mountain. This path descends a ridge with views of its own for 1.1 mile. Then turn left at a junction. For the final 2.7 miles back to your car, the Augspurger Mountain Trail gently spirals halfway around Dog Mountain, like the flight path of an airplane slowly coming in for a landing.

Other Hiking Options

If you're a frequent climber of Dog Mountain, consider tackling Augpurger Mountain instead, a broad, 3667-foot peak with lesser views and less-crowded meadows. Start at the same trailhead, but take the trail to the left 6.1 miles to Augspurger Mountain. Beyond that, the trail descends another 1.7 miles to a powerline access road. A proposed 3.7-mile extension would reach the Grassy Knoll trailhead (see Hike #36), providing a link to the Pacific Crest Trail.

38   Catherine Creek

Easy (3 short hikes)
3.4 miles round-trip
600 feet elevation gain
Open all year
Map: Lyle (USGS)

The first of these three easy hikes follows a paved loop past views of the Columbia Gorge from the Dalles to Hood River. A second hike climbs through Catherine Creek's park-like valley to a natural rock arch. The third walk explores a nearby hillside where mysterious pits in a rockslide are believed to honor the spirits of Indian dead.

Because the trails are so short, it's easy to do them all in a day. If you love wildflowers, you might time your visit to catch the peak displays: grass widows in mid March, blue camas in mid April, and yellow balsamroot in early May.

Start by driving Interstate 84 to Hood River Bridge exit 64. Pay the $1 toll to cross the river. Then turn right onto Washington Highway 14 for 5.8 miles. Just before milepost 71 turn left onto paved Road 1230 around Rowland Lake. After 0.9 mile, when the road climbs a hill, look for a "Road Closed" sign on a spur to the left. This is the trailhead to the Indian pits. To find the trailhead for the first two hikes, continue 0.5 mile along the county road to a large "Catherine Creek" sign on the right.

The first of the three short hikes is a paved, wheelchair-accessible loop that begins on the right, beside the large "Catherine Creek" sign. This wide path tours a dry grassland overlooking the white-capped Columbia River. Scattered ponderosa pines and black oaks provide a bit of shade. Look for Columbia ground squirrels in the fields and cottontail rabbits by the blackberry thickets.

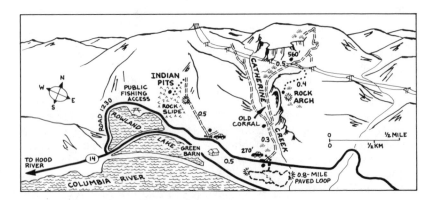

If you keep right at all trail junctions, you'll pass a viewpoint to the west (across the river to Hood River cherry orchards and the top half of Mt. Hood), and a viewpoint to the east (upstream past Memaloose Island to The Dalles), before returning to your car.

For the second hike, walk 50 yards back along the paved county road to a green metal gate on the far side. An abandoned ranch road begins here that explores Catherine Creek's upper canyon. Keep right on the road as it crosses a barren bedrock flat to lusher terrain along the creek. After 0.3 mile go right at a fork and cross the creek. Next the route passes an old corral and stable at the foot of the rock arch—actually a splinter of rimrock on the canyon wall. Then continue up the old road. Just before a powerline you'll reach a meadow where blue lupine blooms in May. This makes a good turnaround point.

Note that the Catherine Creek valley has shrubby clumps of both poison oak and real oak, so pay attention to the difference. The lobed leaves of poison oak are always in clusters of three while real oak has single leaves. At times poison oak can also be identified by white berries or shiny leaves.

For the third short hike (to the Indian pits), return to your car, drive 0.5 mile back west along county Road 1230, and park at the spur on the right marked "Road Closed." Parking is limited here. Walk up the steepish left branch of the spur road for 0.3 mile to a viewpoint where you can see across a huge lava rockslide to Rowland Lake. If you look carefully, you'll notice odd walls and pits in the rockslide. To inspect them, continue 100 yards to the end of the road and rock-hop down the rocky slope. The 5- to 15-foot-wide pits are sometimes clustered in groups of 20 or more within meandering rock walls.

Northwest Indians often built small rock-rimmed meditation sites in places where spirits were thought to be powerful, including many mountain peaks. Young men would fast in such locations in the hopes of receiving a spirit vision to guide their adult life. Are the pits here vision quest sites? Perhaps, since they overlook the Columbia River's Memaloose Island. *Memaloose* means "dead" in the language of the Chinook Indians who once lived here, and the island was an important burial site and spiritual center for that powerful rivergoing tribe.

Catherine Creek's rock arch.   Opposite: The Columbia River from the paved trail.

Columbia Gorge

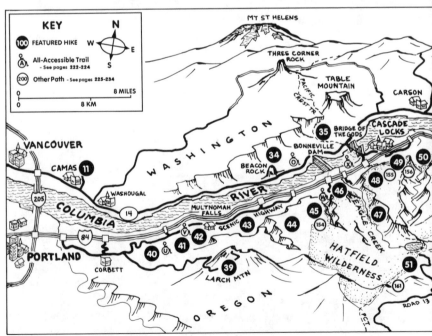

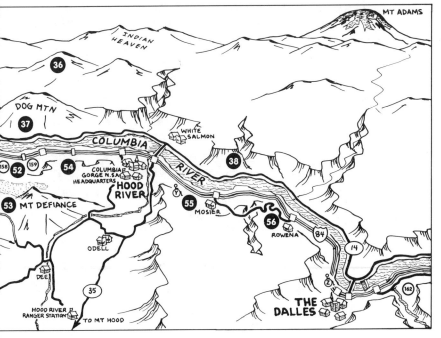

MT ADAMS

INDIAN HEAVEN

36

DOG MTN

37

COLUMBIA

WHITE SALMON

158 52 159 54

COLUMBIA GORGE N.S.A. HEADQUARTERS

HOOD RIVER

RIVER

38

53 MT DEFIANCE

55

MOSIER

56

ROWENA

84

14

ODELL

DEE

35

Y

Z

162

HOOD RIVER RANGER STATION

TO MT HOOD

THE DALLES

39   Larch Mountain Crater

Moderate
6-mile loop
1300 feet elevation gain
Open May through November
Use: hikers, horses, bicycles
Map: Trails of the Columbia Gorge
    (Geo-Graphics)

The panoramic viewpoint atop this 4055-foot volcano deserves its fame. Mount Hood looms across the Bull Run Valley while 4 other snowpeaks mark the horizon. But the charms of Larch Mountain's crater are less well known. A moderate 6-mile loop explores a huge old-growth forest, a meadow of marsh marigolds, and a mossy creek hidden in the throat of the old volcano.

Larch Mountain had a much smaller crater when it stopped erupting some 4 million years ago. During the Ice Age, however, a glacier scoured the peak into an enormous bowl, breached the mountain's north flank, and exposed Sherrard Point—the volcano's central lava plug. When the ice melted, a lake was left that gradually silted in to become a marshy meadow. Trees around the meadow grew to giant size, protected from fire and windstorms by the crater's wall.

Rather than start this loop from the crowded parking area at the summit—which would mean ending the hike with an uphill trudge—it's more fun to start at a secret trailhead near the crater's base.

To find this lower trailhead, take Interstate 84 east of Portland to Corbett exit 22, drive steeply up a mile to Corbett, turn left on the old Columbia River Highway for 2 miles, and then fork to the right on the paved Larch Mountain Road for 11.6 miles. Watch for a sharp curve to the right with a "20 MPH" warning sign and a guardrail. Park along the road's shoulder after the end of the guardrail, but don't block the gate! Then walk past a gate on a small, rough

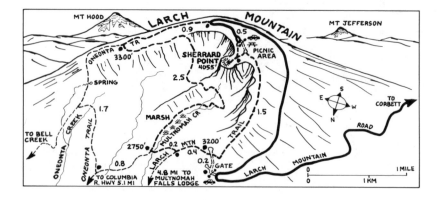

Sherrard Point from inside the crater.   Opposite: Mt. Hood from Sherrard Point.

side road. Keep uphill to the right for a quarter mile. A hundred yards before the road ends you'll see a trail crossing the road. This is the start of the loop.

Turn left on the downhill trail for 0.4 mile. Then turn right onto the Multnomah Creek Way trail and continue down to a 40-foot bridge over Multnomah Creek. The water that later rages over Oregon's tallest falls flows peacefully here amid red cedar, skunk cabbage, and salmonberries. Turn right and follow the creek upstream past a marshy meadow with a view ahead to Sherrard Point's crag. The trail climbs through an ancient grove of hemlock trees.

When you reach a ridgecrest junction, turn right on the Oneonta Trail and climb the ridge. In May this trail is lined with a stunning display of white lilies—both large-leaved trilliums and droopy-headed avalanche lilies. After 0.9 mile the trail ends at the Larch Mountain Road. Walk up the road 0.3 mile to its end and keep right on a paved path to Sherrard Point's railed viewing platform.

To continue the loop, walk back from Sherrard Point but keep right at all junctions. You'll cross a road turnaround, skirt a picnic area, and descend a forested ridge to your car.

Other Hiking Options

To experience the Columbia Gorge from top to bottom, hike from Larch Mountain's 4055-foot summit to the old Columbia River Highway, virtually at sea level. If you can arrange a car shuttle it's a 6.7-mile one-way romp down to the Multnomah Falls Lodge (see Hike #42). Without a shuttle you'll have to start at the bottom— a long, difficult climb.

Lower Latourell Falls.   Opposite: Salmonberry.

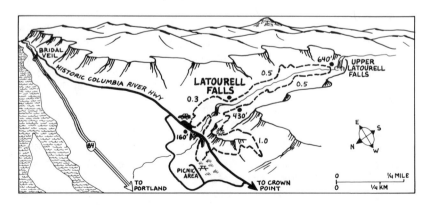

40   Latourell Falls

Easy
2.3-mile loop
600 feet elevation gain
Open all year
Map: Bridal Veil (Green Trails)

Closest to Portland of the Columbia Gorge's great waterfalls, Lower Latourell Falls plunges 249 feet over the lip of an eroded lava flow. An easy 2.3-mile loop trail climbs to the top of the falls, continues to a secluded, 100-foot upper falls, and returns by way of a picnic area.

From Portland take Interstate 84 to Bridal Veil exit 28, turn right on the historic Columbia River Highway, and drive 2.8 miles to the Latourell Falls parking area on the left. If you're coming from Hood River, take exit 35 and follow the old highway 10 miles.

Start on the broad paved path leading *uphill* to the left from the lot. Pavement ends just beyond a first viewpoint. The trail climbs through bigleaf maple woods lush with greenery: delicate black-stalked maidenhair fern, little white-starred candyflowers, stinging nettles, and waterleaf, a low-growing but handsome plant with sharply lobed, foot-wide leaves. In early summer, the trail itself is overhung with edible salmonberries. Shaped like raspberries, these mild-flavored fruits are the pinkish-orange color of fresh salmon.

Pass a viewpoint at the top of the falls and continue upstream. In late spring look here for two closely related pink wildflowers: bleeding hearts (with arching fronds) and corydalis (with tall stalks of pink hoods).

At the 0.8-mile mark the trail crosses a bridge at the splash pool of Upper Latourell Falls, spiraling cascade that arches over a shallow cavern. Continue on the loop trail. The route heads back downstream half a mile and switchback up to a nice viewpoint of the Columbia River. To the west note Rooster Rock, a long splinter of lava that broke off from Crown Point's cliffs only a few thousand years ago and landed upright in the river mud.

Next the loop trail descends to the highway. Cross the road and take the stone steps down to the grassy picnic area. In the middle of the lawn turn right on a paved path that ducks under the 100-foot arch of the highway bridge and emerges at spectacular Lower Latourell Falls. Notice the strangely splayed hexagonal pillars in the falls' cliffy face. This rock began as basalt lava pouring through the Columbia Gorge from Eastern Oregon. Here the lava puddled up. As it slowly cooled, it shrank and fractured into a characteristic honeycomb pattern known as columnar basalt. The resulting splayed pillars are splayed because the surface they cooled against was uneven.

Beyond Lower Latourell Falls, continue on the loop trail up to your car.

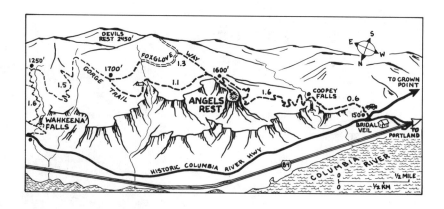

41 Angels Rest

Moderate
4.4 miles round-trip
1500 feet elevation gain
Open all year
Map: Trails of the Columbia Gorge
(Geo-Graphics)

Angels Rest juts like a balcony above the western Columbia Gorge. The trail to this rocky bluff was overswept by a 1991 wildfire, so it traverses an interesting mosaic of forest types. Most of the woods were untouched, while in many areas only the underbrush burned, clearing the forest floor for wildflowers. On a few ridges the trees themselves burned, opening new viewpoints. The changes demonstrate the natural role of fire in Douglas fir forests.

While the viewpoint at Angels Rest makes an excellent goal by itself, it's also tempting to extend the hike by exploring the adjacent plateau. One option is to visit a creekside picnic site by adding an easy 2.4-mile loop. Or better yet, arrange a short car shuttle and continue to beautiful Wahkeena Falls for a 6.4-mile, moderate one-way hike.

From Portland, drive Interstate 84 east, take Bridal Veil exit 28, and park a few hundred yards later at the junction with the old Columbia River Highway. The Angels Rest Trail begins beside a concrete milepost at this intersection. If you're driving here from the east, take exit 35 and follow the old highway 7.3 miles.

The trail starts out uphill through a fern-filled forest where large white trilliums bloom in early spring. After half a mile you'll get a glimpse of 100-foot Coopey Falls. Then the trail climbs past an upper, 30-foot cascade and crosses Coopey Creek on a scenic footbridge. By late spring larkspur crowds the woods here with chest-high stalks of blue flowers.

Beyond Coopey Creek the path climbs in earnest, switchbacking up a ridge and traversing a rockslide. Beware of poison oak growing from beneath the trailside rocks. Finally the trail reaches a windy crest with an unmarked junction. Turn left to Angel Rest's miniature mesa, with views of the Columbia River on three sides. Look for Crown Point's observatory to the west.

If you'd like to continue on the additional 2.4-mile loop, walk back along the ridgecrest past the first junction until you reach a fork in the trail. Keep right, following the sign for Foxglove Way, and ramble onwards through woods carpeted with star-flowered smilacina in May. When the trail joins a dirt road, turn left. The road becomes a trail and then joins the Gorge Trail. Turn left here for 0.4 mile to a lovely campsite and picnic table in a glen with a creek. A side trail to the right leads to a 20-foot cascade. To complete the loop cross the creek and continue 0.7 mile back to Angels Rest.

If you've arranged a car shuttle to Wahkeena Falls, skip the side trip up Foxglove Way. From Angels Rest simply keep left at every junction and you'll pass the creekside picnic site, Wahkeena Spring, and Fairy Falls en route to the Wahkeena Falls trailhead described in Hike #42.

Angels Rest.   Opposite: Larkspur.

42 Multnomah & Wahkeena Falls

Easy (to top of falls)
2.2 miles round-trip
700 feet elevation gain
Open all year
Map: Trails of the Columbia Gorge
  (Geo-Graphics)

Moderate (from Wahkeena Falls)
5-mile loop
1600 feet elevation gain

Oregon's tallest waterfall, Multnomah Falls was the state's most popular tourist attraction until it recently lost that title to a casino. Still, thousands of visitors pull off the freeway each day to snap photos of the 542-foot, two-tiered cascade. Hundreds of them continue up the paved 1.1-mile trail to the top of the falls—a classic little hike. To beat the crowds here, consider the longer, even prettier loop that begins at the quiet Wahkeena Falls trailhead nearby.

For the short hike to the top of Multnomah Falls, drive Interstate 84 east of Portland to Multnomah Falls exit 31, park, and walk under the overpass. The historic stone lodge on your right was built in 1925 for the grand opening of the scenic Columbia Gorge-Mount Hood highway loop. Walk straight toward the falls to find the paved trail switchbacking up to a stone bridge between the two segments of Multnomah Falls' long cascade.

The trail here has seen more than its share of natural drama. In 1991 a forest fire swept across the path, stopping just short of the lodge. In 1996 a bus-sized chunk of the waterfall's cliff broke loose, landed in the splash pool, and sprayed rock splinters past the bridge. In 1998, torrential rainstorms launched a gigantic landslide of rocks, mud, and trees that wiped out the trail and kept it closed for

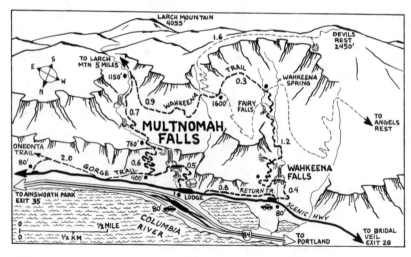

Fairy Falls, along the Wahkeena Trail. Opposite: Wahkeena Falls.

a year. If your courage holds, continue on the reopened path past the stone bridge. Keep right at junctions to climb to a fenced overlook on Multnomah Falls' lip. The dizzying view aims down the cataract to the toy-sized lodge and its ant-like crowds.

If you have the time to try a quieter, prettier route to the top of Multnomah Falls, start at the Wahkeena Falls trailhead instead. To find it, drive the freeway to Bridal Veil exit 28 and turn left along the old Columbia River Highway 2.6 miles to the Wahkeena Falls Picnic Ground pullout on the right.

The Wahkeena Trail starts at a footbridge and climbs to the right 0.2 mile to an elegant stone bridge below Wahkeena Falls, a 242-foot triple cascade in a sculpted chute. Continue on the unpaved, steep path 2.8 miles up to the Larch Mountain Trail. Then turn left along Multnomah Creek for 0.7 mile, passing many smaller falls on the way down to the Multnomah Falls viewpoint. After marveling at the view, continue down the 1.1-mile path to the lodge and turn left along the old highway, where you'll find a return trail back to your car.

Other Hiking Options

Devils Rest is a more challenging goal from Wahkeena Falls, requiring a 7-mile round trip and 2400 feet of elevation gain. Although the summit of this forested knoll has no views, a side trail 0.2 mile before the top leads to a Gorge overlook. Ascend the Wahkeena Trail 1.9 miles until it levels off, and then take the marked Devils Rest Trail to the right.

An even tougher climb is the 13.4-mile round trip from Multnomah Falls to the panoramic view atop 4055-foot Larch Mountain (see Hike #39).

43 Oneonta and Horsetail Falls

Easy
2.7-mile loop
400 feet elevation gain
Open all year
Map: Trails of the Columbia Gorge
(Geo-Graphics)

Next door to busy Multnomah Falls but usually overlooked by tourists, this delightful trail explores a cavern *behind* Ponytail Falls and then loops around Oneonta Gorge, a mossy chasm so narrow that Oneonta Creek fills it wall to wall. What's more, an optional 1.8-mile side trip leads to breathtaking Triple Falls, where three plumes of water plunge 120 feet at once.

Drive Interstate 84 east of Portland to Ainsworth Park exit 35 and follow the old scenic highway 1.5 miles back to the large Horsetail Falls Trailhead parking area. The trail starts beside 176-foot Horsetail Falls and climbs along a mossy slope of little licorice ferns. In late spring tiny white candyflowers and pink geraniums crowd the path.

After 0.2 mile turn right on the Gorge Trail, which soon ducks behind 80-foot Ponytail Falls (alias Upper Horsetail Falls). The lava flow that created this falls' stony lip also buried a layer of soft soil. The falls have washed out the underlying soil, creating the cavern.

Beyond the falls 0.4 mile take a right-hand fork for a quick viewpoint loop out to a cliff edge high above the highway. The view extends up the Columbia to Beacon Rock, but keep children away from the unfenced edge. Then continue on the main trail another 0.4 mile, switchback down to a dramatic metal footbridge above 60-foot Oneonta Falls, and climb to a junction with the Oneonta Trail.

Turn left here if you'd like to take the optional side trip up to Triple Falls and the perfect spot for lunch: a footbridge in a scenic creekside glen at the top of the falls. If you're hiking with children, however, you'd best skip Triple Falls and simply turn right to continue the loop, following the Oneonta Trail 0.9 mile down to the highway.

To complete the loop, walk along the road to the mouth of slot-like Oneonta Gorge. With any luck you'll be able to lounge on the creek's pebble beach here while one of your party runs up the road another third of a mile to fetch the car.

Other Hiking Options

The best way to see the inside of Oneonta Gorge is to put on sneakers and wade knee-deep up the creek from the highway bridge. In late summer when the water's not too deep nor too icy, it's usually possible to trek half a mile through the 20-foot-wide chasm to an otherwise hidden, 100-foot falls.

Another option is a difficult 9.4-mile loop up Rock of Ages Ridge, gaining

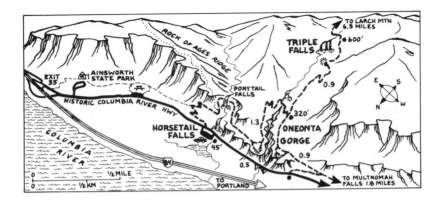

2800 feet. Start as for the main Oneonta-Horsetail loop, but at the ridge end immediately before Ponytail Falls, climb up to the left on an unmaintained user path. The next half mile is a confusion of steep scramble trails. Then follow the view-packed, rocky ridgecrest up to a wooded plateau, turn right on the Horsetail Creek Trail for 3.5 miles, and descend the Oneonta Trail 2.9 miles to the highway.

Triple Falls.   Opposite: Ponytail Falls.

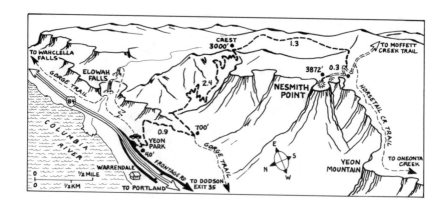

44   Nesmith Point

Difficult
9.8 miles round-trip
3800 feet elevation gain
Open April through November
Map: Trails of the Columbia Gorge
(Geo-Graphics)

Mountain climbers often use the challenging trail to Nesmith Point as a spring conditioning trip because the goal—the highest point in the cliffs lining the Columbia Gorge—is snow-free by April. But this hike offers other rewards than mere exercise. Expect a variety of wildflowers, the solitude of a high valley's natural amphitheater, and of course a bird's eye view across the Columbia to the snowpeaks of Washington.

Nesmith Point's promontory was unnamed until 1915, when the Portland Mazamas club suggested it memorialize James Nesmith, a burly Oregon Trail pioneer whose wagon raft was driven ashore near here by high winds in 1843. Nesmith was forced to wait out the storm reading *The Merry Wives of Windsor.*

If you're coming from Portland on Interstate 84, take exit 35 for Ainsworth Park, turn left toward Dodson for just 200 feet, and turn sharply right onto Frontage Road. (If you miss the Frontage Road turnoff you'll end up back on the freeway.) Then follow Frontage Road 2.1 miles to a big paved pullout on the right—the Yeon Park trailhead for Nesmith Point. If you're driving here from Hood River, take Warrendale exit 37, duck left under the freeway, and turn left for half a mile to the trailhead.

Just after the trailhead the path forks. Keep right, climbing through a lowland forest brightened in summer by chest-high, orange tiger lilies. In 0.9 mile meet the Gorge Trail and turn left. The path climbs relentlessly for the next 2.4 miles, switchbacking up a steep, narrow valley with occasional views out to Beacon Rock and Mt. Adams. Finally climb past huge old-growth cedars in a natural amphitheater at the canyon's head. Then, at a sunny ridgecrest, the forest abruptly shifts to high-elevation fare: small Douglas fir, beargrass, and huckleberries.

After reaching the ridgecrest, climb more gradually along a tilted plateau for 1.3 miles to an abandoned dirt road that leads up to the summit, once the site of a fire lookout tower. Unfortunately trees have grown up, leaving only a view west down the Columbia River to Portland's haze and Silver Star Mountain (Hike #15), the tall brown hump on the horizon. But don't despair; a better viewpoint is nearby. Continue past the old lookout's foundation pier and down into the woods 200 yards. You'll pass the lookout's abandoned outhouse, descend through a forest carpeted with May-blooming trilliums, and emerge at a cliff edge with an aerial view of Beacon Rock's riverside monolith, snowy Mt. Adams, and flat-topped Mt. St. Helens.

Other Hiking Options

By arranging a short car shuttle you can descend on a less steep but longer path that leads to the Oneonta Trailhead described in Hike #43. From Nesmith Point walk down the dirt road 0.4 mile, turn right on the Horsetail Creek Trail for 5.6 miles, and then turn right on the Oneonta Trail for 2.9 miles to the highway. The hike's total length is 13.8 miles.

Hamilton Mountain from Nesmith Point.   *Opposite: Mt. Adams from Nesmith Point.*

45 Wahclella and Elowah Falls

Easy (to Wahclella Falls)
1.8 miles round-trip
300 feet elevation gain
Open all year
Map: Trails of the Columbia Gorge
(Geo-Graphics)

Easy (to Elowah Falls)
3 miles round-trip
600 feet elevation gain

Two of the Columbia Gorge's best waterfalls are hidden in canyons with short trails. The 0.9-mile path to thundering Wahclella Falls loops through a charming, canyon-end grotto. Just down the road, a 0.8-mile trail to airy, 289-foot Elowah Falls features a side path that climbs past a Gorge viewpoint to an additional 100-foot falls. For a quick afternoon stroll, choose just one of the hikes. For a longer walk, try both.

To start the Wahclella Falls hike, drive Interstate 84 to Bonneville Dam exit 40, turn to the south (away from the dam), and keep right for 100 yards to a turnaround and parking area. The trail begins on an old gated road alongside bouldery, maple-shaded Tanner Creek. The old road ends at a small water intake dam for the Bonneville fish hatchery. Continue on a trail into the ever-narrowing canyon. Along the way you'll pass a side creek's 60-foot fan-shaped falls.

When the trail forks after 0.7 mile, keep left for 0.2 mile to the wave-tossed pool at the base of Wahclella Falls. The falls itself has two tiers, with a plunge in an upper slot followed by a 60-foot horsetail. Listen here for the *zeet-zeet* of water ouzels, remarkable robin-sized birds that dive into the creek, flapping their wings underwater so they can run along the streambed eating insect larvae.

Beyond Wahclella Falls, the trail continues on a short downstream loop, ducking under a 20-foot cavern and winding past house-sized boulders left from a 1973 landslide. When the trail recrosses the creek at the end of the loop,

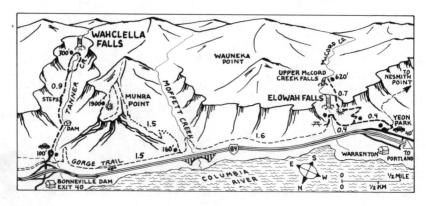

Wahclella Falls.   Opposite: Upper McCord Creek Falls.

turn left to return to your car.

To drive on to the Elowah Falls trailhead after finishing the Wahclella Falls hike, take the freeway 3 miles west to Warrendale exit 37, duck left under the freeway, and turn left for half a mile to a big paved parking pullout on the right. If you're driving to Elowah Falls directly from Portland, however, you'll have to use a different route because the Warrendale freeway exit is only accessible from the east. In this case, take exit 35 for Ainsworth Park, turn left toward Dodson for just 200 feet, and then turn sharply right onto Frontage Road for 2.1 miles.

From the Elowah Falls trailhead, keep left on the level main trail 0.8 mile to an enormous cliff-rimmed amphitheater at the base of the falls, a gauzy ribbon so tall that breezes waft it about. The 7 layers of basalt visible in the cliffs are evidence of the many lava flows that surged down the Columbia Gorge in the past 15 million years only to be cut back by the river.

Then backtrack 0.4 mile from Elowah Falls, turn left at a fork, and switchback up to a dramatic, railed ledge blasted out of sheer cliffs. The aerial view here extends from Elowah Falls across the Columbia to Beacon Rock and Hamilton Mountain (Hike #34). Continue to trail's end at a creekside glen above Upper McCord Creek Falls' twin 60-foot fans.

Other Hiking Options

A nearly level 3.1-mile stretch of the Gorge Trail ambles beside the freeway between the Wahclella Falls and Elowah Falls trails, so you can connect the two trails in a single one-way hike, if you can arrange a short car shuttle. To find this connector trail from the Wahclella Falls parking area, walk 200 feet back toward the freeway and turn left on the Historic Columbia River Highway State Trail across Tanner Creek. Then veer left onto the Gorge Trail.

46 Tooth Rock and Wauna Point

Easy (to Tooth Rock viaduct)
2-mile loop
130 feet elevation gain
Open all year
Use: hikers, bicycles
Map: Trails of Col. Gorge (Geo-Graphics)

Moderate (to Wauna Viewpoint)
4.8 miles round-trip
900 feet elevation gain

Difficult (to Wauna Point)
6.2-mile loop
2200 feet elevation gain

When engineer Samuel Lancaster laid out the original Columbia River Highway in 1913, he decided not to tunnel through Tooth Rock, a basalt shoulder of Wauna Point that juts out over the river. Instead he perched the narrow roadway on a perilous-looking viaduct, a half-bridge clinging to the cliff's face. The resulting viewpoint was so impressive that Model T drivers often stopped to gawk—and were sometimes rear-ended by the next car.

Today, Interstate 84 roars through a modern tunnel in Tooth Rock's base. But high above, the fragile old viaduct has been restored for hikers and bicyclists as part of the Historic Columbia River Highway State Trail. For an easy 2-mile loop, take this paved path across the viaduct and return on an unpaved upper path. For a longer hike, continue up to 1050-foot Wauna Viewpoint. For the best view of all, drive to a rougher upper trailhead and tackle the tough hike to 2160-foot Wauna Point itself.

Start by driving Interstate 84 east of Portland to Bonneville Dam exit 40. Then follow signs half a mile to the Historic Columbia River Highway trailhead's large parking lot. Set off on foot (or by bicycle) on the wide, paved trail to the right, paralleling the noisy freeway 0.8 mile to the viaduct, where views extend across the river from Beacon Rock to the Bridge of the Gods.

Beyond Tooth Rock 0.2 mile the paved path ends at a concrete staircase. But don't go down the stairs. Instead turn uphill to the right at a sign for the Tooth Rock Portage Road Loop. This path follows an even older, dirt roadbed up across the top of Tooth Rock. Beware of 3-leaved poison oak along this route. After climbing 0.4 mile you'll reach a junction, and face a decision. To return to your car, go straight. To continue on the longer hike to Wauna Viewpoint, turn uphill to the left. The upper path climbs 200 yards to the switchback of a gravel road. Keep left to find the continuation of the trail. After another 0.4 mile, turn right at a sign for Wauna Viewpoint and switchback up through the woods. The knoll at trail's end, beside a powerline, features red paintbrush flowers and a view extending from the pools of the Eagle Creek Hatchery to Mt. Adams. There is no direct route from Wauna Viewpoint up to Wauna Point.

To take the more rugged Wauna Point hike, you'll need a car that can handle a rough, steep gravel road. Drive I-84 to Bonneville Dam exit 40, turn briefly south away from the dam, fork left toward the Tooth Rock Trailhead for 0.3 mile

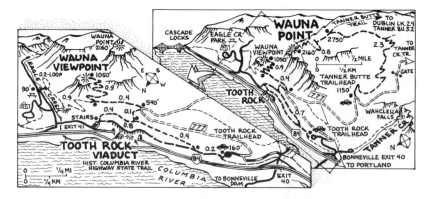

to a T-shaped junction, but then turn right onto (possibly unmarked) Road 777. Follow this frightening gravel track 2 miles and park at a message board on the left beside a creek.

From this upper trailhead, hike up the Tanner Butte Trail past 4 lacy, 20-foot waterfalls in a mossy glen of alder, bleeding hearts, and columbine. The path twice crosses under huge, crackling powerlines and then climbs steadily through Douglas fir woods carpeted in spring with delicate star-flowered smilacina. After 2.3 steep miles the path forks, with the Tanner Butte Trail continuing to the right. If you're headed down the rugged path to Wauna Point, however, keep left past a "Trail Not Maintained" sign for 0.3 mile to another junction. Turn left again on a steep, narrow downhill path that switchbacks under a cliff and scrambles half a mile down a precarious, rocky ridgecrest to Wauna Point, a knife-edge promontory overhanging the Gorge. The dizzying view extends across the river to Table Mountain and Mt. Adams.

Other Hiking Options

For a backpacking trip, try the 10.5-mile loop to Dublin Lake. The challenging loop gains 3200 feet. Start as for Wauna Point, but keep right on the Tanner Butte Trail an extra 2 miles. Continue straight past the Tanner Cutoff Trail junction 150 yards and turn left 0.3 mile down to the woodsy lake. To continue, return to the Tanner Cutoff Trail junction, take this steep trail 2.3 miles downhill, turn right on the Tanner Creek Trail to Road 777, and follow it 2.9 miles back to your car.

The Tooth Rock Viaduct.   Opposite: Marker at the trailhead.

47 Eagle Creek

Easy (to Punchbowl Falls)
4.2 miles round-trip
400 feet elevation gain
Open all year
Map: Trails of Col. Gorge (Geo-Graphics)

Moderate (to High Bridge)
6.6 miles round-trip
600 feet elevation gain

Difficult (to Tunnel Falls)
12 miles round-trip
1200 feet elevation gain

Built in the 1910s to accompany the opening of the Columbia River Highway, the Eagle Creek Trail is one of Oregon's most spectacular paths, passing half a dozen major waterfalls. The trail is also something of an engineering marvel. To maintain an easy grade through this rugged canyon, the builders blasted ledges out of sheer cliffs, bridged a colossal gorge, and even chipped a tunnel through solid rock behind 120-foot Tunnel Falls.

Today the trail is so popular the parking lot fills by 10am on sunny weekends, leaving latecomers to park half a mile away. Although this is a great place to backpack, tenting along the first 7.5 miles is only allowed within 4 designated camp areas, where competition for weekend space is keen. Campfires are strongly discouraged. An additional caution to parents: trailside cliffs make this no place for unsupervised or hard-to-manage children.

If you're coming from the Portland area, take Interstate 84 to Eagle Creek exit 41, turn right, and keep right along the creek for a mile to the road's end. Because the Eagle Creek exit is only accessible from the west, travelers from Hood River will have to take Bonneville Dam exit 40 and double back on the freeway for a mile. Leave nothing of value in your car as break-ins are a problem here.

The trail starts along the creek but soon climbs well above it along a slope of cedars and mossy maples. Look for yellow monkeyflowers and curving fronds

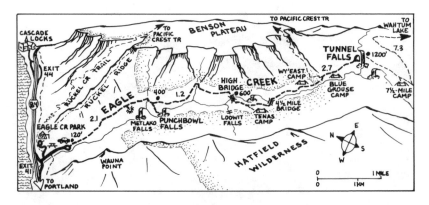

Punchbowl Falls.   Opposite: Cable handrail on the Eagle Creek Trail.

of maidenhair fern overhanging the path. After 0.8 mile the trail traverses a cliff with cables as handrails. At the 1.5-mile mark several short side trails to the right lead down to a viewpoint of 100-foot Metlako Falls in the distance.

Continue on the main trail 0.3 mile to a ridge-end junction with the Lower Punchbowl Trail, a 0.2-mile side trail down to a broad, 15-foot falls with a bedrock bank suitable for sunbathing. Hike upstream to a gravel beach to peer ahead to picturesque, 30-foot Punchbowl Falls in a huge, mossy rock bowl.

If you're game for a longer hike, return to the Eagle Creek Trail and continue 1.2 miles to High Bridge, a metal footbridge across a dizzying, slot-like chasm. Here the creek has exposed a long crack in the earth— the fault along which this valley formed. For a nice lunch spot, continue 0.4 mile to Tenas Campground (on the right) and Skooknichuck Falls (on the left). For a still longer hike continue a couple miles further, duck behind Tunnel Falls, and 200 yards later gain a view ahead to the valley's last great, unnamed waterfall.

Other Hiking Options

A classic 2- to 3-day backpacking trip continues to Wahtum Lake. Snow closes this 26.8-mile loop from mid-November until June. Start by hiking up the Eagle Creek Trail 13.3 miles to Wahtum Lake (see Hike #51). Then veer left on the PCT for 6.3 miles to the Benson Plateau, and turn left to descend the Ruckel Creek Trail (see Hike #48) back to your car.

48   Ruckel Creek

Difficult
9.6 miles round-trip or loop
3700 feet elevation gain
Open April through November
Map: Trails of the Col. Gorge (Geo-Graphics)

The challenging Ruckel Creek Trail climbs nearly 4000 feet to the forested Benson Plateau, passing Indian-dug pits, a clifftop viewpoint, and meadowed slopes dotted with late spring wildflowers. Despite the name, the path approaches Ruckel Creek only twice. Adventurers can turn the hike into a loop by starting out up the Ruckel Ridge Trail, a rough, unmaintained path along a rocky crest with numerous viewpoints.

From Portland, take Interstate 84 to Eagle Creek exit 41, turn right, and park by the restroom at the Eagle Creek Park entrance. Because the Eagle Creek exit is only accessible from the west, drivers coming from Hood River will have to take Bonneville Dam exit 40, duck left through an underpass, and get back on the freeway eastbound for a mile.

From the parking area at the park's entrance, walk up the paved road toward the campground 150 yards to a sign marking the Gorge Trail on the left. Follow this path 0.2 mile up beside the campground to a fork signed for Buck Point. Decide here if you want to tackle the loop up rugged Ruckel Ridge or if you'll skip the loop and take the better-maintained Ruckel Creek Trail both ways.

If you opt for the less difficult Ruckel Creek route, keep straight on the Gorge Trail for 0.3 mile and then turn right on the paved Columbia River Highway Trail. After 200 yards this bike path crosses Ruckel Creek on a picturesque concrete bridge—a remnant of the old scenic highway. Turn right here on a

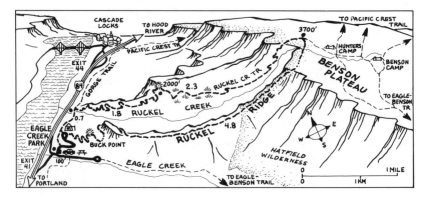

The Ruckel Ridge Trail.   Opposite: Wild iris.

creekside path that switchbacks steeply uphill, heads under a powerline, and 0.3 mile later crosses a strange, hummocky, moss-covered rockslide. The pits here were dug at least 1000 years ago, evidently as vision quest sites for young Indian men.

Next the path switchbacks up for a grueling mile to a viewpoint atop a sheer 500-foot cliff overlooking the Bridge of the Gods, Table Mountain, and Mt. Adams. The trail's next 1.5 miles are relatively level, through grassy slopes of purple cluster lilies and red paintbrush. Finally climb very steeply again to the Benson Plateau. After just 150 yards through this level forest the trail forks. Turn right past a "Trail Not Maintained" sign for another 150 yards to splashing Ruckel Creek—a perfect lunch spot and turnaround point.

If you want to convert the hike into a loop, you'd best start out differently. Back at the junction beside the Eagle Creek Campground you'll want to turn right, cut through the campground to site #5, and hike up to the right past a big sign for the Buck Point Trail. This path climbs 0.6 mile to Buck Point, a viewpoint beneath a powerline. Continue down to the right past a "Trail Not Maintained" sign to a rockslide. Scramble straight up this slide, following cairns and watching for loose rocks. Traverse left around the base of a cliff and then climb steeply to a viewpoint on the ridgecrest. From here on the unofficial Ruckel Ridge Trail is clear enough, although you'll have to step over a few logs and occasionally use your hands as you clamber up and down along the narrow crest for another 3 miles. When you finally gain the level Benson Plateau, follow cairns and blazes 0.3 mile left to the Ruckel Creek crossing described above. Shortly afterwards, turn left on the Ruckel Creek Trail to complete the loop.

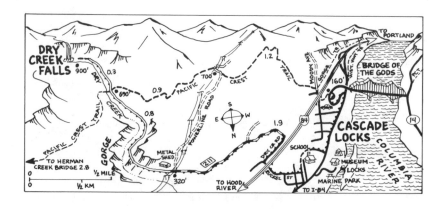

Dry Creek Falls.   Opposite: The Bridge of the Gods in Cascade Locks.

49   Dry Creek Falls

Moderate
5.4-mile loop
710 feet elevation gain
Open all year
Use: hikers, horses
Map: Trails of the Columbia
Gorge (Geo-Graphics)

This surprisingly convenient, yet often overlooked portion of the Pacific Crest Trail starts within a stone's throw of a busy freeway, but then leads through quiet woods to one of the Columbia Gorge's least visited waterfalls. To make a loop, return on backroads through the village of Cascade Locks.

Drive Interstate 84 to Cascade Locks exit 44 and follow signs toward the Bridge of the Gods. A hundred yards before the bridge's toll booth, pull into a small forested park on the right. Park by the restrooms and walk back across the road to a sign marking the Pacific Crest Trail.

Follow the PCT to the left 200 yards, turn right on a paved street that ducks under the freeway, and fork to the right on gravel Moody Avenue. After 50 yards, turn left onto the continuation of the trail at a sign "PCT South." The path now enters a mossy Douglas fir forest with pink bleeding heart blooms in summer and scarlet vine maples leaves in fall. At the 1.2-mile mark, turn right for 50 yards on a powerline access road with a view of distant Mt. Adams' tip. Then veer left onto the trail's continuation.

In another 0.9 mile the PCT crosses a dirt road alongside Dry Creek—here, a rushing torrent. Turn right up the old road 0.3 mile to the base of Dry Creek Falls, a 50-foot plunge from a slot in a 300-foot cliff. The cliff's contorted rock layers are Columbia River basalt, lava flows that repeatedly surged westward through the Columbia Gorge 10-17 million years ago. Look among the misty boulders below the falls for yellow monkeyflower, giant ladys fern, and delicate maidenhair fern. Also expect to see a water ouzel, an ordinary-looking, dark gray bird with a surprising skill. The ouzel dives into whitewater and stays submerged for as long as two minutes, running along the bottom of raging streams in search of insects.

An old diversion dam below the plunge pool has fallen into disuse, but the city of Cascade Locks still has water rights here, and keeps a rough access road open for official vehicles. To return on a loop, follow this quiet road 2 miles down along the creek to town. Along the way you'll pass a rocky lower gorge where Dry Creek really does run dry in summer. When Dry Creek Road finally ends at a T-shaped junction, turn left on Ruckel Street under the freeway. Follow Ruckel Street 3 blocks to its end, turn left on a short gravel path, and walk through a parking lot behind a school. When you reach the main highway, turn left through downtown 4 blocks to the Bridge of the Gods and your car.

50 Herman Creek

Easy (to Herman Creek bridge)
2 miles round-trip
500 feet elevation gain
Open all year
Use: hikers, horses
Map: Trails of Col. Gorge (Geo-Graphics)

Moderate (to forks of Herman Creek)
8.4 miles round-trip
1700 feet elevation gain

Difficult (to Indian Point)
8-mile loop
2600 feet elevation gain

Herman Creek's huge canyon and nearby Nick Eaton Ridge offer hiking options for nearly everyone. There's an easy walk to a bridge over the alder-shaded creek. There's a moderate hike to the confluence of the creek's forks deep in the wilderness. And finally, there's a more difficult loop that climbs to the viewpoint atop Indian Point's rock pinnacle, returning through the steep wild-flower meadows of Nick Eaton Ridge.

From Portland, take Interstate 84 to Cascade Locks exit 44 and drive straight through town 2 miles. Just when you reach the on-ramp for the freeway east, go straight onto a paved road marked "To Oxbow Fish Hatchery." Follow this road 2 miles, turn right at Herman Campground, and drive up through the campground to the trailhead parking loop at the far end. If you're driving from Hood River it's quicker to take Herman Creek exit 47 and head toward the Oxbow Hatchery for 0.6 mile to the trailhead turnoff.

The trail begins in a cool forest of Douglas fir and bigleaf maple. Look for white inside-out flowers and bold orange tiger lilies in summer. Keep left at an unmarked fork near the start, switchback up across a powerline access road

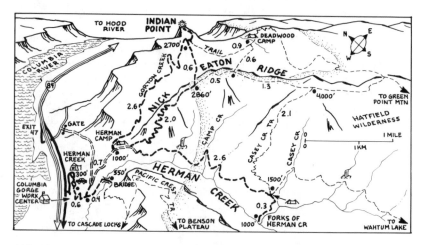

Indian Point.   Opposite: Herman Creek.

fringed with poison oak, and then climb another 0.4 mile to a well-signed fork.

If you're interested in the easy hike option, veer right onto the Herman Creek Bridge Trail and descend slightly for 0.4 mile to the 75-foot metal span, where you can relax beside the rushing stream's bouldery banks. If you're aiming for a longer hike, however, keep left at the fork and continue up the Herman Creek Trail. The path soon joins an old dirt road and follows it uphill to the right for 0.6 mile to Herman Camp, a primitive tentsite.

For the moderate hike option, continue straight past Herman Camp. The road soon becomes a trail again and contours through old-growth woods with Herman Creek audible far below. Cross several side creeks, one with a 100-foot waterfall, and finally meet the Casey Creek Trail. Turn right here and descend steeply 0.3 mile to a mossy bower where two creeks join.

If you'd prefer the difficult loop hike to Indian Point, turn left when you reach Herman Camp and take the signed Gorton Creek Trail. This path climbs steadily for 2.6 miles before switchbacking up to a junction on a ridge end. To continue the loop you'll turn uphill to the right here on the Ridge Cutoff Trail, but first continue straight 50 yards on the Gorton Creek Trail to find a small, unmarked side path to the left that leads 0.1 mile down to Indian Point, where views extend from Hood River to Mt. St. Helens. The final 30-foot scramble up an exposed rock pinnacle requires the use of your hands. Turn back here if you're uncertain.

To complete the loop return to the Ridge Cutoff Trail, follow it 0.6 mile, and take the Nick Eaton Trail down a steep ridgecrest through rock gardens of summer blooms: purple penstemon, blue lupine, red paintbrush, and lavender plectritis. Views include the tip of Mt. Hood and Bonneville Dam.

Other Hiking Options

For a weekend backpacking trip try the 26.4-mile loop to Wahtum Lake. Hike 11.2 miles up the Herman Creek Trail and turn left on the Pacific Crest Trail 1.6 miles to the lake (see Hike #51). Then turn around and take the PCT 12.1 miles north across the Benson Plateau to the Herman Creek Bridge Trail.

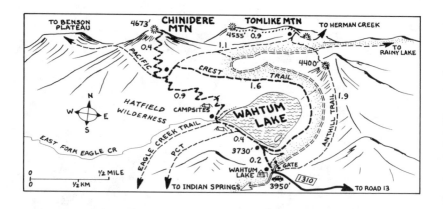

51   Wahtum Lake

Moderate (to Chinidere Mountain)
4.1-mile loop
1100 feet elevation gain
Open June to mid-November
Use: hikers, horses
Map: Trails of the Columbia Gorge
    (Geo-Graphics)

The loop around this scenic lake climbs on the Pacific Crest Trail past patches of huckleberries and wildflowers to Chinidere Mountain, arguably the best viewpoint in the Hatifled Wilderness.

Drive Interstate 84 to West Hood River exit 62, head into Hood River 1.1 mile, turn right on 13th Street, and follow signs for Odell for 3.4 zigzagging miles. After crossing the Hood River Bridge take a right-hand fork past Tucker Park for 6.3 miles. Then fork to the right again toward Dee, cross the river, and turn left on the road to Lost Lake. After 4.9 miles veer right at a "Wahtum Lake" pointer, follow 1-lane paved Road 13 for 4.3 miles, and finally veer right again onto Road 1310 for 6 miles to a pass with primitive Wahtum Lake Campground.

Park by the message board and take the "Wahtum Express Trail" down 252 steps to the lake. Turn right on the Pacific Crest Trail and climb gradually away from the shore through a hemlock forest dotted with blue huckleberries in August. Earlier in summer expect wildflowers: 4-petaled white bunchberry, big trilliums, bleeding hearts, mint, and columbine. The rarest bloom of all is cutleaf bugbane, which grows here and at Lost Lake (Hike #69), but nowhere else on earth. Look for its salmonberry-like leaves and 5-foot plumes of tiny white starbursts.

After 1.6 miles the PCT forks. Head uphill to the right past a "Chinidere

Mountain" sign on a steepish 0.4-mile switchbacking path to the former lookout site's bare summit amid alpine wildflowers: blue gentian, red paintbrush, and purple aster. The 360-degree view includes the entire route of your hike, as well as snowpeaks from Jefferson to Rainier. Mt. St. Helens rises above the broad Benson Plateau, while Mt. Adams looms above Tomlike Mountain's barren ridge. *Chinidere* was the last reigning chief of the Wasco Indians, and his son was named *Tomlike.* Appropriately, *Wahtum* is an Indian word for lake.

To finish the loop, return to the PCT, head left for 100 feet, and turn right on a continuation of the Chinidere Mountain Trail. This path switchbacks 0.9 mile down past several campsites, crosses Wahtum Lake's log-jammed outlet creek, and joins the Eagle Creek Trail. Turn left past some more campsites, join the PCT, pass a nice bathing beach, and then turn right to climb back to your car.

Other Hiking Options

For a slightly wilder 6.6-mile loop, visit Tomlike Mountain instead. Descend to Wahtum Lake, turn right on the PCT for 1.5 miles and turn right on the Herman Creek Trail for 1.1 mile to a junction with the Anthill Trail. Continue straight 300 feet to a switchback at a ridge end. Leave the trail at this corner and bushwhack left, straight out the ridgecrest. The first few hundred yards are a tangle of small trees, but then it's easy walking along the open rock crest 0.9 mile to the summit. To complete the loop, return via the Anthill Trail, which has a nice viewpoint of Wahtum Lake.

Backpackers often stop at Wahtum Lake on 2- or 3-day loop trips via Eagle Creek (see Hike #47) or Herman Creek (see Hike #50). Camping is banned on the fragile lakeshore, but nice sites have been designated nearby.

Wahtum Lake from Chinidere Mountain.   Opposite: Cutleaf bugbane.

52 Mount Defiance North

Easy (to Hole-in-the-Wall Falls)
2.5-mile loop
600 feet elevation gain
Open all year
Map: Trails of the Columbia Gorge
(Geo-Graphics)

Very Difficult (to summit)
11.8-mile loop
4800 feet elevation gain
Open mid-June through October

One of the most physically demanding paths in Oregon, the Mount Defiance Trail gains nearly 5000 feet of elevation on its way to the highest point in the Columbia Gorge. Ironically, the trail begins with an easy option—a short loop that visits waterfalls, viewpoints, and creek valleys at the mountain's base.

Take Interstate 84 east of Cascade Locks 10 miles to Starvation Creek Trailhead exit 55. (If you're coming from Hood River, you'll have to take Wyeth exit 51, turn around, and drive back on the freeway 3 miles to access Starvation Creek Trailhead exit 55.) The parking lot here once served as a popular wayside rest stop for freeway travelers, but the restrooms' septic system proved inadequate.

While you're here, be sure to take the 100-yard paved path past the closed restrooms to the base of 186-foot Starvation Creek Falls. The falls earned their name when two trains were trapped near here in an 1884 blizzard. Stranded passengers were offered $3 a day to dig out the track while waiting for skiers to arrive with food from Hood River.

To find the Mount Defiance Trail, walk back toward the freeway and follow its noisy shoulder west. The trail veers into the woods, passes mostly-hidden Cabin Creek Falls, and after 0.8 mile crosses a footbridge below Hole-in-the-Wall Falls, which plummets 100 feet from a tunnel. This oddity was created in 1938 when the Oregon Highway Department, upset that Warren Creek Falls wetted the old Columbia River Highway, diverted the creek through a cliff.

In another 0.1 mile reach a junction with the Starvation Ridge Trail. Turn left if you'd like to take the easy loop. This path climbs to a crossing of Warren Creek and then switchbacks up over a grassy ridge to a cliff overlooking the parking area, the river, and Dog Mountain (Hike #37). Continue across Cabin Creek and soon veer left on the Starvation Cutoff Trail to return to your car.

If you'd prefer the difficult loop, follow the Mount Defiance Trail from Hole-in-the-Wall Falls straight 0.2 mile to 20-foot, fan-shaped Lancaster Falls. After another level half mile the trail suddenly launches upward, climbing 3 miles along a densely wooded ridgecrest. Finally reach a junction with the Mitchell Point Trail (route of the return loop). Continue uphill to the right for 0.2 mile, watching carefully for an unmarked side trail to the right. Take this new scenic route across massive rockslides overlooking Bear Lake, and curve left up to the microwave relay towers at the summit.

To return on a slightly shorter loop, walk past the fenced microwave building

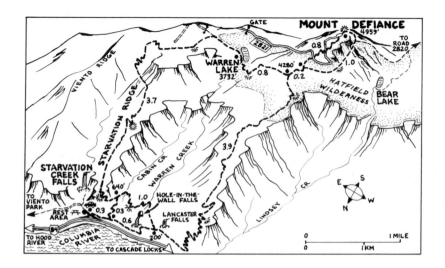

and a smaller tower to an old wooden trail sign, Take a path downhill that crosses a dirt road twice. When you return to the Mitchell Point Trail junction turn right toward Warren Lake. This route descends 0.8 mile to the pretty lake, rimmed with rockslides and pines. Though mud-bottomed, Warren Lake is a fine spot to swim or camp.

Beyond the lake the trail continues straight and level for half a mile to an important but unmarked junction where you'll want to turn left onto the Starvation Ridge Trail. If you miss the turnoff, the Mitchell Point Trail ends 50 yards later at a dirt road. The Starvation Ridge Trail, on the other hand, barrels down a wooded ridgecrest for over 3 miles, passing two excellent viewpoints. At the bottom turn right on the Starvation Cutoff Trail to return to your car.

Mt. Hood from Mt. Defiance.   *Opposite: The Columbia River from Starvation Ridge.*

53   Mount Defiance South

Easy (to Bear Lake)
2.6 miles round-trip
400 feet elevation gain
Open June to mid-October
Use: hikers, horses
Map: Trails of Col. Gorge (Geo-Graphics)

Moderate (to Mount Defiance)
4.8-mile loop
1500 feet elevation gain

Mt. Defiance was named because it remains defiantly snowclad until June, and not, as hikers might suggest, because the grueling Mount Defiance Trail from Interstate 84 (see Hike #52) is defiantly difficult. If you'd like an easier route to the summit, try starting at this more remote trailhead on the mountain's south side. Here you'll also find a short side trail that leads to a small campsite at swimmable Bear Lake.

Drive Interstate 84 to West Hood River exit 62, head toward Hood River 1.1 mile, turn right on 13th Street, and follow signs for Odell for 3.4 miles. After crossing the Hood River Bridge take a right-hand fork past Tucker Park for 6.3 miles. Then fork to the right again toward Dee, cross the river, and turn right, following signs for Rainy Lake. Go straight on paved Punchbowl Road for 1.4 miles and continue on washboard gravel Road 2820 for 10 miles to a sign on the right for the Mount Defiance Trail. Park on the shoulder.

Hike 200 feet, turn right at a junction, and follow the trail up through a hemlock and fir forest with beargrass and huckleberry bushes. The path forks after half a mile. To visit Bear Lake, veer left onto a rocky trail that descends gradually to the lodgepole pine-rimmed lake, with its view up to Mt. Defiance. The shallow water is relatively warm. The shore, lined with flat rocks and a few logs, is fine for wading or a quick dip.

To climb the mountain, return to the Mount Defiance Trail and continue uphill

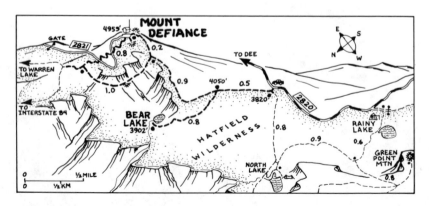

Rockslide on Mount Defiance.   Opposite: Bear Lake from Mount Defiance.

0.9 mile to a junction on an old rockslide. Turn right to reach the summit, where you'll find a microwave relay building and an admirable view of Mt. Hood. For a view in the other direction, walk left past the fenced station and follow a short path through the trees to a cliff edge. From here you can see Bear Lake, the town of Carson, and three Washington snowpeaks.

To return on a loop, walk past the small radio tower on the far end of the summit to find a wooden sign for the old Mountain Defiance Trail. Take this path down through the woods, cross a dirt road twice, and 400 yards later *watch carefully for a small, unmarked side trail that leads uphill to the left*. Take this path and traverse around the mountain, climbing across view-filled rockslide slopes. After a mile turn right on the trail back to the car.

54   Wygant Trail

Moderate (Chetwoot loop)
5.1-mile loop
800 feet elevation gain
Open all year
Map: Hood River (Green Trails)

Moderate (to upper viewpoint)
6.1-mile loop
1200 feet elevation gain

From the base of Mitchell Point, a landmark of the eastern Columbia Gorge, the Wygant Trail follows a stretch of the old Columbia River Highway, explores the Perham Creek canyon, and climbs to a clifftop viewpoint. Hikers with a bit more energy can continue up the slopes of Wygant Peak to an even more spectacular viewpoint at the 1350-foot level. Wear long pants, as the paths here pass poison oak.

From Cascade Locks take Interstate 84 east 14 miles to the Lausman State Park rest area at exit 58. Since this rest area is only accessible from the west, travelers from Hood River will have to take Viento Park exit 56 and double back on the freeway 2 miles.

Park at the rest area but don't walk up the obvious, paved path. Instead walk back toward the freeway and take an old gated road that parallels the freeway. The overgrown foundations below this road are the remains of Sonny, an oddly named railroad stop. The place's inhabitants tried to call it Mitchell, but Oregon already had a town by that name. Next they chose Little Boy after a local ranch, but this was rejected as awkward to telegraph. Sonny seemed the next best thing.

At a corner in the road, trail signs direct you onto a path that crosses Mitchell Creek and joins an abandoned section of the old Columbia River Highway for 0.3 mile. In autumn the Douglas fir forest here is bright with red vine maple. Snowberry bushes flaunt white but inedible fruit. In spring look for white sprays

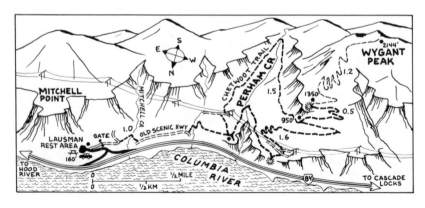

Columbia River from the Wygant Trail.   Opposite: Snowberry.

of large smilacina and yellow clusters of Oregon grape.

At the 1-mile mark continue straight past a junction with the Chetwoot Trail, the loop's return route. Ignore a side trail to an overgrown viewpoint on the right and continue to a bridge over rushing, fern-lined Perham Creek.

In another half a mile the trail reaches a viewpoint almost 300 feet directly above the freeway, overlooking 20 miles of the Columbia River. From here the trail ducks straight back into the woods and climbs for over a mile to a junction. The loop route continues straight onto the Chetwoot Trail, but if you have the energy for a worthwhile side trip, turn uphill to the right and climb half a mile in 4 switchbacks to an excellent ridge-end viewpoint across the Gorge to the top of Mt. Adams. Although this trail continues 1.2 miles up Wygant Peak, the route beyond this viewpoint is in disrepair and the overgrown lookout site at the top has no view.

To complete the loop, follow the Chetwoot Trail on a long traverse across Perham Creek's canyon. This rough, infrequently maintained path may have a few trees across it. When you reach a powerline access road, look 50 feet to the right to find the continuation of the path down to the Wygant Trail and the route to the car.

Chetwoot means black bear in Chinook jargon, the old trade language of Northwest Indians. The Chetwoot Trail, built by Portland-area volunteers, was named for a rare sighting of a bear.

55 Mosier Twin Tunnels

Easy (from east trailhead)
1.8 miles round-trip
160 feet elevation gain
Open all year
Use: hikers, horses, bicycles
Map: White Salmon, WA (USGS)

Moderate (entire trail)
9.4 miles round-trip
960 feet elevation gain

Tunnels with gracefully arched rock windows pierce the basalt cliffs high above the Columbia River at Mosier. The twin tunnels were built in 1919-21 for the historic Columbia River Highway, one of America's earliest and most beautiful pleasure drives. When falling rocks from the cliffs above damaged several cars in 1953, engineers backfilled the tunnels and rerouted traffic onto a new, river-level route—now Interstate 84.

Still, many people remained nostalgic for the old highway, with its daring tunnels, grand panoramas, graceful curves, delicate bridges, and stonework railings. And so in 1995, work began reopening portions of the original route as the Historic Columbia River Highway State Trail. Much of this paved path is best toured by bicycle, but the twin tunnels near Mosier are interesting enough to attract hikers as well.

To start, drive Interstate 84 east of Hood River 5 miles to Mosier exit 69. Head south 0.2 mile to the village of Mosier and turn left on Rock Creek Road for 0.7 mile to the large Hatfield Trailhead on the left. A machine here accepts bills or credit cards for the area's $3-per-car fee. Follow a paved path back along the shoulder 200 yards and cross the road to a gate where the actual trail begins.

The "trail," of course, is a paved highway that's closed to traffic. The engineers who designed this pioneer road specified that it be 14 feet wide, with a minimum 100-foot radius on curves, and a maximum grade of 5 percent. Though unusually generous for 1921, such specifications now make the highway seem narrow and twisty.

This portion of the old road sets off across a strange, hummocky landscape of basalt rock piles. Shade is scarce so remember to bring a hat. The rockfield was formed by the crumbling rimrock above, and has been colonized only by a few Douglas firs, ponderosa pines, and oaks. If you look carefully, you might notice that some of the rock piles are not natural. Thousands of years ago, native tribes arranged the rocks in walls and pits. These are believed to be vision quest sites, where young men fasted to obtain guidance from the spirit world.

After 0.8 mile you'll enter the tunnels. The first is 288 feet long, with two windows carved out of the cliff wall. The windows overlook a rocky island in the river below, with the town of Bingen and the Hood River toll bridge in the distance. Sailboarders ride the windy river's whitecaps far below.

The shorter, second tunnel was connected to the first by a concrete roof in 1999. Engineers built this roof—and the concrete shed covering the road for 700

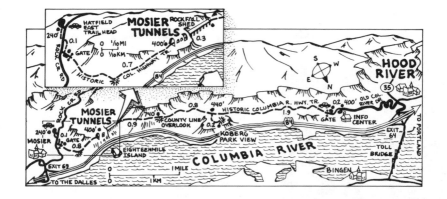

feet beyond the tunnels—to protect trail users from rockfall. Because the structures also had to keep rocks from bouncing down onto the railroad tracks and freeway below, they were designed with massive, flat roofs capable of catching a 5000 pound rock that has fallen 200 feet.

If you're not ready to turn back yet, consider continuing up to County Line Overlook, where the old highway skirts a tall riverside cliff near the border of Wasco and Hood River counties. Still not tired? Then sally onward another 0.8 mile and turn right on a 0.2-mile side path to a viewpoint knoll overlooking Koberg Beach State Wayside.

If you plan to hike (or bike) the entire 4.7-mile trail, you might want to start from the Hood River side, where two former gravel pits have been converted to trailhead parking lots with visitor facilities. To find this trailhead, drive Interstate 84 to the east end of Hood River, take exit 64 and follow "Government Camp" signs 0.3 mile to a stop sign. Then turn left onto Old Columbia River Drive for 1.3 miles to road's end.

The view from one of the tunnels' rock windows.   Opposite: Inside the tunnels.

56   Tom McCall Preserve

Easy (to plateau ponds)
2.2 miles round-trip
300 feet elevation gain
Open all year
Map: brochure at trailhead

Moderate (to McCall Point)
3.4 miles round-trip
1100 feet elevation gain
Open May 1 to October 30

This cliff-edged plateau of oak grasslands and wildflowers is one of the Nature Conservancy's most dramatic preserves. The conservancy is a non-profit private organization that quietly purchases ecologically sensitive land. Their preserve here has two trails. A path easy enough for children explores several ponds on a lower plateau overlooking the Columbia River, while a steeper trail climbs to the breathtaking mountain viewpoint atop McCall Point.

The best time to visit this dry eastern end of the Columbia Gorge is spring, when flowers dot the slopes. Grass widows are at their showiest in mid March, while yellow balsamroot and blue lupine peak in early May. Avoid the heat of July and August. And remember to wear long pants if you're taking the upper trail, as it passes poison oak.

Take Interstate 84 east from Hood River to Mosier exit 69 and follow "Scenic Loop" signs 6.6 miles to the Rowena Crest Viewpoint parking area. If you're coming from The Dalles, take Rowena exit 76 and follow a winding section of the historic Columbia River Highway up to the viewpoint. Because this is a nature preserve, dogs, horses, and bicycles are not allowed. Camping and flower picking are also banned. Hikers must stay on designated trails.

The easy path to the lower plateau starts at a stile and signboard on the opposite side of the highway from the viewpoint's entrance road. During the spring wildflower season, look here for sunflower-like balsamroot, purple

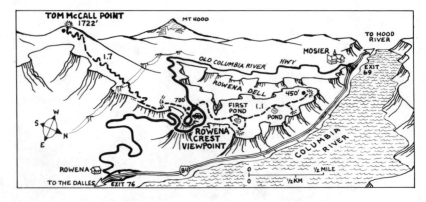

View from McCall Point.   Opposite: Cluster lily.

vetch, blue bachelor buttons, and white yarrow. Ten-inch-long ground squirrels zip about the fields from February to June but hibernate the other 7 months. Where the path crosses a narrow neck leading to the plateau notice the old stone wall that once fenced sheep.

After 0.3 mile take a right-hand fork of the trail around a pond full of lilypads and cattails. Listen for the melodious warble of redwing blackbirds. The trail loops past a cliff-edge viewpoint and returns to the main trail. Continue out the plateau past a smaller, poison-oak-fringed pond, and reach trail's end at a cliff with a view across the Columbia to the town of Lyle at the mouth of the Klickitat River. Note the 8 layers of basalt in the opposite cliffs, evidence of the repeated lava floods that deluged the Columbia Basin and created this plateau 10-17 million years ago.

To try the steeper path up McCall Point (open May through October), return to the parking area and look for a trail sign on the right at the start of the parking loop. This path joins an ancient road and turns left along the rim edge. When the trail forks at a large signboard, switchback up to the right on a steep path. Here the lower-elevation wildflowers are joined by red paintbrush and blue lupine. The trail switchbacks steeply up the ridgecrest through scrub oak (and poison oak) to a summit meadow with glorious views of Mt. Hood, Mt. Adams, and the entire eastern Columbia Gorge.

Mount Hood
West

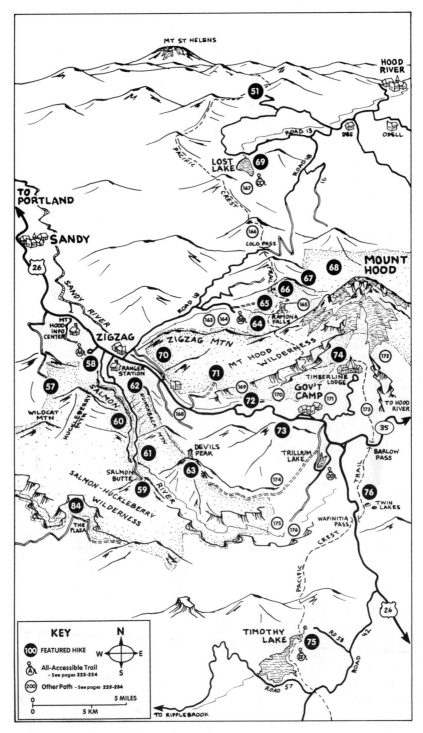

Opposite: Mt. Hood from Lost Lake (Hike #69).

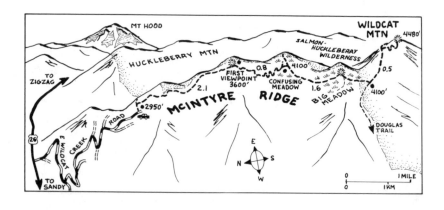

Wildcat Mountain from McIntyre Ridge.   *Opposite: Beargrass.*

57   Wildcat Mountain

Moderate
10 miles round-trip
1800 feet elevation gain
Open May to mid-November
Use: hikers, horses
Map: Salmon-Huckleberry (USFS)

Wildcat Mountain tops one of the westernmost ridges of the Cascades, with views extending from the Willamette Valley to Mt. Hood. The trail to this lookout site is surprisingly uncrowded, although it is less than an hour from Portland. In early summer, rhododendrons bloom in the trailside forest and beargrass plumes brighten the ridgecrest meadows.

From Portland, take Highway 26 east toward Mt. Hood 35 miles. Beyond Sandy 11 miles, just after the Shamrock Motel, turn right onto East Wildcat Creek Road for 4.1 miles. This gravel logging road has many unmarked forks, so always stick to the larger, uphill branch. Once you turn off Highway 26 you'll need to keep left after 0.3 mile, keep left again at 1.5 and 2.1 miles, switchback to the right at 2.8 miles, keep left at 3.1 miles, keep right at 3.4 miles, and veer left at 3.6 miles. Park at road's end in an old clearcut regrowing with hemlock and noble fir. Hike up to the left on an undrivable track 100 yards and then veer to the right on the McIntyre Ridge Trail.

The path soon enters old-growth mountain hemlock forest on McIntyre Ridge's rim. In June these woods feature pink rhododendrons, star-flowered smilacina, and the tiny white blooms of shamrock-leaved oxalis. After some ups and downs, the path climbs in earnest to the 2.1-mile mark and a viewpoint of Mt. Hood rising above Huckleberry Mountain (Hike #58).

After climbing another 0.8 mile the trail forks in a small but confusing beargrass meadow. Don't take the left fork, which leads to an old overgrown viewpoint. Fork to the right on a faint path for 200 feet, meet a larger trail, and turn right. Study this obscure junction so you can find it when you return.

Beyond the first meadow 0.3 mile the trail enters a much larger and grander field of beargrass extending along the ridgecrest to a small rocky rise with a sweeping view of Mt. Hood, Mt. Jefferson, and Wildcat Mountain ahead. The Coast Range's silhouette stretches south to the tall hump of Marys Peak.

The beargrass in these meadows is not actually grass at all, but rather a disguised lily that blooms on a 2- or 3-year cycle, filling the early summer fields with white plumes only in certain years. Bears eat the starchy roots and Indians once wove with the grass-like leaves.

Continue straight along the ridge another mile, turn left at the junction with the Douglas Trail, and climb 0.4 mile until the path crests. Here take a marked side trail uphill to the right 100 yards to a partly overgrown viewpoint at the old lookout site atop Wildcat Mountain.

58   Wildwood Area

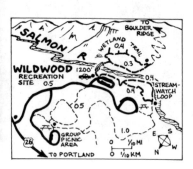

Easy (Wildwood loops)
1.5-mile loop
No elevation gain
Open all year

Difficult (Boulder Ridge Trail)
10.6 miles round-trip
3100 feet elevation gain
Use: hikers
Open May to mid-November
Map: Salmon-Huckleberry (USFS)

Difficult (Bonanza Trail)
11.6 miles round-trip
3000 feet elevation gain

Two very easy and two very hard hikes begin along the Salmon River near the village of Wildwood. If you're hiking with children, stick to the two easy, paved loops in the Bureau of Land Management's park-like Wildwood Recreation Site. For a more athletic challenge, tackle the Boulder Ridge or Bonanza Trails instead. They both rocket 3000 feet uphill to a rocky ridgecrest atop Huckleberry Mountain, where a view of four snowpeaks awaits.

From Portland, take Highway 26 east toward Mt. Hood 39 miles. Beyond Sandy 15 miles, turn right at a large sign for the Wildwood Recreation Site. The gate here is locked at sunset each day. It's also locked in winter, but hikers can always park here and walk half a mile to the trailhead. If the gate's open, keep left for half a mile and park beside the restrooms in the trailhead parking area. Expect to pay a $3 parking fee at a machine here.

Both of the short paths are wheelchair-accessible. The paved, 0.8-mile Cascade Streamwatch Trail starts to the right of the restrooms, ambles along the Salmon River, and explores a small side creek before looping back to the parking lot. Along the way you'll pass interpretive signs, a window with an underwater creek view, and a gravel beach suitable for sunbathing.

The next short walk, the Wetland Trail, starts to the left of the parking area's restrooms and crosses a 300-foot bridge over the Salmon River. On the far shore, turn left onto a boardwalk that skirts a slough in an alder forest. Explore 4 short spurs to the left to find viewpoints of cattails, skunk cabbage, and marsh wildlife. At the end of the boardwalk you can either turn right to return to your car, or you can turn left onto the rugged Boulder Ridge Trail.

If you're ready for a workout, follow the Boulder Ridge Trail. This path switchbacks steeply up through a Douglas fir forest. At the 1.8-mile mark, you'll gain a first glimpse of Mt. Hood and enter the Salmon-Huckleberry Wilderness. After another grueling half mile, a 20-foot path to the left leads to a cliff edge with an impressive view across Wemme and Zigzag Mountain (Hike #70) to Mt. Hood. This viewpoint makes a good turnaround point for a moderate hike. If you're still going strong, continue 2 miles up Boulder Ridge and turn right on the Plaza Trail for a mile to the superior view from a rocky crest atop Huckleberry Mountain.

Footbridge across the Salmon River.

Despite its steepness, the Boulder Ridge Trail sees heavy use. The nearby Bonanza Trail offers a quieter route to the same viewpoint, and it passes an explorable old mining tunnel along the way. To find the Bonanza Trail, drive Highway 26 a mile east from the Wildwood Recreation Site to the stoplight at Wemme. Turn right on Welches Road for 1.3 miles, keep left at a fork, continue another 0.7 mile to a junction, and go straight past a "One Lane Bridge" sign. Drive across a bridge, take the second gravel street to the left, and follow East Grove Lane a few hundred yards to a fork. The road straight ahead, closed by a cable, is the start of the trail. But parking is vehemently forbidden here or anywhere else nearby. To avoid being towed, drive back to a small parking space on the far side of the bridge or to the barely parkable shoulder of Welches Road.

Once you've parked and hiked back to the trailhead, walk up the road 200 yards to a sharp curve and continue straight on a path. This trail is easy for the first 1.6 miles, ambling through dappled alder woods along Cheeney Creek. Then it switchbacks up for 1.1 mile to the rusting ore-cart rails of the Bonanza Mine. A level, 6-foot-tall tunnel beside the trail extends back 100 feet. To continue, follow the Bonanza Trail up another 2.4 miles and turn right on the Plaza Trail along Huckleberry Mountain's ridgecrest. After 0.3 mile you'll pass a saddle with a view, but the best panorama is 0.2 mile beyond.

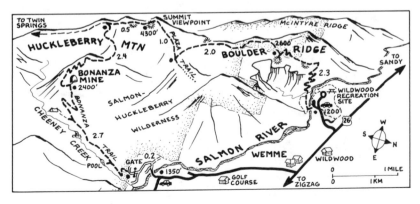

59   Salmon Butte

Difficult
8.8 miles round-trip
2840 feet elevation gain
Open mid-May to mid-November
Use: hikers, horses
Map: Salmon-Huckleberry (USFS)

Rhododendrons grow 15 feet tall along the trail to Salmon Butte, a lookout site smack in the midst of the Salmon-Huckleberry Wilderness. Even if you miss the rhodies' flower show in June, consider taking this remarkably well-graded trail for the summit's view across the Salmon River Canyon to Mt. Hood.

Drive Highway 26 to Zigzag (about 42 miles east of Portland) and turn south on the Salmon River Road for 4.9 paved miles and an additional 1.7 gravel miles to a (possibly unsigned) pullout on the left. Park here and walk up a narrow, partly barricaded dirt road to the right for 300 yards, keepihg straight at junctions. The trail proper starts on the left, at a turnaround area just before road's end.

The path climbs, steeply at first, into a forest of Douglas fir, red cedar, salal berry bushes, and Oregon grape. At the 1.4-mile mark you'll reach a bare ridge-end with a view ahead to Salmon Butte's green knob and Mack Hall Creek's valley.

Beyond this viewpoint the trail traverses a slope full of colossal rhododendrons. Chosen as Washington's state flower, rhodies cannot withstand a sharp freeze, and so only grow wild along the ocean shore where winters are mild and in the high mountains where snow falls deep enough to insulate them. Although countless colors of rhodies have been bred for city gardens, in the wild these huge, deceptively tropical-looking blooms only come in pink, or rarely, white.

At the 3.5-mile mark pass a first viewpoint of Mt. Hood. Continue 0.6 mile to a long-abandoned road, turn right, and follow the spiraling road to the summit.

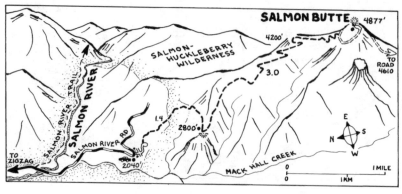

Melted glass and rusty nails are all that remain of the lookout tower that burned here. Mt. Hood looms above Devils Peak's green ridge (Hike #63), with snowy Mt. Adams, faint Mt. Rainier, and flat St. Helens to the left. On the southern horizon Mt. Jefferson seems surprisingly close, with all Three Sisters peering over his right shoulder.

Mt. Hood and Devils Peak from Salmon Butte.   Opposite: Oregon grape.

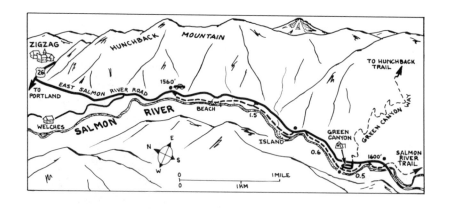

Salmon River Trail.   Opposite: Salmonberry flower.

Lower Salmon River

Easy
5.2 miles round-trip
100 feet elevation gain
Open all year
Use: hikers, bicycles
Map: Salmon-Huckleberry (USFS)

One of the most accessible old-growth forests in Oregon towers above this portion of the Salmon River. The popular riverside trail here not only passes 10-foot-thick red cedars, it also leads to small sandy beaches with deep green pools suitable for a chilly summer swim. And since a paved road parallels the route, it's easy to arrange a car shuttle so you can hike the 2.4-mile trail one way.

From Portland, take Highway 26 toward Mount Hood for 42 miles. At Zigzag turn right at a sign for the Salmon River Road and follow this paved route 2.7 miles. Two hundred yards beyond the national forest boundary sign, park at a pullout on the right for the Old Salmon River Trail.

The trail promptly descends to the river—a clear, 40-foot-wide mountain stream. In this ancient forest, huge Douglas firs filter sunlight for an understory of vine maple, sword fern, shamrock-shaped sourgrass, and deep green moss. Look for "nursery logs," fallen giants that provide a fertile platform above the brush for rows of seedling trees to catch light and take root.

Many side paths lead to the water's edge from the heavily used main trail. After 0.5 mile a particularly noticeable cross-path leads to a beach beside a 10-foot-deep pool in the river. Just upstream from this pleasant picnic site the river tumbles over two 4-foot falls.

Continue on the main trail to the 1.3-mile mark. Then watch for another worthwhile side trail to the right. This one crosses a bouldery, mostly dry oxbow slough to a forested island with pebbly river beaches.

Just 250 yards after the side trail to the island, the main trail joins the paved road. Walk along the road's shoulder 200 yards until the riverside trail continues. After another half mile you'll pass the campsites of Green Canyon Campground. Stay on the graveled path past the campground and an adjacent picnic area. Another 0.2 mile beyond, the trail joins the paved road for 200 yards and then ducks back into the woods for 0.2 mile to an upper trailhead parking area at the Salmon River Bridge.

Other Hiking Options

If you'd like to extend your hike once you reach the Salmon River Bridge, simply cross the road and continue on the longer, wilder portion of the Salmon River Trail described in Hike #61.

61 Central Salmon River

Easy (to Rolling Riffle Camp)
4.0 miles round-trip
200 feet elevation gain
Open all year
Map: Salmon-Huckleberry (USFS)

Moderate (to canyon viewpoint)
7.2 miles round-trip
900 feet elevation gain

This popular portion of the Salmon River Trail begins with a riverside stroll among huge old-growth trees. After 2 miles, the path leaves the river and climbs to a bluff with a view of the Salmon River's rugged upper canyon. Inaccessible waterfalls roar far below. Backpackers or hardy day hikers can continue on a demanding 15.7-mile loop to the Devils Peak lookout tower.

Start by driving Highway 26 to Zigzag, 42 miles east of Portland. Turn south at a sign for the Salmon River Road and follow this paved route 4.9 miles to a pullout on the left just before a bridge. Start at the "Salmon River Trail" sign on the left and hike upriver through a Douglas fir forest. Large white trilliums bloom here in spring. After 0.4 mile pass a deep, green river pool with bedrock banks. Beyond this point the forest is even grander, with 8-foot-thick, moss-draped firs.

At the 2-mile mark pass a signed "Toilet Area" on the left and Rolling Riffle Camp on the right. The Forest Service asks backpackers to confine camping in this area to the 10 sites along the riverbank. Space is tight on weekends and campfires are strongly discouraged.

If you're out for an easy day hike, you might want to turn back 0.2 mile further at a footbridge over a side creek, where the big old-growth trees end and the trail leaves the river. If you'd like a longer hike, however, continue 1.4 miles uphill to a fork in the trail at a "Fragile Area" sign. Veer right for a viewpoint

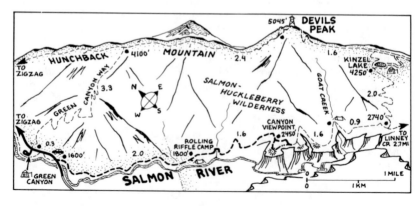

The Salmon River Canyon.   Opposite: The Salmon River.

loop across a grassy slope overlooking the Salmon River's huge canyonland. Do not venture off the trail, because the steep, pebble-strewn slopes are deceptively slippery. After 300 yards the narrow path reenters the woods and climbs steeply to rejoin the main trail.

The roar in this canyon is caused by a string of waterfalls. Up the Salmon River Trail another 0.2 mile, a side trail to the right leads down to a grassy knoll, from which a rugged scramble path to the right descends 0.3 mile to a partly obscured overlook of aptly named Vanishing Falls, Frustration Falls, and Final Falls. This slippery, unprotected scramble trail has caused at least one fatal accident and is not recommended.

Other Hiking Options

If you'd like to tackle the difficult, 15.7-mile loop to Devils Peak, continue up the Salmon River Trail 2.5 miles and turn left on the Kinzel Lake Trail. After climbing 2 miles, ignore a side trail to the right to Kinzel Lake's car campground. Continue uphill on a faint trail to Road 2613 and turn left on the Hunchback Trail to Devils Peak (see Hike #63). Beyond the lookout 2.4 miles take the steep Green Canyon Way left 3.3 miles to the road, 0.3 mile from your car.

For a less strenuous backpacking trip, arrange a car shuttle to the upper end of the Salmon River Trail (see Hike #176) and hike up the wilderness river a total of 14.4 miles.

62 Hunchback Mountain

Moderate (to rimrock viewpoint)
4.2 miles round-trip
1700 feet elevation gain
Open late April to mid-November
Use: hikers
Map: Salmon-Huckleberry (USFS)

Difficult (to Great Pyramid)
9 miles round-trip
2900 feet elevation gain

Handy for a bit of exercise, this trail switchbacks from the Zigzag Ranger Station up the long, wooded ridge known as Hunchback Mountain. After climbing steeply for 2.1 miles, the path passes a rimrock viewpoint overlooking the forested valleys of the Salmon-Huckleberry Wilderness. For a better look east to Mt. Hood, continue up and down along the ridgecrest to three other viewpoints.

Start at the Zigzag Ranger Station, 42 miles east of Portland on Highway 26. As you drive into the entrance from the highway, veer left into a large parking area. Park near the far end by a sign for the Hunchback Mountain Trail.

After hiking 50 yards you'll cross a side trail, pass a spring house, and head uphill. The first mile, with 8 long switchbacks, is so well graded it's never very steep. Deep moss, lady ferns, sword ferns, and vine maple make the Douglas fir forest here lush and jungly. Traffic noise from the highway slowly fades.

Then the trail suddenly steepens. The second mile, with 10 switchbacks, is a grueling climb. Notice the shamrock-shaped leaves of oxalis covering the forest floor. This April wildflower is also known as sourgrass because its leaves have a tart, refreshing citrus flavor when chewed—in small doses, a temporary thirst-quencher while climbing.

The rimrock viewpoint at 2.1 miles makes a good goal. From the rim of a 100-foot cliff, views extend across castle-like crags to the green-fluted canyons

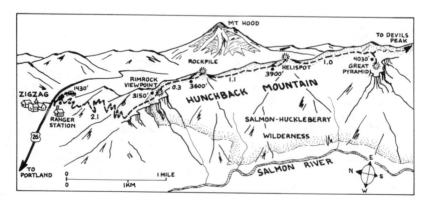

of the Salmon River. The top half of Mt. Hood protrudes to the east.

After this viewpoint the poorly graded trail roller-coasters along the ridge-crest. Though views are few from the trail itself, three short side trails scramble up to panoramas. At the 2.4-mile mark, you can follow a "Viewpoint Rockpile" sign 100 steep yards to the right to a rocky crest with a full frontal view of Mt. Hood. After another 1.1 mile along the Hunchback Trail a sign for "Viewpoint Helispot 260" marks a steep 200-yard side trail to a summit with a similar view. And after yet another mile along the Hunchback Trail, a signed side trail leads to Great Pyramid, a narrow rock promontory jutting out above the Salmon River Valley.

Other Hiking Options

The Hunchback Trail continues past Great Pyramid with some steep ups and downs for 3.6 miles to the Devils Peak lookout tower. While this would be a very difficult 16.2-mile round trip from Zigzag, the hike can be shortened by shuttling a car to one of the three trailheads nearer to Devils Peak: Green Canyon Campground, the Cool Creek Trailhead, or the Hunchback Trailhead near Kinzel Lake. These routes are described in Hikes #61 and #63.

Ridge alongside the trail.   Opposite: Mt. Hood from Rockpile viewpoint.

63   Devils Peak Lookout

Easy (from Road 2613)
2.4 miles round-trip
600 feet elevation gain
Open June to mid-November
Use: hikers, horses
Map: Salmon-Huckleberry (USFS)

Difficult (via Cool Creek Trail)
8.2 miles round-trip
3200 feet elevation gain

The unstaffed lookout tower atop Devils Peak, with a view from Mt. Hood to Mt. Jefferson, is maintained by volunteers as a cozy shelter and lunch spot for hikers. Getting there, however, poses a dilemma. The trail from Road 2613 is short, easy, and scenic—but the drive to the trailhead is a nightmare on a seemingly endless dirt road. The other trailhead is easily accessible—but the hike itself is 3 times longer and demands 5 times more climbing.

If you opt for the easy walk (and the hard drive), take Highway 26 to the Trillium Lake turnoff 3 miles east of Government Camp. Follow paved Road 2656 for 1.7 miles—passing the campground entrance—and then keep right on Road 2612 around the lake. After another 1.5 miles turn left onto Road 2613 and follow this narrow, bouldery, rough dirt road for 10 miles to its end at the Hunchback Mountain Trailhead. High-clearance 4-wheel-drive vehicles can navigate these final miles well enough, but passenger cars will find them slow and punishing.

The trail starts beside the ruin of an old garage and traverses a forest full of pink rhododendrons (in June), beargrass blooms (in July), and ripe blue huckleberries (in August). After 0.4 mile emerge from the woods at a ridgecrest with a stunning view of Mt. Hood to the north. Be sure to peer south over the ridgecrest, too, into the Salmon River's wilderness valley. Next the path switchbacks twice up the side of Devils Peak, passes the steep Cool Creek Trail on the

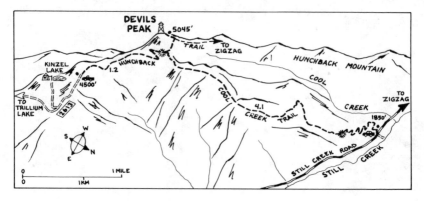

Mt. Hood from the lookout door.   Opposite: The Devils Peak lookout.

right, and 100 yards later meets a trail on the left to the lookout tower. The tower itself is generally unlocked, with battened windows, a wood stove, and two cots. Since the site is no longer used for fire spotting, trees have grown up, limiting the view somewhat.

If you prefer to get here on a more rugged hike (but an easier drive), take Highway 26 to the Still Creek Road turnoff 1.4 miles east of Zigzag. Follow this road 2.6 miles to the end of pavement and continue on good gravel 0.3 mile to the crossing of Cool Creek. Drive slowly another 300 yards, watching for an inconspicuous "Cool Creek Trail" sign on the right. Park near here, beside a short spur road leading down to the shore of Still Creek.

Despite its name, the Cool Creek Trail never approaches a creek. Instead it launches up a ridge at a grueling grade. After 0.7 mile the path emerges from the woods to a slope with June-blooming rhododendrons and vistas of Mt. Hood. Then the trail climbs again through woods until the 3.5-mile mark, when it reaches a bare ridgecrest with a view extending all the way to Mt. Adams. After another half mile turn right onto the Hunchback Trail for 100 yards to the lookout path.

Other Hiking Options

By arranging a car shuttle, you can descend from Devils Peak on the 8-mile Hunchback Trail to the Zigzag Ranger Station (see Hike #62).

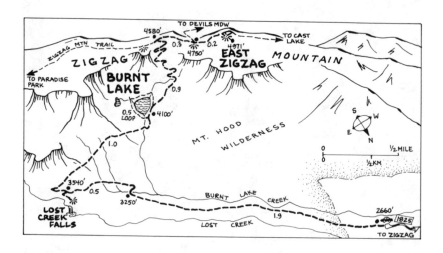

64   Burnt Lake

Moderate (to Burnt Lake)
6.8 miles round-trip
1500 feet elevation gain
Open June through October
Map: Mt. Hood Wilderness (Geo-Graphics)

Difficult (to East Zigzag)
9.6 miles round-trip
2370 feet elevation gain

Dragonflies dip into Burnt Lake's reflection of Mt. Hood, splitting the snowy volcano into ripples. This is one of the cherished sanctums of the Mt. Hood Wilderness, just far enough from the world of roads to keep casual tourists at bay. A well-graded trail to the lake passes a waterfall, wildflowers, and huckleberries. For a longer hike, continue up to East Zigzag, a former fire lookout site with a bird's-eye view of the magic mountain.

The Forest Service is planning a permit system to keep Burnt Lake uncrowded, perhaps beginning in 2003. Day hikers and campers would be required to apply for a free permit in advance, either online at *www.fs.fed.us/r6/mthood* or from the Mt. Hood Information Center on Highway 26 (1-888-622-4822).

To find the trailhead from Portland, take Highway 26 toward Mt. Hood for 42 miles. At the village of Zigzag, turn left onto East Lolo Pass Road. After 4.2 miles turn right onto paved Road 1825 for 0.7 mile, and then turn right across the Sandy River bridge. Follow Road 1825 another 2.1 miles to the Lost Creek Campground entrance. Then veer left onto a gravel road for 1.4 miles to its end at a parking area.

The trail sets off through a stile designed to enforce a ban on bicyclists and horses. For the next half mile the path traverses second-growth woods with ancient stumps, white bunchberry flowers, and plenty of blue huckleberries (ripe in late August). Then sally into uncut stands of Douglas fir, hemlock, and cedar. Note the 18-inch leaves of spiny devils club among the undergrowth.

After 1.9 miles the path crosses Burnt Lake Creek on stepping stones and passes several gigantic cedar snags. Hollowed by the 19th-century fire that gave Burnt Lake its name, the blackened 10-foot-wide trunks are large enough for children to stand inside. In another half mile the trail forks. Detour briefly 100 yards down to the left to see Lost Creek Falls, a series of four mossy cascades in a contorted rock gorge. Then continue on the main trail and climb steadily for a mile to Burnt Lake. If you're stopping at the lake, hike the half-mile path that loops around its shore. Backpackers should expect to search a bit to find the area's approved campsites. Fires are banned within half a mile.

If you're continuing to East Zigzag, keep right past the lake for 0.9 mile up to a junction in a wooded saddle. Turn right on a steep path that traces a ridgecrest toward ever grander vistas of Mt. Hood, distant Mt. Adams, and truncated Mt. St. Helens. Along the way you'll traverse a subalpine rock garden with cushions of lavender phlox, plumes of beargrass, fuzzy cats ears, red paintbrush, and purple larkspur. Continue straight up the ridge half a mile to East Zigzag's summit, where the view opens south past the green swaths of Multorpor Mountain's ski runs to ghostly Mt. Jefferson.

Mt. Hood from Burnt Lake.   Opposite: Burnt Lake from East Zigzag.

65   Ramona Falls

Moderate (to Ramona Falls)
7.1-mile loop
1000 feet elevation gain
Open late April through October
Use: hikers, horses
Map: Mt. Hood Wilderness (Geo-Graphics)

Difficult (to Bald Mountain)
13.2-mile loop
2000 feet elevation gain
Open June through October

Like white lace, 120-foot Ramona Falls drapes across a stair-stepped cliff of columnar basalt. It's understandably one of the most popular hiking goals in the Mount Hood area, even though a 1997 flood and road closure lengthened the round-trip tour by 2.6 miles. Hikers can return from the falls on either of two loop paths: a shortcut horse trail along the Sandy River or a challenging section of the Pacific Crest Trail past Bald Mountain's dramatic view of Mt. Hood.

To drive here from Portland, take Highway 26 toward Mt. Hood for 42 miles. At the village of Zigzag, turn left onto East Lolo Pass Road. After 4.2 miles turn right onto paved Road 1825, and in 0.7 mile turn right across the Sandy River bridge. Continue 1.8 miles on what is still Road 1825, and then fork left onto Road 100 for half a mile to a large parking area at road's end.

The trail starts at the right-hand side of the parking area and ambles through a mossy forest of small alders and hemlocks beside the Sandy River's bouldery outwash plain. The pioneers who named this river thought its milky color was caused by sand. In fact the stream carries glacial silt, rock that has been powdered by the grinding weight of Mt. Hood's glaciers.

After 1.2 miles the path crosses the Sandy River on a temporary bridge. Forest Service crews remove the bridge each year near the end of October and replace it each spring, usually in late April, after the danger of floods has lessened.

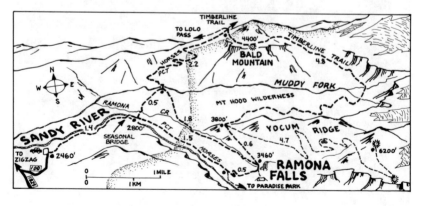

Mt. Hood from the Sandy River crossing.   Opposite: Ramona Falls.

A few hundred yards beyond the bridge you'll reach a trail junction with signs marking the start of the loop. The shortest route to the falls is the horse trail to the right, but it's much less scenic, so leave it as a possible return route. Instead go left. This path crosses a creek and traverses a lodgepole pine forest to the wild Muddy Fork of the Sandy River. Here, turn right on a path that soon follows the mossy bank of Ramona Creek—a delightful woodsy stream that leads up to the base of the falls.

If you're backpacking, note that camping is banned within 500 feet of Ramona Falls. A side path leads to a designated camping area just south of the falls.

Hikers at Ramona Falls have to decide whether to take the moderate or the difficult loop back. For the short loop, turn right at the falls and keep right on a horse trail.

If you have the energy for the longer, prettier loop to Bald Mountain, however, turn left at the falls and follow the Timberline Trail around Yocum Ridge 3 miles to Muddy Fork, a milky, glacial outwash river. The bridgeless crossing is tricky in June and on summer afternoons, when snowmelt swells this two-branched torrent. Horses are banned on this trail, largely because of this crossing.

After negotiating both branches of Muddy Fork, the Pacific Crest Trail climbs steadily to a cliff-edged meadow on Bald Mountain, where Mt. Hood dominates a sweeping view. Half a mile beyond the viewpoint turn sharply left at a 4-way trail junction, following signs for the Pacific Crest Trail's horse route. This path descends in 7 long switchbacks to a 60-foot bridge over the Muddy Fork. Cross the bridge and keep right to complete the loop back to your car.

66　McNeil Point

Easy (around Bald Mountain)
2.2-mile loop
400 feet elevation gain
Open June to early November
Use: hikers, horses
Map: Mt. Hood Wilderness (Geo-Graphics)

Moderate (to ponds below McNeil Point)
6.8 miles round-trip
Open mid-July through October
1500 feet elevation gain

Wildflowers, tumbling brooks, and craggy mountain vistas lend alpine splendor to this ridge on Mt. Hood's northwest shoulder. An easy loop circles Bald Mountain to a picture-postcard view of Mt. Hood. But for real alpine drama, climb the Timberline Trail to a pair of ponds reflecting massive McNeil Point.

Turn north off Highway 26 at the Zigzag store (42 miles east of Portland) onto East Lolo Pass Road. After 4.2 miles turn right onto paved Road 1825. In 0.7 mile go straight onto Road 1828 and follow signs for "Top Spur Trail No. 785" for another 7.1 miles to a pullout on a good gravel road.

The Top Spur Trail starts in a patch of blue huckleberries (ripe in August), and climbs through a forest of hemlock and Douglas fir. Look for bunchberry, carpeting the ground with white blooms in June and red berries in fall.

After 0.5 mile turn right on the Pacific Crest Trail for 60 yards to a big, 4-way trail junction that can be confusing. *Go uphill to the right* on the Timberline Trail (formerly the Pacific Crest Trail's hiker route). Don't go left, and don't take the Pacific Crest Trail horse route to the far right. The correct path soon emerges from the woods onto the steep, meadowed face of Bald Mountain, with views ahead to Mt. Hood and west to the distant Willamette Valley.

After 0.4 mile through these meadows, watch carefully for the unmarked loop trail around Bald Mountain. When the trail reenters the woods after the second, smaller meadow, continue 100 yards to a fork in a draw, just beyond a former

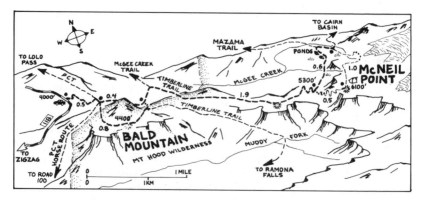

Mt. Hood from Bald Mountain.   Opposite: McNeil Point shelter.

campsite on the left. *Take the unmarked left-hand fork* over a ridge 100 yards to an unsigned junction with another section of the Timberline Trail. For the easy loop, turn left here to return to the car. If you'd like a longer hike, turn right.

If you turn right on this portion of the Timberline Trail (heading *clockwise* around Mt. Hood this time), you'll climb up a ridgecrest with wind-dwarfed firs, summer-blooming beargrass, and mountain views. After 1.9 miles the trail switchbacks 4 times up a steep wildflower meadow and passes an unmarked scramble trail on the right. Keep straight on the Timberline Trail, which now passes a creek and two reflecting ponds amidst a dazzling display of early August wildflowers: red paintbrush, blue lupine, and the fuzzy seedheads of old-man-of-the-mountain (western pasque flower). From the ponds, sharp eyes can spot the McNeil Point shelter high on the ridge above.

If you're backpacking, be sure to camp out of sight in the woods and not on the fragile meadows or shore. Bring a stove, as campfires are banned within 500 feet of the shelter and are discouraged anywhere near timberline.

Other Hiking Options

No marked trails lead through the alpine landscape to McNeil Point's shelter, but a 1.5-mile user path makes a rugged loop possible. To try the loop, continue 0.2 mile past the ponds to an unmarked junction at a creek crossing. Go straight on the path up the creek toward Mt. Hood. This path fades somewhat in 0.3 mile at the base of a snowfield, but climb steeply left to a ridgecrest and then traverse to the right across a rockslide or snowfield. In a mile the path reaches the 10-foot-square stone shelter, built in the 1930s by the CCC and later named to honor Portland newspaperman Fred McNeil (1893-1958). The extremely steep, final portion of the unofficial loop trail dives 0.5 mile down a rocky ridge-end from the shelter to the Timberline Trail. Only attempt this dangerous section if you're prepared to use your hands and watch for loose rocks.

67 Mazama Trail

Diffiicult (to ridge viewpoint)
8.4 miles round-trip
2500 feet elevation gain
Open Open mid-July through October
Map: Mt. Hood Wilderness (Geo-Graphics)

The Mazamas, Portland's first outdoor club, held its inaugural meeting on top of Mt. Hood in 1893, when 155 men and 38 women trekked to the snowy summit to elect the club's first president. A century later the club decided to give something back to its baptismal peak by restoring an abandoned trail on the mountain's beautiful, less-visited north flank.

The newly completed Mazama Trail may not be the quickest route to Mt. Hood's alpine glories—both Hikes #66 and #68 describe nearby routes with 1000 feet less elevation gain—but as the Mazamas proved with their 1893 meeting on Mt. Hood's summit, easier is not always better.

From Portland, drive Highway 26 toward Mt. Hood 42 miles. At the Zigzag store, turn left onto East Lolo Pass Road (Road 18) and follow this paved route 10.5 miles to Lolo Pass. Here turn right onto gravel McGee Creek Road 1810 for 5.5 miles. Just before Road 1810 becomes paved, turn right on gravel Road 1811 for 2.5 miles to a parking pullout on the left in a ridgecrest saddle.

The Mazama Trail sets off toward Mt. Hood through a 1990 clearcut regrowing with rhododendrons, beargrass, and noble fir. Soon the path enters old-growth hemlock woods and launches up the face of Cathedral Ridge. Ancient blazes on the lichen-draped trees show that the track once scrambled straight up this slope. Thousands of hours of Mazama volunteer trailwork have replaced that bobsled run with switchbacks. It's still a thigh-burning climb. When you pause

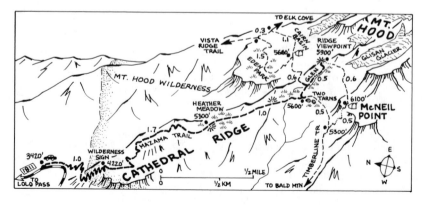

to catch your breath, take time to pick a few huckleberries (if it's August), or to admire the millions of white avalanche lilies that bloom in these woods (in July).

After climbing 2.7 miles the path levels off across a heather meadow with a Mt. Hood view. The trail's final mile is relatively easy. When you reach the Timberline Trail, so many alpine wonders lie near at hand that it's hard to decide which way to turn. To the right you could tackle a very rugged 2.1-mile loop to McNeil Point's stone shelter (described in Hike #66). To the left you could take a long 4.1-mile loop across raging creeks to Cairn Basin and Eden Park (described in Hike #68).

Considering that you've already climbed 2200 feet, however, why not settle for a couple of closer goals? First explore the Timberline Trail 200 yards to the right to discover a pair of tarns with first-rate reflections of Mt. Hood and McNeil Point. Then backtrack to the junction and take the Timberline Trail 200 yards the other direction. At a creek, veer right on an unmarked path up through a gorgeous glen of wildflowers: white beargrass plumes, red paintbrush, blue lupine, and pink heather. After 0.3 mile this trail climbs left beside a snowfield to a satisfying turnaround point—a sunny ridgecrest with a close-up view of Mt. Hood.

Mt. Hood from the ridge viewpoint.   Opposite: Avalanche lilies.

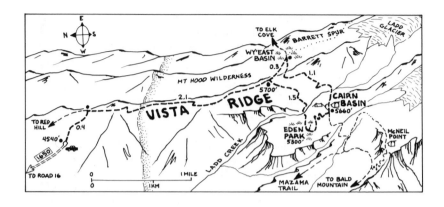

68   Cairn Basin

Moderate
7.9-mile loop
1700 feet elevation gain
Open mid-July through October
Use: hikers
Map: Mt. Hood Wilderness (Geo-Graphics)

This alpine trail up Vista Ridge not only has views of Mt. Hood's craggy north face, it also loops through three wildflower-packed vales: Wy'East Basin, Cairn Basin, and Eden Park.

From Highway 26, turn north at the Zigzag store onto East Lolo Pass Road (Road 18) and follow this paved route 10.5 miles to Lolo Pass. Here turn right onto gravel McGee Creek Road (Road 1810) for 7.7 miles until it rejoins Road 18. Then continue on pavement 3.2 miles and turn right onto Road 16. From here on, signs for "Vista Ridge Trail No. 626" will direct you 9 miles along Roads 16 and 1650 uphill to the trailhead. The final 0.7 mile of Road 1650 is rough but still passable for passenger cars.

The trail begins along an old cat road but soon dives into a lichen-draped forest of hemlock and Douglas fir. After 0.4 mile turn right and ascend a long, forested ridge. Blue huckleberry bushes here mingle with false huckleberry (mock azalea), recognizable by its bigger bell-shaped flowers and larger whorled leaves.

After 2.1 miles, reach a trail junction on a meadowed ridge with views of 4 mountains: Hood, Adams, St. Helens, and Rainier. The alpine wildflowers—best in early August—include red paintbrush, pink heather, blue lupine, and entire hillsides of delicate white avalanche lilies.

Turn left at this junction for 0.3 mile to a basin called Wy'East—after Mt. Hood's legendary Indian name. Turn right in Wy'East Basin's lupine-filled meadow following a sign for Cairn Basin. This path crosses a ridge and switchbacks down to a bridgeless crossing of Ladd Creek. Look up and down this sometimes raging stream for the safest place to cross. On the far shore the path leads into the forested but badly trammeled Cairn Basin area. A 10-foot-square stone shelter stands on the left, while a path to the right leads to a designated camping area.

The main trail is confused here by overuse, but continue on the level through the trees to a trail junction beside a wildflower-lined creeklet. Turn right and switchback down 0.3 mile to Eden Park's meadowy bowl. Just beyond Eden Park, recross bridgeless Ladd Creek as best you can. On the far shore the path scrambles upstream a bit before climbing back to the Vista Ridge Trail and the route back to the car.

Other Hiking Options

The alpine country around Cairn Basin invites exploration. One option is to take the 2.7-mile loop west along the Timberline Trail to McNeil Point (see Hike #66). Another possibility is to climb cross-country from Wy'East Basin up a series of meadows and bluffs to Barrett Spur, an open ridge with breathtaking views of the Coe and Ladd Glaciers. The topmost viewpoint accessible without climbing gear is 1.3 miles from Wy'East Basin and a grueling 2000 feet up.

Avalanche lilies and Mt. Hood from Vista Ridge.   Opposite: Cairn Basin's shelter.

69   Lost Lake

Easy (around the lake)
3.4-mile loop
100 feet elevation gain
Open mid-May through October
Use: hiker only
Map: Bull Run Lake (USGS)

Moderate (to Lost Lake Butte)
3.8 miles round-trip
1300 feet elevation gain

An old-growth forest circles Lost Lake, the classic setting for picture post-cards of Mt. Hood. For an easy loop, try the 3.4-mile lakeshore trail. If this isn't enough exercise, climb a neighboring volcanic butte to a former lookout site with a broader panorama.

Lost Lake was known to the Hood River Indians as E-e-kwahl-a-mat-yam-ishkt, or "Heart of the Mountains." When an expedition of white men had trouble finding the legendary lake in 1880 they declared they were not lost; the lake was. Today the lake is quite definitely found. Forest Service projects have restored the overused lakeshore, added a half-mile-long boardwalk through an old-growth cedar grove, and expanded the campground to one of the largest in Northwest Oregon.

To find the lake from Portland, take Highway 26 for 42 miles, turn left at the Zigzag store onto East Lolo Pass Road (Road 18) and follow this paved route 10.5 miles to Lolo Pass. Here turn right onto gravel McGee Creek Road (Road 1810) for 7.7 miles until it rejoins Road 18. Continue on pavement 7 miles and then turn left onto Road 13 for 6 miles to the Lost Lake entry station booth.

To find the lake from Interstate 84, take West Hood River exit 62, drive into town 1.1 mile, turn right on 13th Street, and follow signs for Odell 5 miles. After crossing a bridge, fork to the right past Tucker Park for 6.3 miles. Then fork to the right to Dee and follow signs 14 miles to Lost Lake. Travelers from Portland will find

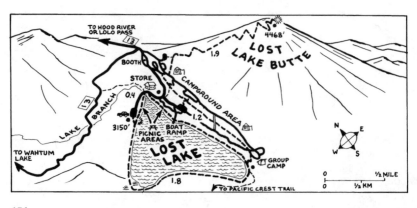

The Lost Lake Old Growth Trail.   Opposite: Mt. Hood from Lost Lake.

this route 10 miles longer than the route via Lolo Pass, but entirely paved.

Drive past the Lost Lake entry booth, follow signs to the rustic general store, and continue right around the lake to a picnic area parking lot at road's end. The lakeshore trail begins at the far end of the parking lot, where the view of Mt. Hood is at its finest. Numbered posts along the trail correspond to numbers in a nature trail booklet available at the store for a quarter.

The broad lakeshore path sets out through a forest of big hemlocks and cedars. Count on seeing striped Townsend's chipmunks, orange-bellied Douglas squirrels, gray jays, and pointy-hooded Stellar's jays, all of which are accustomed to gleaning crumbs from the nearby picnic area. Small white wildflowers dot the forest floor in early summer: queen's cup, bunchberry, and vanilla leaf. After 0.6 mile a boardwalk crosses the lake's marshy inlet creek, where huge-leaved skunk cabbage puts out yellow blooms.

At the 1.8-mile mark, the Huckleberry Trail joins from the right. A hundred yards later veer to the right on the Old Growth Trail. This graveled path switchbacks twice to a campground road. Follow the road 100 feet to find the continuation of the trail—a remarkable half-mile boardwalk through a grove of 8-foot-thick cedars. Decked pullouts have benches and interpretive signs. Beyond the end of boardwalk 0.3 mile turn left, make your way down through the campground, and follow the lakeshore path onward to your car.

You can climb Lost Lake Butte either at the end of the lakeshore loop or as a separate trip. The butte's trail begins at the entrance to Campground Loop B and climbs steadily through woods thick with rhododendrons and beargrass. The old lookout tower has been reduced to a pile of boards, but the view is intact: huge Mt. Hood to the south, a glimpse of Lost Lake to the west, Adams and Rainier to the north, and the brown Columbia River Plateau far to the east.

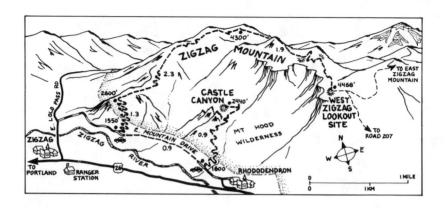

70   West Zigzag Mountain

Easy (to Castle Canyon)
1.8 miles round-trip
800 feet elevation gain
Open all year
Map: Mt. Hood Wilderness (Geo-Graphics)

Difficult (to lookout site)
11 miles round-trip
Open May through November
Use: hikers, horses
3100 feet elevation gain

Forests cloak this steep ridge in the westernmost corner of the Mt. Hood Wilderness, but two convenient trails lead to viewpoints above the trees. The first is a short but very steep path to a collection of craggy rock towers. The second is a strenuous conditioning hike—a 3000-foot climb at a steady grade to the clifftop site of a former lookout building.

From Portland, drive Highway 26 toward Mt. Hood 44 miles. For the short hike to Castle Canyon, turn left in the village of Rhododendron, just after milepost 44, onto East Littlebrook Lane. Keepl laft on a small paved road 0.3 mile, and then turn left on gravel, following a "Barlow Road Route" pointer for 0.4 mile to the trailhead sign on the right. Park on the left-hand shoulder just before the trail.

As you start up the Castle Canyon Trail, you'll switchback through a young Douglas fir forest with a smattering of little vine maple trees that turn brilliant red in autumn. The most common bush here is salal, whose tough blue berries were valued by Northwest Indians. Nineteenth-century botanist David Douglas so admired this evergreen shrub that he popularized its use as an ornamental in England's formal gardens.

After half a mile of stiff climbing you'll pass the first of this canyon's mossy rock outcroppings. Just before the trail peters out at the 0.9-mile mark, contour left to a rocky spine among the towers. Footing is hazardous here, so hang onto children. The barren bluff of the West Zigzag lookout site is visible above to the east while Hunchback Mountain (Hike #62) looms across the Zigzag Valley.

If you'd prefer a tougher climb to the better view at the West Zigzag lookout site, start your hike at a different trailhead instead. To find it, drive back to Highway 26, head west toward Portland 2 miles to the village of Zigzag, and turn north onto East Lolo Pass Road for 0.4 mile. Then turn right onto East Mountain Drive, a potholed gravel lane. After 0.2 mile, keep right at a fork by a telephone pole. In another half mile look for a sign on the left marking the Zigzag Mountain Trail. Park on the shoulder a few hundred feet back.

The Zigzag Mountain Trail climbs relentlessly for its first 3.6 miles, yet it is so well graded that it manages to gain more than 3000 feet without being unbearably steep. On the way up you'll leave the vine maple / salal zone, pass through a level where pink rhododendrons bloom in June, and finally enter a high-altitude fir forest with beargrass and manzanita.

The final 1.9 miles to the lookout site follow the ridgecrest up and down, sometimes skirting cliffs with views east to Mt. Hood or west down the Sandy River toward Portland. Four concrete piers mark the site of the old fire lookout on a dramatic bluff high above the crags of Castle Canyon and the towns of Rhododendron and Zigzag. Flag Mountain looks like the green back of a crocodile sleeping in the Zigzag Valley below, while the tip of Mt. Jefferson peers over the shoulder of Devils Peak (Hike #63).

Cliffs near West Zigzag's lookout site.   Opposite: Salal flowers.

71   East Zigzag Mountain

Moderate (to East Zigzag)
8-mile loop
1700 feet elevation gain
Open mid-May to mid-November
Use: hikers, horses
Map: Mt. Hood Wilderness (Geo-Graphics)

Difficult (to East and West Zigzag)
11.4-mile loop
2400 feet elevation gain

The meadow atop East Zigzag Mountain offers a full frontal view of Mt. Hood and glimpses of four more distant Cascade peaks. From the trailhead in Devil Canyon you can hike to East Zigzag's summit via either of two loops: a moderate route or a more difficult loop that extends along a ridgecrest to West Zigzag's lookout site. In either case it's tempting to take the short, nearly level detour to Cast Lake, a nice lunch stop.

To find the trailhead from Portland, take Highway 26 toward Mt. Hood 47 miles. At a junction 1.5 miles beyond the village of Rhododendron (and 100 yards before milepost 46), turn left onto paved Road 27 for 0.6 mile. Then turn left onto gravel Road 207 for 4.5 narrow, winding miles to a parking area at road's end. The final half mile of this road is very rough and rocky. Passengers cars should proceed with caution.

Start on the Burnt Lake Trail, which for its first 2 miles is actually an ancient road leading to a long-abandoned campground at Devils Meadow. In June expect pink rhododendrons, delicate twinflowers, and tiny white starflowers blooming in the quiet trailside forest. Devils Meadow is a bracken-filled slope with July flowers: purple aster, red paintbrush, yellow goldenrod, and an occasional tiger lily.

Follow "Burnt Lake Trail" signs up from Devils Meadow and straight past a junction with the Devils Tie Trail (the short loop's return route). You'll switch-

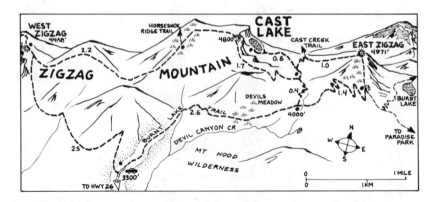

Cast Lake.   Opposite: Mt. Hood from the trail junction near East Zigzag.

back up through drier woods, gaining views south to Hunchback Mountain (Hike #62), Devils Peak (Hike #63), and Mt. Jefferson. Then crest a ridge to a trail junction with a terrific view of Mt. Hood. Notice Burnt Lake (Hike #64) below the peak and Paradise Park (Hike #74) on the mountain's right shoulder.

Turn left along the ridgecrest, following the Zigzag Mountain Trail steeply up to the East Zigzag lookout site, where the view widens to include Mt. St. Helens, the distant flats of the Willamette Valley, and the entire route of your hike. Then continue downhill 0.7 mile, turn left at a junction with the Cast Creek Trail, and 300 yards later reach the Cast Lake junction. Unless you're truly exhausted, it's worth it to detour 0.6 mile over a little pass to Cast Lake, a remarkably crawdad-filled pool with a sometimes island and a glimpse of Mt. Hood's tip.

When you continue on the Zigzag Mountain Trail past the Cast Lake turnoff, you'll soon reach a junction with the Devils Tie Trail. For the moderate 8.1-mile loop, go left on the trail that switchbacks down to Devils Meadow and the path back to the car. For the longer loop via West Zigzag, go uphill to the right.

This next portion of the Zigzag Mountain Trail climbs steeply to a clifftop overlooking Cast Lake, then dips across a forested saddle to the scenic beargrass meadows at the junction of the Horseshoe Ridge Trail. Continue 2.2 viewless miles on the sometimes rocky, brushy Zigzag Mountain Trail to a junction with the West Zigzag Trail that leads back down to your car—but don't go to your car yet! First continue 0.2 mile on the ridgecrest trail to the dramatic clifftop site of West Zigzag's former lookout, now marked by concrete piers.

Laurel Hill

Easy (to 2 viewpoints)
2.4 miles round-trip
400 feet elevation gain
Open March to mid-December
Map: Mt. Hood Wilderness (Geo-Graphics)

Moderate (Pioneer Bridle Trail)
8.2 mile round-trip
900 feet elevation gain
Use: hikers, horses, bicycles

For a walk through history, explore the trails on this forested ridge near Government Camp. A one-mile tour visits a pioneer wagon chute on the old Barlow Road. A 1.4-mile loop follows an abandoned portion of the 1921-vintage Mt. Hood highway to Little Zigzag Falls. For a longer hike across Laurel Hill, take the Pioneer Bridle Trail, a portion of the Barlow Trail that was converted to a hiking path by Civilian Conservation Corps workers in 1935.

Sam Barlow laid out his wagon road from The Dalles to Sandy in 1845 to spare Oregon Trail pioneers the dangers of rafting the Columbia River. Most travelers ended up cursing Laurel Hill, where Barlow's brushy route plunged so steeply

Little Zigzag Falls.   *Above: Tunnel beneath old Mt. Hood Highway.*

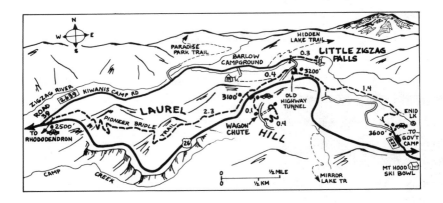

into the Zigzag River Valley that wagons had to be unhitched and winched
down backwards. Ironically, the rhododendrons that now delight hikers with
pink blooms in early summer only infuriated the pioneers, who typically passed
here in bloomless October and mistook the tough-limbed brush for laurel.

For a quick look at Laurel Hill's infamous wagon chute, drive Highway 26
east from Portland toward Mt. Hood. Just before milepost 51, park at an "Oregon
History" signboard on the right. A trail leads 200 yards to an abandoned section
of the old Mt. Hood loop highway. Turn right a few yards to the bottom of the
rocky chute. Then continue, following signs, to switchback 0.4 mile up through
the woods to the top of the chute, where Barlow Trail wagon ruts are still visible.
Then return to your car.

A slightly longer loop from the same roadside pullout visits more of the
historic roadway and a lovely waterfall as well. To find this path, walk 200 yards
downhill along the shoulder of Highway 26 and carefully cross the busy
highway. At the end of a guardrail, head into the forest on a path marked "Route
of the Barlow Road." After 0.1 mile, at a T-shaped junction, turn right on the
Pioneer Bridle Trail. When this path ducks through a tunnel, turn left onto
another abandoned section of the old Mt. Hood loop highway. In just 200 yards
you'll reach the Little Zigzag Falls trailhead. Turn right on this streamside path
for 0.3 mile to its end at the falls' 30-foot fan. Then return to the abandoned
highway and follow it back the way you came. To complete the loop, continue
on the old road straight past the tunnel to the shoulder of Highway 26, a few
steps from your car.

For a more substantial trip across Laurel Hill, hike a 4.1-mile section of the
Pioneer Bridle Trail. This route is open to bicycles and horses too. If you can
arrange a shuttle, plan on doing this section of trail one way. To leave a shuttle
car (or bicycle) at the upper trailhead, drive Highway 26 to between mileposts
52 and 53, a mile west of Government Camp. Opposite the western entrance to
Mt. Hood Ski Bowl, turn north off the highway onto Road 522 for 0.2 mile to the
Glacier View Sno Park, where signs point out the Pioneer Bridle Trail. To start
your hike at the lower trailhead, drive Highway 26 to between mileposts 48 and
49. Just 200 yards before the intersection with Road 39, park on the north side
of the highway by a "Pioneer Bridle Trail" sign. When you reach the middle of
the 4.1-mile trail, you might want to detour on hiker-only side paths to see the
wagon chute and Little Zigzag Falls.

73 Mirror Lake

Easy (to Mirror Lake)
3.2 miles round-trip
700 feet elevation gain
Open mid-May to mid-November
Map: Mt. Hood Wilderness (Geo-Graphics)

Moderate (to summit viewpoint)
6.4 miles round-trip
1500 feet elevation gain

Avoid this popular hike on summer weekends, when the unmarked parking area is jammed and the trail crowded. But on weekdays or in the off-season, the trip is hard to beat. The relatively easy path starts at a waterfall and climbs to a subalpine lake mirroring Mt. Hood. Hikers with weary soles can stop to reflect by the lake while more energetic hikers chug on up through the wildflowers to an even more spectacular viewpoint atop Tom Dick & Harry Mountain.

Drive Highway 26 to between mileposts 51 and 52, about 2 miles west of Government Camp. Park on the highway's south shoulder by a footbridge and (usually) a cluster of other cars. The footbridge spans Camp Creek just above Yocum Falls, a long, lacy cascade overhung with yellow monkeyflowers. Cross the bridge and enter a deep, cool forest. In early summer expect pink rhododendrons and numerous white woodland wildflowers: 6-leaved bunchberry, wild lily-of-the-valley, and star-flowered smilacina.

After 0.4 mile traverse a rockslide where you're almost certain to hear the cheeping cry of pikas; with patience, you'll spot one of these little round-eared "rock rabbits." Then switchback up another mile to a trail junction. Keep right around the lakeshore.

Heavy use has brought some restrictions here. Do not enter areas that have been roped off to allow plants to regrow. If you're backpacking, tent well away from the shore. Six sites are designated.

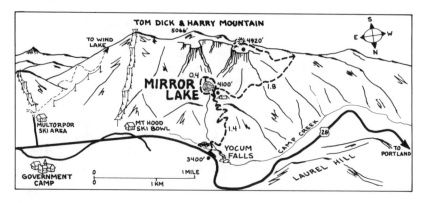

Mirror Lake from Tom Dick & Harry Mountain.   *Opposite: Mt. Hood from Mirror Lake.*

The first little beach you pass is the best for swimming. The lake bottom is muddy, but the water warms by late summer. Another 100 yards past the beach the trail forks. Keep left if you'd like to circle the lake (and discover some quieter picnic spots). Turn right if you're headed to the viewpoint atop Tom Dick & Harry Mountain.

The viewpoint path traverses a slope cleared of trees by winter avalanches. In summer the hillside sports alpine wildflowers, masses of huckleberries (ripe in late August), and views of the Zigzag Valley. After climbing 0.8 mile, turn sharply left at a monstrous 6-foot rock cairn. The trail grows fainter and rockier on this wooded ridge, and after 0.7 mile ends altogether at a summit rockpile. Continue 100 yards up to a 3-sided rock windbreak atop the shaley summit. Purple penstemons and a shaggy brown marmot live here. Views extend south across the green ridges of the Salmon-Huckleberry Wilderness to Mt. Jefferson, and north across Mirror Lake to Government Camp and Mt. Hood.

Tom Dick & Harry Mountain was named for its three distinct summits. The trail ends at the westernmost of the tops. The other two are off-limits to protect peregrine falcon habitat.

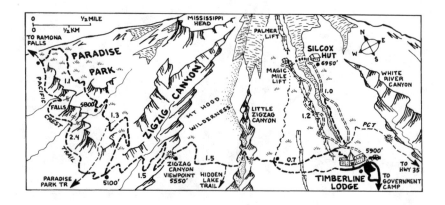

74   Timberline Lodge Trails

Easy (to Zigzag Canyon)
4.4 miles round-trip
500 feet elevation gain
Open mid-July through October
Use: hikers, horses
Map: Mt. Hood Wilderness (Geo-Graphics)

Moderate (to Silcox Hut)
2.2-mile loop
1100 feet elevation gain

Difficult (to Paradise Park)
12.2-mile loop
2300 feet elevation gain

Mt. Hood's Timberline Lodge began as a Depression-era make-work program, but by the time President Roosevelt dedicated this elegantly rustic hotel in 1937 it had become a grand expression of Northwest art. Surprisingly, few visitors venture very far into the scenic alpine landscape that lured hotel builders here in the first place. Three particularly tempting goals await hikers: the Silcox Hut, Zigzag Canyon, and Paradise Park. To reach the trailhead from Portland, drive Highway 26 toward Mt. Hood 54 miles. On the far side of Government Camp, turn left for 6 miles up to the lodge's huge parking lot.

The Silcox Hut served as upper terminus for Timberline's original Magic Mile ski lift from 1939 to 1962. Reopened as a chalet in 1992, it now offers overnight bunks and a limited cafe in the European alpine tradition. To hike there, walk past the right-hand side of the Timberline Lodge and follow a paved walkway uphill 200 yards. Turn right on the Pacific Crest Trail across a snow gully for 100 feet and then turn uphill onto the Mountaineer Trail, a braided path through wind-gnarled firs and August-blooming blue lupine. After 0.6 mile, join a dirt road for the remainder of the climb to the hut. To return on a loop, contour 100 yards across a snowfield from the Silcox Hut to the new Magic Mile chairlift and follow a service road back down to the lodge. Tenderfeet should note that the lift is open to non-skiing passengers 10am to 1:30pm from Memorial Day to Labor Day—for a fee, of course.

For a more wilderness-oriented hike, take the Pacific Crest Trail to Zigzag Canyon or Paradise Park. From the patio behind Timberline Lodge, follow a "Timberline Trail" pointer up a paved path amidst lupine and cushion-shaped clumps of white phlox. Keep uphill until pavement ends and the path ducks left under a chairlift. Next the trail contours through gorgeous wildflower meadows with views south to Mt. Jefferson and the Three Sisters. At the 1-mile mark the path dips into a 200-foot-deep gully to cross the Little Zigzag River on stepping stones (a possible turnaround point for hikers with small children). Continue another easy 1.2 miles to an overlook of Zigzag Canyon, a 700-foot-deep chasm gouged into Mt. Hood's cindery flank by the glacier-fed Zigzag River.

If you're headed for Paradise Park, continue 1.5 grueling miles on the PCT, which switchbacks across the huge gorge. At a trail junction on the far side, turn right onto the Paradise Loop Trail and climb another mile to meadows stuffed with August wildflowers: beargrass, paintbrush, lupine, and avalanche lilies. If you're backpacking, tent under the trees and *not* in the fragile meadows.

To complete the loop, keep straight on the Paradise Loop Trail until it crosses a big creek and reaches a bare area—the site of a stone shelter smashed by a falling tree in 1994 and painstakingly removed. From the shelter site, head uphill to find a path traversing left below a cliffy bluff. This path leads 1.1 mile through heather fields before descending to the PCT. Then turn left for 2.4 miles to return to Zigzag Canyon and the route back.

Other Hiking Options

For a shorter walk than any of these, follow the PCT east from Timberline Lodge and descend half a mile to an overlook of the White River Canyon.

For a 3- to 5-day backpack, try hiking the entire 37.6-mile Timberline Trail around Mt. Hood. The route starts out along the PCT to Paradise Park.

The Silcox Hut.   Opposite: Mt. Hood from Zigzag Canyon.

75 Timothy Lake

Easy (to Timothy Lake viewpoint)
4.4 miles round-trip
100 feet elevation gain
Open May through November
Maps: Mt Wilson, Timothy L. (Green Trails)

Difficult (around Timothy Lake)
12-mile loop
200 feet elevation gain
Use: hikers, horses

This hike starts at sapphire Little Crater Lake and follows the Pacific Crest Trail to the forested shore of Timothy Lake, one of the Cascades' larger and more scenic reservoirs. Hikers interested in a longer loop can continue all the way around Timothy Lake, passing four campgrounds, several beaches, and views of Mt. Hood and Mt. Jefferson.

Little Crater Lake may only be 100 feet across, but it's as blue and as geologically unusual as its bigger National Park cousin. For centuries an artesian spring has been welling up in a wildflower meadow 15 miles south of Mt. Hood. The cold, gushing water has gradually worn away an underlying layer of soft siltstone, leaving a 45-foot-deep funnel of astonishingly clear blue water.

From Portland, drive Highway 26 past Mt. Hood to a turnoff 3.4 miles east of Wapinitia Pass (between mileposts 65 and 66). At a sign for Timothy Lake, turn onto paved Skyline Road 42 for 4 miles. Then turn right onto paved Abbott Road 58 for 1.4 miles to Little Crater Campground. Park at the far end of the campground loop by a trail sign.

The short paved path to the lake crosses a meadow with blue gentians and a view of Mt. Hood. Go right around the little lake, cross a fence on a stile, enter an old-growth forest of big Douglas firs, and reach the Pacific Crest Trail. Turn left onto this wide trail for 0.3 mile to a junction marking the start of the Timothy Lake loop. Keep left on the PCT.

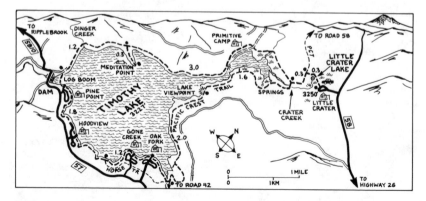

Timothy Lake and Mt. Hood.   *Opposite: Log boom near the dam.*

After this junction the PCT promptly crosses swift, 50-foot-wide Crater Creek on a scenic footbridge—a possible turnaround point for hikers with small children. For the next mile, occasional springs gush out beside the trail. Several side trails to the right lead into lakeshore meadows dotted with stumps and grazing cows. Beyond Crater Creek 1.6 miles the trail climbs through woods to a "Timothy Lake" sign and your first view across the main body of the lake. This makes a good stopping point, particularly if you bushwhack 100 yards down to a scenic peninsula.

If you'd like to hike all the way around the lake, continue 2 miles on the PCT and turn right on the Timothy Lake Trail. Follow this path across the lake's main inlet (the Oak Grove Fork Clackamas River) and then keep right, sticking to the lakeshore. In the next 3 miles you'll pass a number of car campgrounds, boat ramps, and bathing beaches. Finally reach a planked boom of floating logs, chained end to end across the reservoir's mouth to protect the dam. While this precarious boom is open to hikers, it's safer to cross on the dam.

On the far shore, continue on the lakeshore path 1.2 miles before detouring to the right to explore Meditation Point, a peninsula with a boater campground. Then continue 3 miles around the lake to complete the loop.

Other Hiking Options

You can also drive to Timothy Lake from the Clackamas River side. Take Highway 224 east of Estacada 25.6 miles to the bridge at Ripplebrook, turn left onto paved Road 57, and follow signs to Timothy Lake. In this case, it's quicker to start your hike at the dam. Equestrians should also start the lake loop here.

Mount Hood
East

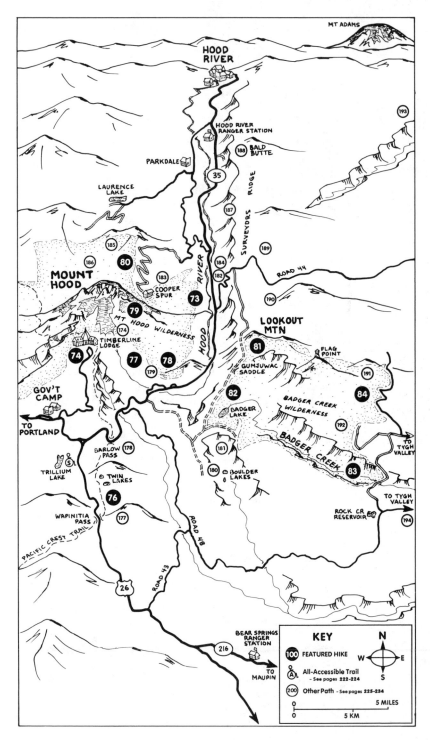

Opposite: Mt. Hood from Gnarl Ridge (Hike #77).

76   Twin Lakes

Easy (around Lower Twin Lake)
5.1 miles round-trip
700 feet elevation gain
Open June to early November
Use: hikers, horses
Map: Mt. Hood Wilderness (Geo-Graphics)

Moderate (to Palmateer Point)
9.1-mile loop
1500 feet elevation gain

Children like Lower Twin Lake for lots of reasons. The hike isn't too long, the water's swimmable, the beach has logs for climbing, campsites are plentiful, and there's a path around the lake for exploring. Adults will appreciate the option of a longer loop hike past less-visited Upper Twin Lake and Palmateer Point, a cliff-edge viewpoint of Mt. Hood and the historic Barlow Creek Valley.

Drive Highway 26 to milepost 62 (east of Government Camp 8 miles), and turn at the Frog Lake Sno-Park. Park at the far left-hand end of this huge lot.

The trail starts beneath a brown skier-symbol sign and promptly meets the Pacific Crest Trail. Turn right onto this wide path and keep straight on it for 1.4 miles. Along the way you'll climb gradually from a mountain hemlock forest into woods dominated by firs. The forest is recovering naturally from a bud-worm infestation that killed a few of the firs. The extra sunlight has allowed the understory to thrive. Expect ripe huckleberries in late summer and the blooms of rhododendrons and beargrass in early summer.

Turn right at a trail junction, following a pointer for Lower Twin Lake. This path crests a saddle and slowly descends to a junction near the far end of the lake. Turn right for 100 yards to the lakeshore and a camping area.

To continue on a longer loop, return to the lake-end trail junction and take the 0.7-mile path to Upper Twin Lake, a shallower pool with a view of Hood's head. Keep right around the shore for 100 yards and then veer to the right onto

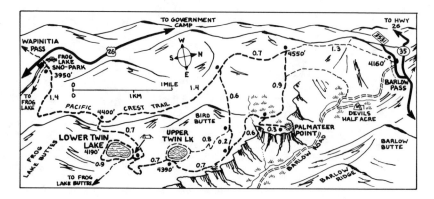

Upper Twin Lake.   Opposite: Old Pacific Crest Trail marker.

Palmateer View Trail #482. A bit narrower and rockier, this path passes the rim of a 100-foot cliff with a full-length view of Mt. Hood.

Continue straight 1.3 miles until the trail crosses a small creek and enters a meadow. A small "Viewpoint" sign here marks the 0.3-mile side trail up to Palmateer Point, overlooking a dramatic, glacially carved valley that served as the route for the 1845 Barlow Road between The Dalles and Sandy. The meadow visible far below (now a primitive campground with an outhouse) was one of the highest campsites used by covered wagon pioneers on Sam Barlow's rugged trail. Travelers named the meadow the Devil's Half Acre because of its wintry weather early in autumn.

To complete the loop, return to the main trail and follow it up through the meadow and a lodgepole pine forest to the PCT. Turn left here for 3.5 easy miles back to the car.

Other Hiking Options

With a shuttle car you can hike one-way from Wapinitia Pass to Barlow Pass in just 6.9 miles and still visit both Twin Lakes and Palmateer Point. Drive Highway 35 to Barlow Pass and turn briefly south on Road 3531 to the PCT trailhead parking area.

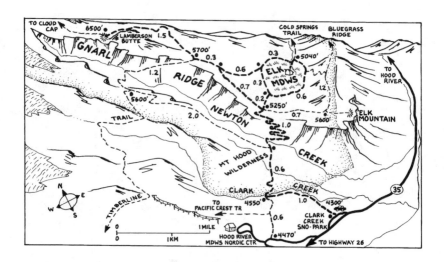

77   Elk Meadows

Moderate (to Elk Meadows)
6.8 miles round-trip
1400 feet elevation gain
Open late June through October
Use: hikers, horses
Map: Mt. Hood Wilderness (Geo-Graphics)

Difficult (to Gnarl Ridge)
10.2 miles round-trip
2400 feet elevation gain
Open mid-July through October

Two of Mt. Hood's most scenic hiking goals are tucked away on the mountain's southeast flank: a rustic shelter amidst Elk Meadows' wildflowers, and Gnarl Ridge's breathtaking cliff-edge viewpoint amid wind-dwarfed pines. Visit either destination, or take a slightly longer loop and visit both.

From Portland, drive Highway 26 past Government Camp and take Highway 35 toward Hood River for 8.3 miles. Beyond the main Mt. Hood Meadows turnoff 1.5 miles, turn left on the Clark Creek Sno-Park loop for 0.3 mile to the second pullout. The trail starts on the left by a sign for Elk Meadows. (From Hood River, drive Highway 35 south for 32 miles and turn right onto the Clark Creek Sno-Park loop for 0.1 mile.)

The trail sets off through a fir forest with blue lupine blooms in July and ripe blue huckleberries in August. In places, floods from Clark Creek have left gravel beds in the woods. After a mile, turn right at a T-shaped junction and cross Clark Creek on a footbridge. Continue nearly level for another 0.6 mile. Then ignore the Newton Creek Trail on the left, and cross raging Newton Creek on logs. This crossing can be tricky in the high water of summer afternoons.

The path now launches up a wooded ridge in eight long switchbacks, finally reaching a 4-way trail junction at a saddle. If you want the shortest route to Gnarl Ridge, turn left here and stick to the ridgecrest for 2.5 uphill miles.

But if you're headed for Elk Meadows, go straight. After 400 yards, turn right on the Elk Meadows Perimeter Trail, a 1.2-mile circuit designed to keep hikers from tramping through the fragile meadows in the middle. If you're backpacking, note that although tents are banned in the meadows (and in tree islands within the meadows), the perimeter trail passes several usable campsites in the woods. After 0.6 mile the perimeter trail turns left at a junction beside a creek. Forty yards later reach an unmarked fork. Keep left here to find a three-sided shelter with a picture-postcard view across the meadows to Mt. Hood.

To return to the car, simply follow the perimeter trail the rest of the way around the meadows. If you still have the energy to climb to Gnarl Ridge, however, hike 0.3 mile from the shelter along the perimeter trail and turn right at a sign, "To Gnarl Ridge." This route climbs 0.9 mile to the Timberline Trail. Follow the "Cloud Cap" pointer to the right and climb 1.5 miles into an alpine landscape where views extend from Mt. Adams to the Three Sisters. Finally pass the remains of a stone shelter on the left and reach a colossal cliff edge overlooking Newton Creek's 800-foot-deep chasm. Cowering whitebark pines form a gnarled mat along the rim. Turn back here—or, if you're feeling sprightly, scramble up Lamberson Butte, a rocky outcrop 400 yards to the south.

Other Hiking Options

If you're heading for Elk Meadows, it's only 1.4 miles further to make a loop via the old lookout site at Elk Mountain. Turn right at the 4-way trail junction just before the meadows, climb 0.7 mile to a spur trail leading to the viewpoint, and return along Bluegrass Ridge.

If you've hiked to Gnarl Ridge, it's only 1.2 miles further to return on a dramatic loop across Newton Creek's canyon. Just stay on the Timberline Trail as it descends to Newton Creek (bridgeless, so use caution). Then climb briefly to the Newton Creek Trail junction and turn left.

Mt. Hood from Elk Meadows.   Opposite: Elk Meadows' shelter.

Tamanawas Falls

Easy (direct to falls)
3.8 miles round-trip
500 feet elevation gain
Open late April through November
Map: Mt. Hood Wilderness (Geo-Graphics)

Moderate (via Polallie Overlook)
5.6-mile loop
900 feet elevation gain

The Northwest Indians believed everyone has a *tamanawas*—a friendly guardian spirit. Tamanawas Falls seems as though it might be Mt. Hood's guardian, an inspiring 100-foot curtain of white water in a green canyon at the mountain's eastern base.

The path to the falls is a delight, with scenic footbridges and lots of access to mossy-banked Cold Spring Creek. There's even a pack of cute golden-mantled ground squirrels at the falls for extra entertainment. Children will enjoy hiking the same trail both directions, but adults may prefer returning on a slightly

Tamanawas Falls.   Above: East Fork Hood River.

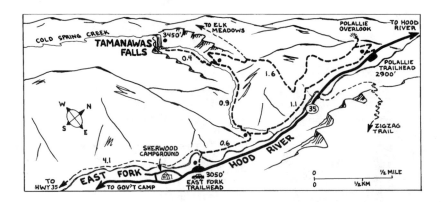

longer 5.6-mile loop past the Polallie Overlook.

Drive Highway 35 around Mt. Hood to the well-marked East Fork Trailhead near milepost 72, about 0.2 mile north of Sherwood Campground. Park by a message board at the north end of the pullout. Although the path is unclear near the parking area, simply walk 200 feet to the East Fork Hood River, a bouldery torrent milky with the silt of Hood's glaciers. Cross on an impressive footbridge and turn right on the East Fork Trail.

The mountain hemlock forest here is carpeted with twinflower, a tiny double-belled white wildflower with shiny little leaves. This delicate flower's Latin name is *Linnaea borealis* because it was a favorite of Linnaeas, the 18th-century Swedish botanist who invented the system of identifying plants with two Latin names.

After 0.6 mile on the East Fork Trail, turn left and follow a path up Cold Spring Creek 1.3 miles to the base of Tamanawas Falls. The falls spills over the lip of an old lava flow. The same basalt forms the canyon walls and is visible as a cliff of hexagonal columns along the East Fork Hood River.

If you'd like to return on the 5.6-mile loop, hike back 0.4 mile from the falls. Just after the footbridge turn left and switchback up to a ridgetop trail junction. Turn right (following the Polallie Campground pointer), descend gradually for a mile, and then take a 150-yard detour to the Polallie Overlook. The cliff-top view of brushy Polallie Creek is only impressive if you know the creek's history. In 1980 an 80-foot-deep flash flood roared past here, destroying an old growth forest and 6 miles of Highway 35. (To see the flood's origin, a raw canyon headwall 4 miles upstream, take Hike #79 to Cooper Spur.)

To complete the loop, continue 200 yards on the main trail and turn right onto the East Fork Trail.

Other Hiking Options

For a longer riverside hike from the same trailhead, cross the footbridge near Sherwood Campground and turn left on the East Fork Trail for 4.1 miles to an upper trailhead on Highway 35. This route is open to mountain bikes, and although it passes a few old clearcuts, it offers quiet river views and backpacking campsites. The upper trailhead, between mileposts 68 and 69 of Highway 35, is at the gated entrance road to the former Robin Hood Campground, closed since a 1999 flood.

79 Cooper Spur

Moderate (to shelter)
3-mile loop
1000 feet elevation gain
Open mid-July to mid-October
Use: hikers
Map: Mt. Hood Wilderness (Geo-Graphics)

Difficult (to Tie-In Rock)
8.2-mile loop
2800 feet elevation gain

The highest hiking trail on Mt. Hood switchbacks up Cooper Spur's cindery shoulder to Tie-In Rock, where mountain climbers traditionally rope up. From this vertiginous perch, peaks from Mt. Rainier to the Three Sisters dot the horizon. The massive Eliot Glacier writhes below, a splintered river of ice. And if the thought of a 2800-foot ascent leaves you winded, Cooper Spur has a much easier hiking option: a 3-mile loop to a historic stone shelter at timberline.

Drive Highway 35 around Mt. Hood to the Cooper Spur Ski Area turnoff between mileposts 73 and 74. Head west on Cooper Spur Road for 3.3 miles to Tilly Jane Junction, turn left onto Road 3512 toward Cloud Cap, and follow signs 10.3 miles up to Cloud Cap Campground in a high saddle. The last 9 miles are on a steep, narrow, winding gravel road.

Park beside a sign on the right for the Timberline Trail and walk across the primitive campground 200 feet to a message board beside a trail junction. Go straight, following the Timberline Trail's "Gnarl Ridge" pointer uphill. In 100 yards keep left as the path forks twice (the unmarked right-hand branches lead to the toe of Eliot Glacier). Continue on the Timberline Trail, which half a mile later climbs into a bouldery gully at the head of Tilly Jane Creek. The only plants able to grow here are alpine partridge foot and sand verbena. Large rock cairns mark the path up through the sand. Then the path climbs through a patch of twisted whitebark pines to a trail crossing in a broad field of blue lupine.

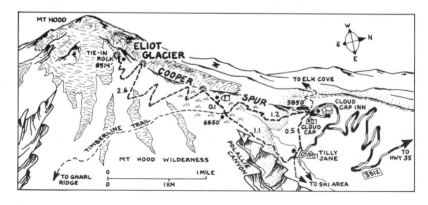

Mt. Hood from Cooper Spur.   Opposite: The Cooper Spur shelter.

Turn right at this junction, taking the Cooper Spur Trail up 200 yards to a hidden 10-foot-square stone shelter built in the 1930s by the Civilian Conservation Corps. The view here extends from Mt. Adams and the Hood River Valley to the brown scablands of the Columbia River Plateau. Lookout Mountain (Hike #81) tops a green ridge to the east.

If you're interested in the tougher 8.2-mile hike, continue up past the shelter on a remarkably well-graded trail with occasional overlooks of Eliot Glacier. After 2.6 switchbacking miles reach a crest with four low stone windbreaks and a rock commemorating a 1910 Japanese climbing party. This makes a good stopping point, or you can continue 500 yards along the ridge to Tie-In Rock, a big boulder. But unless you have climbing equipment *do not* venture onto the deceptively dangerous snowfields beyond.

To complete the loop, hike down from the Cooper Spur shelter and go straight at the Timberline Trail junction, following the pointer toward Tilly Jane Campground. This path descends along the rim of Polallie Canyon, a quarter-mile-wide bowl created in December 1980 when rains launched a colossal landslide and flash flood. After 1.1 mile reach a trail junction near a windowless plank cookhouse built by the American Legion in 1924. Turn left, passing the historic Tilly Jane Guard Station and climbing gradually half a mile to your car.

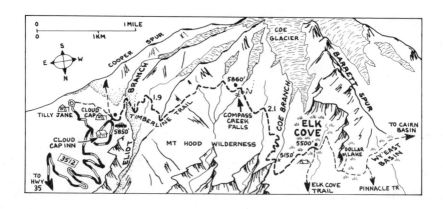

Mt. Hood from Elk Cove.   Opposite: Western pasque flower (old man of the mountain).

80   Elk Cove

Easy (to Compass Creek Falls)
3.8 miles round-trip
800 feet elevation gain
Open mid-July through October
Use: hikers, horses
Map: Mt. Hood Wilderness
(Geo-Graphics)

Moderate (to Elk Cove)
8 miles round-trip
2000 feet elevation gain

The Timberline Trail on Mt. Hood's north slope is a parade of wildflower meadows, mountain viewpoints, and tumbling brooks. By starting at the mile-high Cloud Cap trailhead you needn't climb much to reach these wonders, either. The path contours 1.9 miles to a pretty picnic spot above the 60-foot falls of Compass Creek, a good goal for hikers with children. Beyond that the trail drops sharply to cross a canyon before climbing to Elk Cove, a broad bowl of wildflowers.

Drive Highway 35 around Mt. Hood to the Cooper Spur Ski Area turnoff between mileposts 73 and 74. Head west on Cooper Spur Road for 3.3 miles to Tilly Jane Junction, turn left onto Road 3512 toward Cloud Cap, and follow signs 10.3 miles up to Cloud Cap Campground in a high saddle. The last 9 miles are on a steep, narrow, winding gravel road.

Park beside a sign on the right for the Timberline Trail, walk across the primitive campground 200 feet to a message board beside a trail junction, and turn right. The path sets out through a fir forest where blue lupine bloom in mid-summer and blue huckleberries ripen in late summer. But after 0.2 mile the trail suddenly traverses into the raw, V-shaped canyon of Eliot Branch, a roaring stream whose milky color betrays its glacial origin. The footbridge has a view across the Hood River Valley to Mt. Adams.

Wildflowers decorate the trailside from here on, especially in early August. Near creeks look for yellow and pink monkeyflower. Where snow melted late, expect the dishmop-shaped seed heads of western pasque flower. In drier areas look for blue lupine, purple daisy-like asters, and red paintbrush.

After 1.5 miles cross the first of Compass Creek's three branches. For the easy hike, stop at the third fork, where a 10-foot waterfall below the trail swirls through a rock bowl (and often into a snow cave). To see the much larger waterfall below, continue 200 yards on the trail to a viewpoint.

If you're continuing on to Elk Cove, the Timberline Trail descends gradually for 0.9 mile before switchbacking steeply down to a footbridge across a frothing, 20-foot-wide creek: the Coe Branch. Then the path climbs a wooded ridge to Elk Cove, a cliff-rimmed basin with lupine, paintbrush, and a view of Mt. Hood. Tenting is prohibited in the meadows. If you're backpacking, turn right at the Elk Cove Trail junction for 100 yards to find approved sites among the trees.

81   Lookout Mountain

Easy (to summit)
2.4 miles round-trip
600 feet elevation gain
Open July through October
Use: hikers, horses
Map: Badger Creek Wilderness (USFS)

Moderate (to Oval Lake)
6.2 miles round-trip
1800 feet elevation gain

This summit not only overlooks every Cascade peak from the Three Sisters to Mt. Rainier, it also offers a rare panorama of the Columbia River Plateau and the Badger Creek Wilderness.

Most people climb to Lookout Mountain on a grueling path switchbacking up 3000 feet from Highway 35 via Gumjuwac Saddle. But there's a much easier route, starting at High Prairie's wildflower meadow. And if you take this shortcut you might well have enough energy left to continue along the Divide Trail to seldom-visited Oval Lake and the commanding rock pinnacles at Palisade Point.

Drive Highway 35 around Mt. Hood to the turnoff for Dufur Mill Road 44 (between mileposts 70 and 71, or just north of Nottingham Campground). Turn east on this paved road for 3.8 miles and then turn right onto gravel High Prairie Road 4410. After another 4.7 miles—always keeping uphill—reach a T-shaped intersection where the gravel road turns to dirt. Turn left on High Prairie Road for 200 yards and park at the trailhead on the right. Posts block vehicles from the old summit road—now a hiking trail.

As you start up this trail-like road you'll hike through a subalpine meadow with purple asters, fuzzy-leaved yarrow, and a few spire-topped firs. Also look for the foot-long, boat-shaped leaves of false hellebore, an odd plant with a stalk of green flowers. Indians believed the plant's poisonous root could ward off evil spirits.

Follow the old road up a long switchback to a signed trail junction in a high saddle. Take the Divide Trail left 200 yards to Lookout Mountain's summit.

If you'd like to visit Oval Lake, continue east on the Divide Trail as it descends (at times steeply) along a lovely alpine ridgecrest. After a mile the path descends through hemlock woods to a junction with the Fret Creek Trail. Turn left here for 0.2 mile to Oval Lake, a forest-rimmed pool reflecting several crag-topped bluffs. To continue to the view at Palisade Point, return to the Divide Trail and follow it 0.3 mile east up to a saddle. Beyond the saddle 60 yards take a short scramble trail to Palisade Point, a rock ledge overhanging the Badger Creek Valley.

Other Hiking Options

The Flag Point lookout tower, visible to the east from Palisade Point, is a more distant goal. It's another 2 miles down the trail at the end of gated Road 200. When not in use by lookout staff, the tower is available for rent from the Barlow

Mt. Hood from Lookout Mountain.   *Opposite: Oval Lake.*

Ranger District. For prices and reservations, call (541) 467-2291.

If you'd like a lot more exercise and a little less driving on your way to Lookout Mountain, start at the Gumjuwac Trailhead, beside a bridge on Highway 35 between mileposts 68 and 69. It's 2.4 steep miles up to Gumjuwac Saddle, where you cross a road and bear left onto the Divide Trail for the final 2.2-mile climb to the summit.

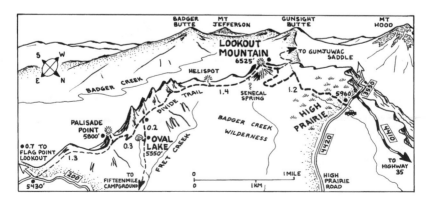

82   Badger Lake

Moderate (via Badger Creek)
6.7-mile loop
1300 feet elevation gain
Open late June through October
Use: hikers, horses
Map: Badger Creek Wilderness (USFS)

Moderate (via Gunsight Butte)
8.5-mile loop
1600 feet elevation gain

Difficult (from Highway 35)
11.5-mile loop
3300 feet elevation gain

Three different paths lead down to Badger Lake from the Gumjuwac Saddle trailhead, so hikers have a choice of loop options. If you take the steepish trail down to Badger Creek you'll amble to the lake through a towering old-growth forest. If, however, you start with a climb along the Gunsight Trail you'll tour the valley rim past viewpoints of Mt. Hood. In either case, it's easiest to return from the lake on the middle of the three paths, the well-graded Divide Trail.

Rugged, high-clearance vehicles can reach the trailhead at Gumjuwac Saddle, but hikers with passenger cars should plan on parking instead at a lower trailhead, at the north end of a bridge between mileposts 68 and 69 of Highway 35. From there, the hike begins on a switchbacking trail that gains 1700 feet of elevation in 2.4 miles to Gumjuwac Saddle. It's a workout, but views of Mt. Hood emerge along the way.

If you're confident your vehicle can handle the rough road to Gumjuwac Saddle, drive around Mt. Hood on Highway 35 to the turnoff for Dufur Mill Road 44 (between mileposts 70 and 71, or just north of Nottingham Campground). Turn east on this paved road for 3.8 miles and then turn right onto gravel High Prairie Road 4410. After another 4.7 uphill miles, turn right onto dirt Bennett Pass Road 3550 for 3.3 miserably bumpy miles. Park by a large sign explaining the origin of the name Gumjuwac Saddle (from Gum Shoe Jack, a rubber-booted shepherd).

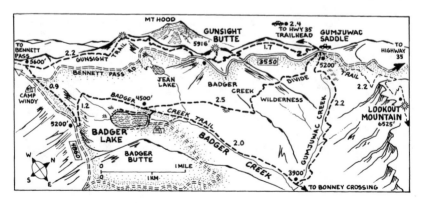

Mt. Hood from the Gunsight Trail.   Opposite: Badger Lake from the Divide Trail.

If you've opted for the 6.7-mile loop via Badger Creek, take Gumjuwac Trail #480, immediately to the left of the big Gumjuwac Saddle sign. This path dives down through a meadow. After losing 1300 feet in 2.2 miles, turn right on the Badger Creek Trail and climb gradually through a valley-bottom forest of big Douglas firs. In another 2 miles a spur trail to the left leads down to an old earthen dam and a primitive car campground at Badger Lake.

The dam was built in the 1930s as part of an irrigation project. Today both the dam and the dirt access road are surrounded by designated Wilderness. Explore the lakeshore on a path to the right. Although this fisherman's trail dead ends in 0.5 mile, it passes several wooded campsites. To complete the Badger Creek loop, return to the Badger Creek Trail, continue 200 yards to a junction with the Divide Trail, turn right, and climb 2.5 miles back to Gumjuwac Saddle.

If you'd rather take the 8.5-mile Gunsight Butte loop, start out on the opposite side of the Road 3550 from the big Gumjuwac Saddle sign. Take an unmarked path 30 feet and then fork left, following a small "Gunsight Trail" pointer. This path climbs for 1.5 miles past the wooded summit of Gunsight Butte, joins the dirt Bennett Pass Road for 400 feet, and then continues along the ridgecrest—a series of natural rock gardens where red paintbrush and purple penstemon bloom. Mt. Hood dominates the view, although you can also spot Mt. Adams and Mt. Jefferson.

At the 3.9-mile mark descend to a wooded saddle and turn left onto the Camp Windy Trail. This somewhat rough path crosses Road 3550 and continues 0.8 mile to a pullout beside dirt Road 4860. At the far end of the pullout take the Badger Creek Trail downhill to the left for 1.2 miles to the Divide Trail junction just above Badger Lake. Take a side trip here to explore the lake and then return to the Divide Trail for the 2.5-mile climb back to Gumjuwac Saddle.

If you've left your car at the trailhead on Highway 35, of course, you'll still have to walk 2.4 miles downhill to complete your hike.

Badger Creek

Easy (to creekside boulders)
5.8 miles round-trip
400 feet elevation gain
Open all year
Use: hikers, horses
Map: Badger Creek Wilderness (USFS)

Moderate (to Pine Creek)
11.4 miles round-trip
900 feet elevation gain
Open late March to mid-December

Badger Creek's wilderness canyon climbs from the sagebrush flats of Central Oregon to the alpine forests of Mt. Hood. In the middle it crosses a strange, mixed zone known as a pine-oak grassland. This hike along Badger Creek focuses on this botanically fascinating middle zone, rich with wildflowers from both the high desert and the mountains.

If you're driving here from Portland, take Highway 26 past Mt. Hood. Shortly after milepost 68 turn left onto paved Road 43 at a sign for Wamic. After 6 miles turn right onto paved Road 48 and continue 15.2 miles. Then turn left onto Road 4810, following signs toward Bonney Crossing Campground from here on. After just 0.2 mile, be sure to follow Road 4810's unmarked right-hand turn to avoid ending up at Rock Creek Reservoir. Then take Road 4810 another 1.9 miles, veer right onto paved Road 4811 for 1.2 miles, and turn right onto narrow, roughish gravel Road 2710 for 1.8 miles. The trail starts on the left, just beyond Bonney Crossing Campground and a bridge, but parking is tight here, so park in a large lot along the campground entrance road and walk 200 feet to the trailhead.

If you're driving here from The Dalles, take Highway 197 south 34 miles to Tygh Valley and turn right. Follow signs for Wamic, then for Rock Creek Reservoir, and finally for Bonney Crossing Campground.

The trailside wildflower show is at its best from April to June. In dry, grassy areas look for sunflower-like balsamroot, little purple larkspur, erratic-petaled white prairie star, blue lupine, and wild strawberry. In moister conifer woods expect trilliums, twinflower, and smilacina. If you didn't know orchids grow in Oregon, look for the little pink hoods of the rare lady's slipper orchid beside the trail register at the 0.2-mile mark. Hikers with children should remind them not to pick any plants.

Although the creek is never far away, one of the nicest access points comes after 2.6 miles, when the creek squeezes between a pair of 10-foot boulders, creating a pool and a tiny pebble beach. Hikers with children can turn back here, or perhaps continue 0.3 mile past a scenic cliff to another pair of creekside boulders and a 5-foot waterfall.

Hikers interested in a longer trip can continue another 2.8 miles to an old campsite on a riverbend opposite the cascading confluence of Pine Creek. Here the music of the creeks is particularly sweet, beneath a canopy of ancient red cedar and grand fir. Because this old campsite is too close to the creek and the

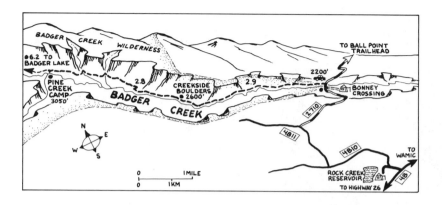

trail for modern low-impact tenting, backpackers should choose more remote flat spots on the far side of the creek.

Other Hiking Options

Backpackers can continue 6.2 miles past Pine Creek to Badger Lake, where there are several possible side trips and loop options (see Hike #81).

Ponderosa pine tree at the Wilderness boundary.   *Opposite: Badger Creek.*

84   Ball Point

Moderate (to helispot)
7.2 miles round-trip
1400 feet elevation gain
Open late March to mid-December
Use: hikers, horses
Map: Badger Creek Wilderness (USFS)

In the rain shadow of the Cascades, the Badger Creek Wilderness not only has better weather than nearby Mt. Hood, it's also much less crowded. The hike to Ball Point shows just how attractive these eastern foothills can be, with slopes full of early summer wildflowers and with sweeping views from rock pinnacles.

If you're driving here from Portland, take Highway 26 past Mt. Hood to a turnoff shortly after milepost 68. Following signs for Wamic, turn left onto paved Road 43 for 6 miles and turn right onto paved Road 48 for 15.2 miles. Then, following signs for Bonney Crossing Campground, turn left onto Road 4810 for 2.1 miles, veer right onto paved Road 4811 for 1.2 miles, and turn right onto Road 2710. Follow this narrow gravel road for 6.7 miles toward Tygh Valley before turning left onto paved Road 27 for 2.1 miles to a pullout and sign on the left for the School Canyon Trail.

If you're driving here from the east, take Highway 197 between Maupin and The Dalles to milepost 33, opposite the Tygh Valley Rodeo Grounds. Turn west onto Shadybrook Road for 1 mile, turn left onto Fairgrounds Road for 1.1 mile, and then turn right onto Badger Creek Road. After 6.4 miles on this gravel road, turn right onto paved Road 27 for 2.1 miles to the School Canyon Trailhead.

The School Canyon Trail begins as an ancient jeep track through a remarkable pine-oak grassland, where gnarled old oaks mingle with stately ponderosa pines amid park-like fields of wildflowers. In May and June expect masses of

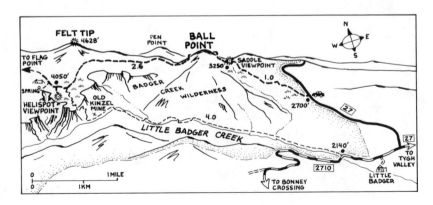

Ball Point.   Opposite: Death camas.

red paintbrush, sunflower-like balsamroot, blue lupine, and lobed white prairie star. After 0.8 mile the road becomes a trail that leads up to a saddle viewpoint. The panorama extends to Mt. Jefferson and the Three Sisters. To the east are the Pine Hollow Reservoir and the farmfields of Wamic.

Next the trail ducks into a more conventional Douglas fir forest, bypasses Ball Point, and slowly climbs for a couple of miles to a plateau meadow with pinemat manzanita bushes. The Little Badger Trail takes off downhill to the left here, but continue 300 yards to a short side trail to a helispot—an old firefighter landing site surrounded by weird-shaped rock pinnacles. The leftmost set of spires is particularly fun to explore.

If you're backpacking, return to the main trail and continue 100 yards to a campsite on the left. A path down through the campsite leads to a mossy glen with a hidden spring.

Other Hiking Options

By arranging a 3.6-mile car shuttle you can return on the Little Badger Trail, which switchbacks steeply downhill and then follows Little Badger Creek to Road 2710.

Clackamas
Foothills

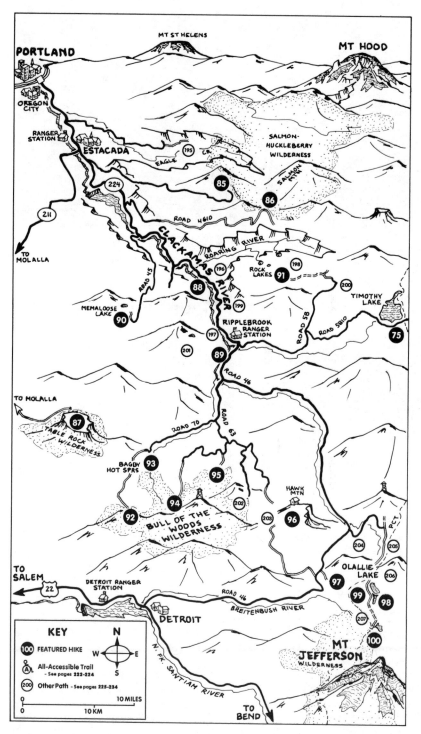

Opposite: Jefferson Park (Hike #100).

Mt. Hood from Squaw Mountain's lookout site.   Below: Bunchberry.

85   Squaw Mountain

Moderate (to Squaw Mountain)
4.4 miles round-trip
1020 feet elevation gain
Open June to mid-November
Use: hikers, horses, bicycles
Map: Salmon-Huckleberry (USFS)

Moderate (to Old Baldy)
7.7 miles round-trip
1200 feet elevation gain

Less than an hour's drive from Portland on a paved road, the delightful viewpoint trails to Squaw Mountain and Old Baldy remain surprisingly uncrowded—despite their recent fame. National media attention focused here in 1999 when environmental activists barricaded the access road at the Old Baldy trailhead to protest logging of the area's old-growth forest. Forest Service officials responded by building a gate of their own 4.4 miles down the road. The controversy led timber sale buyers to shelve their logging plans. For now, the protesters are gone and the gate is open.

From Interstate 205 near Oregon City, take exit 12 and follow signs east 18 miles to Estacada. Go straight through town, continuing 1.6 more miles on Highway 224. Just after milepost 25, turn left on Surface Road for 1.1 mile, and then turn right on Squaw Mountain Road. Follow this paved, two-lane road (which becomes Road 4614) for a total of 13.4 miles. Along the way, make sure you keep right at an unmarked Y-junction at the 9.5-mile mark, and keep straight at an unmarked junction at the 9.8-mile mark. You'll pass the Forest Service's massive green gate at the 10-mile mark.

If you're heading for Squaw Mountain, drive past the green gate 3.4 miles.

Where the paved road climbs a steep hill and curves sharply left, turn right onto a small gravel road, marked only by the tilted, rusty metal posts of a former gate. Drive 200 yards to the signed Fanton Trail on the left, just before the road ends at an old clearcut.

The Fanton Trail to Squaw Mountain climbs through an ancient forest of oichen-draped hemlocks and firs. Expect pink rhododendron blossoms and white bunchberry wildflowers in June, tall beargrass plumes in July, and scarlet vine maple leaves in fall.

The path follows a creek past a campsite and a marsh. Keep right at trail junctions for 1.7 miles to reach Squaw Mountain's old lookout service road. Long closed to cars, the overgrown track has been rutted by motorcycles. Climb to the left along it a hundred yards to the concrete stairs of the vanished lookout tower. The panorama sweeps from Mt. Hood to Mt. Jefferson, with the vast green canyons of the Roaring and Clackamas rivers seemingly at your feet.

If you'd rather visit Old Baldy instead, it's easiest to start at the trailhead where the protesters once camped. To find it, drive paved Road 4614 past the green gate 4.4 miles—or 1 mile past the Fanton Trailhead turnoff. Just 0.2 mile after the road finally starts going downhill, park in a forested saddle at a poorly marked driveway-like pullout onthe right. At the end of the 20-foot driveway look for a small wooden sign announcing the Old Baldy Trail.

Follow the trail left around the shoulder of Githens Mountain 1.6 miles, fork to the right in a glen, and traverse a mile to a forested rim with rounded crags resembling stacks of giant, mossy muffins. When the trail crests beside a stump with a rock cairn, bushwhack 30 feet to the right to a mossy clifftop with the area's best viewpoint. Note forested Wildcat Mountain (Hike #57) between the snowy peaks of Mt. Hood and Mt. Adams.

Beyond this viewpoint the trail to Old Baldy sweitchbacks briefly downhill. Keep right at junctions for 0.9 mile to trail's end at a former lookout site, its view now largely blocked by trees.

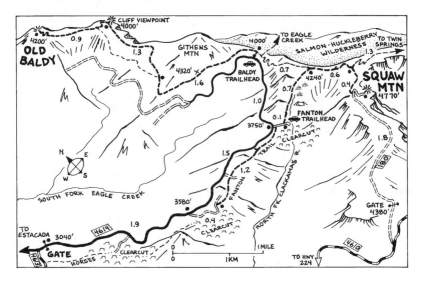

86   Sheepshead Rock

Easy (to Sheepshead Rock)
2.8 miles round-trip
500 feet elevation gain
Open mid-June to early November
Use: hikers, horses
Map: Salmon-Huckleberry (USFS)

Difficult (to Salmon Mountain)
10 miles round-trip
1800 feet elevation gain

In the early 1900s, when the newly created National Forests were threatened by sheepherders and timber thieves, the government built a guard station atop a remote mile-square plateau called The Plaza. By the 1930s wildfire seemed a bigger threat, so rangers strung telephone wires from The Plaza to lookout towers on half a dozen neighboring peaks.

Now that most of The Plaza's forests lie within the protected Salmon-Huckleberry Wilderness, the guard station and lookout towers are gone. The old trails, however, remain.

For an easy sample of these historic paths, hike the Plaza Trail past the original guard station site to Sheepshead Rock, a crag with a view from Mt. Hood to Portland. For a more rugged adventure, continue on an old lookout trail along Salmon Mountain's ridge to an even better viewpoint at one of Northwest Oregon's most remote places.

From Interstate 205 near Oregon City, take exit 12 and follow signs east 18 miles to Estacada. Go straight through town, continuing 6.5 miles on Highway 224. Opposite Promontory Park turn left at a sign for Silver Fox RV Park and veer left onto Road 4610. Stick to this mostly gravel and sometimes rough road for a total of 18.4 miles, following signs for "4610" or "Plaza Trail." The signs may be missing, so watch the odometer and fork to the left at the 7.1-mile mark, turn right at the 8-mile mark, and fork to the left at the 17-mile mark. Then look

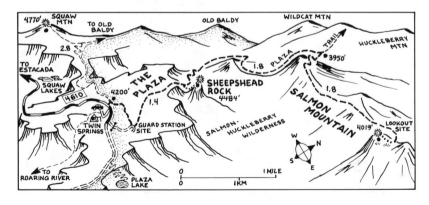

Salmon Mountain's lookout site.   Opposite: Looking down from Sheepshead Rock.

for a trailhead sign on the left. Since there is no room to park here, continue a hundred yards to the primitive Twin Springs Campground on the right, and walk back to the trailhead.

Hike up the Plaza Trail 100 feet to a junction and turn right. The sparse mountain hemlock forest here lets in enough sunlight that rhododendrons and huckleberries thrive. Expect big pink blooms in early summer and loads of ripe blue fruit at summer's end. After 0.3 mile the trail briefly joins an abandoned road at the old guard station site and then veers left into the woods again.

After 1.2 miles reach the edge of The Plaza's plateau and start going downhill. Just 100 feet before the first switchback, take an unmarked side path up to the right. This path scrambles up Sheepshead Rock's bare, lumpy crag to the edge of a 100-foot cliff. From here Salmon Mountain's ridge looks like a green arm reaching toward Mt. Hood. To the west, look down the valley of Eagle Creek (Hike #196) to the flats of Portland.

If you're ready for a much more rugged hike, continue down the Plaza Trail 1.8 miles to a signed junction and turn right on the Salmon Mountain Trail. This path clambers up and down along a rhododendron-choked ridgecrest for 1.8 miles, growing steadily fainter and more brushy. Just before reaching a bare knoll the path angles down to the left across a brushy slope and then ends altogether at a saddle. Turn right and bushwhack 200 yards up the open ridgecrest to the old lookout site, with its view of four snowpeaks and the entire Salmon-Huckleberry Wilderness.

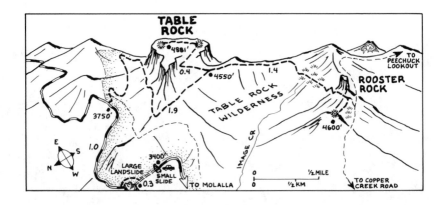

87 Table Rock

Moderate (to Table Rock)
7.2 miles round-trip
1500 feet elevation gain
Open June to mid-November
Use: hikers, horses
Map: Bull of the Woods Wilderness (USFS)

Difficult (to Rooster Rock)
10 miles round-trip
2600 feet elevation gain
Left: Rooster Rock and Mt. Jefferson.

This fortress-shaped plateau, centerpiece of a pocket Wilderness near Molalla, offers a formidable panorama of 10 Cascade snowpeaks and the Coast Range. A relatively easy trail skirts a 1996 landslide and ducks below huge columnar basalt cliffs before switchbacking up the plateau's gentle western slope. Rhododendrons flag the route pink in early summer, while gentians dot it with blue in late summer. For a longer hike, continue on a slightly rougher path to Rooster Rock's picturesque crag.

Start by driving to Molalla, either by heading south from Interstate 205 at Oregon City or by heading east from Interstate 5 at Woodburn. From Molalla drive half a mile toward Estacada on Highway 211, turn right onto South Mathias Road for 0.3 mile, turn left on South Feyrer Park Road for 1.6 miles, and then turn right onto South Dickey Prairie Road. Follow this road past several jogs for a total of 5.3 miles to a poorly marked junction with South Molalla Forest Road. Turn right on a bridge across the Molalla River, follow the paved road 12.8 miles to a fork, veer left onto gravel Middle Fork Road for 2.6 miles, and then turn right at a pointer for the Table Rock Trailhead. After 2 more miles, veer left at a fork with another pointer. A final 2.4 miles brings you to the trailhead, where a small landslide blocks the road to cars.

Park at the small landslide and hike ahead on the abandoned road. The track is gradually regrowing with alder, ox-eye daisies, and penstemon. After 0.3 mile the road ahead crumbles into a chasm left by a much larger landslide. Both of these slides were launched by the roadcut itself. The second slide grew so large because it was in an old clearcut, with no tree roots to hold the soil. To detour around the large slide, turn right on a new trail that scrambles 150 yards through the trees. Then continue a mile up the road to the pre-1996 trailhead, where a genuine trail heads into an old-growth forest on the right.

After 100 yards on the trail you'll reach a confusing junction. Don't turn right on a wide trail; it's actually an old cat road. Instead go straight, climbing at a steady grade through lichen-draped hemlocks and firs. After a mile you'll traverse below Table Rock's dramatic north cliff—a cutaway view of 7 basalt lava flows, 16 to 25 million years old. Here the trail crosses a rockslide where snow patches linger into July. Listen for the peeping cry of the rabbit-like pikas that store dried plants under the boulders for winter.

After 1.9 miles turn left at a junction in a ridgecrest saddle and switchback up to the summit. Lined up to the east are Cascade peaks from Mt. Rainier to the Three Sisters. Beyond the quilt of Willamette Valley farmfields to the west, the Coast Range silhouette stretches from the Tualatin Hills to Marys Peak.

To continue to Rooster Rock, return to the saddle junction and go straight, following the rough ridgecrest up and down. The path drops to a thimbleberry meadow before climbing steeply to an open saddle. Turn right and hike 100 yards up to a rocky knoll with a view across Rooster Rock to the High Cascades.

88   Clackamas River Trail

Moderate (with shuttle)
7.8 miles one-way
1300 feet elevation gain
Open all year
Map: Fish Creek Mtn. (Green Trails)
Right: The Narrows.

This all-year trail through the Clackamas River's canyon features hidden beaches, mossy forests, and whitewater viewpoints. A highway unobtrusively follows the river's far shore, making it easy to arrange a car shuttle and hike the 7.8-mile trail one way. If you can't find a second car to shuttle, try a 7.2-mile round-trip hike to Pup Creek Falls, a good picnic spot and turnaround point.

From Interstate 205 near Oregon City, take exit 12 and follow signs 18 miles east to Estacada. Go straight through town, continuing 14.4 miles on Highway 224. Beyond milepost 39, and just after crossing the second of two green bridges, turn right onto Fish Creek Road 54. Follow this paved road 0.2 mile, cross the Clackamas River on yet another green bridge, and park at a big lot on the right. The trail starts at the far end of the parking lot and crosses the road. (To leave a shuttle car at the upper trailhead you'll have to drive another 7 miles up

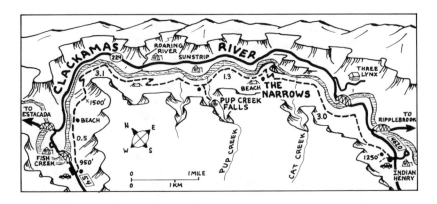

Highway 224 to a final green bridge, go straight at a sign for Indian Henry Campground, follow Road 4620 for 0.6 mile, and park on the right, opposite the campground entrance.)

Starting from the lower trailhead on Fish Creek Road, you'll follow a path lined with thousands of April-blooming oxalis. This white wildflower's shamrock-shaped leaves have such a tart flavor they're also called sourgrass. Spring brings trilliums and yellow wood violets to these woods, too. After half a mile the trail accesses a lovely stretch of riverbank. The sandy beach here is suitable for wading, and the mossy bedrock invites summer sunbathing.

Beyond the beach the trail spends a mile climbing through the forest to avoid riverside cliffs. Then the path continues gradually up and down along the shore, crossing an occasional powerline clearing. At the 3.6-mile mark (just before crossing 8-foot-wide Pup Creek on stepping stones), turn right on a 200-yard side trail through an alder grove to a view of Pup Creek Falls.

If you continue on the main trail, you'll reach another side path in 0.9 mile that leads left across a plank to a campsite by a whitewater riffle—the last beach access of the hike. Next the trail climbs a bluff with a view of The Narrows, a 20-foot-wide river gorge. Continue down the far side of the bluff and take a side trail to the left to see this chasm close up. In the final 2.9 miles to Indian Henry Campground, the trail ducks beneath a cliff's overhang, passes a side creek's thin waterfall, and contours through an old-growth forest of 5-foot-thick cedars.

The Clackamas River.   Opposite: Riverbar rocks.

89 Riverside Trail

Easy (to Rainbow Campground)
5.2 miles round-trip
300 feet elevation gain
Open all year
Use: hikers, bicycles
Map: Fish Creek Mtn. (Green Trails)

A classic old-growth forest flanks this popular portion of the Clackamas River. Explore it on the Riverside Trail, visiting secluded beaches and clifftop viewpoints. Because private concessionaires operate the campgrounds on either end of the trail—and charge $6 or more for day-use parking—plan to start at the new Riverside Trailhead along Road 46 instead.

From Interstate 205 near Oregon City, take exit 12 and follow signs east 18 miles to Estacada. Go straight through town, continuing 26 miles on Highway 224 to the bridge at Ripplebrook. Then fork right onto Road 46 for 1.8 miles to a small Riverside Trailhead sign and pull into a parking lot on the right.

The path sets off toward the river amid big Douglas fir and hemlock. The forest understory includes vine maple and Oregon grape, whose clustered yellow blooms are Oregon's state flower. After 100 yards, turn right on the Riverside Trail to a blufftop viewpoint of the curving stream below. Continue north along the trail, switchbacking down through a magnificent grove of ancient 5-foot-thick Douglas fir to a footbridge over Mag Creek.

Half a mile beyond Mag Creek the trail dips to a lovely river beach, just before a second footbridge. If you're hiking with kids, you might make this beach your destination. The riverbend of sand and cobbles, palisaded by giant firs, is a perfect spot to skip rocks, read a book, or sunbathe.

If you continue beyond the beach on the main trail, you'll cross the Tag Creek

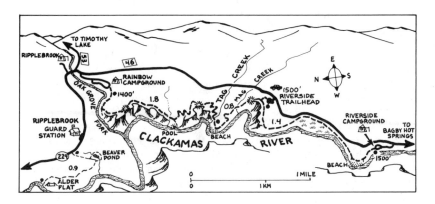

bridge and climb over a hill 0.8 mile to another interesting river access, just before the trail's third footbridge. Turn left on a side path here to discover a small sandy cove beside a chilly but swimmable 50-foot pool, protected from the river's swift current by a large rock. Beyond this turnoff, the Riverside Trail skirts tall clifftops overlooking the Clackamas River. Then the path follows the smaller Oak Grove Fork to trail's end at Rainbow Campground.

Other Options

If you're not yet tired after returning to your car, continue south on the other portion of the Riverside Trail. This 1.4-mile segment follows within a stone's throw of Road 46 for a half mile. Then the path curves out around a pretty riverbend with a large beach before ending at the Riverside Campground loop.

Although mountain bikes are discouraged on the Riverside Trail because of heavy use by hikers, you might bring a bicycle to use as a shuttle. Here's the plan: Stash a bike at Riverside Campground, drive back to the Riverside Trailhead, hike 1.4 miles along the trail to your bike, ride 3 miles downhill on paved Road 46 to Rainbow Campground, and then hike the river trail 2.6 miles back to your car.

90   Memaloose Lake

Easy (to Memaloose Lake)
2.6 miles round-trip
700 feet elevation gain
Open mid-June to early November
Use: hikers, horses, bicycles
Map: Fish Creek Mtn. (Green Trails)

Moderate (to South Fork Mountain)
4.6 miles round-trip
1400 feet elevation gain

This popular path is only 20 miles from Estacada, yet has the feel of the High Cascades. Hike 1.3 miles through a grand old-growth forest to a mountain lake in the woodsy cirque of a long-vanished glacier. If you like, continue up to the former lookout site atop South Fork Mountain for a view from the Three Sisters to Mt. Rainier.

From Interstate 205 near Oregon City, take exit 12 and follow signs 18 miles to Estacada. Go straight through town and continue 9.2 miles on Highway 224. Between mileposts 33 and 34, turn right across a green bridge onto Memaloose Road 45. Drive 11.2 paved miles on this road and then keep right on gravel for another mile to the trailhead sign on the left, just before Memaloose Creek.

The route of the hike lies within a single, isolated square mile of ancient forest, but the valley's steep walls make it seem as though the big woods extend forever. White wildflowers bloom in here in May, and for the rest of summer their delicate green leaves remain to blanket the forest floor. Look for vanilla leaf's three large triangular leaves. Oxalis resembles a shamrock, bunchberry has

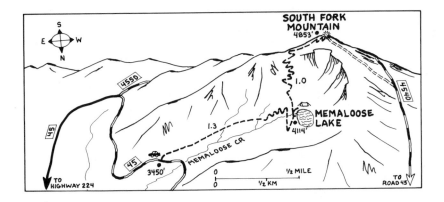

leaves in clusters of 6, and star-flowered smilacina's leaflets are arched fronds.

The path crosses a couple of creeklets overhung with elegant lady ferns before switchbacking up to a picnic table at the shallow lake. When you reach the shore, turn left and cross the outlet creek's bed. On your right you'll find a forested flat with several campsites. Directly in front of you is the unmarked (and unmaintained) path to South Fork Mountain.

If you're interested in a quick climb, follow this path as it switchbacks up into a higher elevation forest with huckleberries, beargrass, and rhododendrons. The trail crests a ridge and follows it up to the old lookout site. A bit of searching will locate all four foundations, inscribed with a 1931 date.

To be sure, an ungated dirt road occasionally brings cars to this summit. But this does not diminish the view. To the right of Mt. Jefferson look for pointy Three-Fingered Jack, Broken Top, and all Three Sisters. To the left of Mt. Hood look for Mt. Adams, Mt. Rainier, and Mt. St. Helens.

Memaloose Lake.   Opposite: Trail to Memaloose Lake.

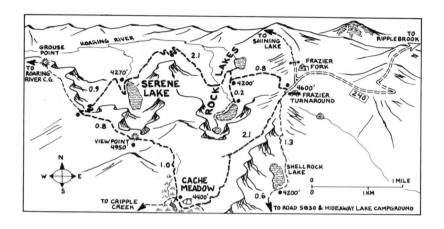

91   Rock Lakes

Easy (to Middle Rock Lake)
2 miles round-trip
500 feet elevation loss
Open mid-June to early November
Use: hikers, horses, bicycles
Maps: High Rock, Fish Creek Mtn.
   (Green Trails)

Moderate (to Serene Lake)
7.7-mile loop
1500 feet elevation gain

During the Ice Age, glaciers gouged high, bowl-shaped valleys into the tableland between the Clackamas and Roaring Rivers. Now mountain lakes fill these forested dales. An easy, mile-long trail descends to the Rock Lakes, a collection of three pools in the glaciers' footprints. If you continue on a 7.7-mile loop, you'll also get to visit larger Serene Lake, a viewpoint of Mt. Hood, and an old shelter at Cache Meadow.

From Interstate 205 near Oregon City, take exit 12 and follow signs east 18 miles to Estacada. Go straight through town, continuing 26 miles on Highway 224 to the bridge at Ripplebrook. Then fork left onto paved Road 57 (toward Timothy Lake) for 7.4 miles, turn left onto Road 58 for 6.9 miles (following signs to High Rock), turn left onto Abbott Road 4610 for 1.3 paved miles, and go straight onto dirt Road 240 at a sign for Frazier Fork. Follow this unmaintained, rocky, bumpy, slow road for 4.4 grueling miles, keep left at an unmarked fork (beside primitive Frazier Fork Campground), and continue 0.2 mile to road's end at Frazier Turnaround.

Start on the Serene Lake Trail. This path descends through Douglas fir woods where white wildflowers bloom in early summer: beargrass plumes, bunchberry, and queen's cup. After 0.8 mile turn left for a few hundred yards to a campsite at Middle Rock Lake. If you'd like to do a little exploring, go right at this campsite, cross the lake's outlet creek, follow a faint path to the far end of the lake, and hike up a slope to discover Upper Rock Lake in the Ice Age glacier's rocky cradle. To find the third lake in this valley, return to the main trail, continue downhill 500 feet, and follow a pointer 500 feet to the right to Lower Rock Lake.

If you're taking the loop hike, continue on the main trail 2 miles (with some downs and ups) to large, green, very deep Serene Lake. A fork to the left ends at the lake's bouldery east shore, while the main trail continues to a forested campsite on the west side. Here the trail turns uphill and climbs for most of a mile to a trail junction on the edge of a high, forested plateau. Go left. In 0.8 mile you'll traverse a 1-acre clearcut with a super view of Serene Lake, Mt. Hood, and three Washington snowpeaks.

Next the trail descends a mile to a 4-way trail junction at Cache Meadow, with its lakelet and flowers. Turn left for 200 yards to the ruin of a small log shelter from the early 1930s. The old shelter was once one of many primitive backcountry guard stations used by Forest Service rangers on their rounds. To complete the hike, continue past the shelter 300 yards, fork left on trail 517, climb for a mile to an ancient road, and follow it right for a mile to your car.

Other Hiking Options

If you hesitate to take your car on the final 4 miles of bad dirt road to the Frazier Turnaround trailhead, why not start from a good road near Hideaway Lake instead? This route adds about 3.5 miles to your hike (and 500 feet of elevation gain), but you pass Shellrock Lake and August huckleberry fields on the way. From Ripplebrook, drive Road 57 for 7.4 miles, turn left onto Road 58 for 3 miles, and turn left onto paved Road 5830 for 5 miles. If you're staying at the Hideaway Lake Campground, start the Shellrock Trail there. Otherwise drive Road 5830 past the campground entrance 0.3 mile to where the Shellrock Trail crosses the road, and start there.

Upper Rock Lake.   Opposite: Mt. Hood and Serene Lake.

92 Whetstone Mountain

Moderate
4.8 miles round-trip
1100 feet elevation gain
Open mid-June to early November
Use: hikers, horses
Map: Bull of the Woods Wilderness (USFS)

From Whetstone Mountain's rocky summit, the famous old-growth forests of Opal Creek's valley look like a rumpled green blanket. Eastward the forests roll up into the Bull of the Woods Wilderness, a protected cluster of green peaks. Glinting on the horizon are snowpeaks from Mt. Rainier to the Three Sisters. Though the view is panoramic, the climb to this old lookout site is relatively easy, and the trail passes through great patches of pink rhododendrons in early summer and huge blue huckleberries in August.

From Interstate 205 near Oregon City, take exit 12 and follow signs east 18 miles to Estacada. Go straight through town, continuing 26 miles on Highway 224 to the bridge at Ripplebrook. Then, following signs for Bagby Hot Springs, keep straight on paved Road 46 for 3.6 miles, turn right onto paved Road 63 for 3.5 miles, and turn right onto paved Road 70. Drive 9 miles on Road 70, and then follow signs for the Whetstone Mountain Trail, turning left onto Road 7030 for 5.6 miles, and turning right onto Road 7020 for 0.7 mile. Just before Road 7020 ends, turn left onto spur Road 028 to a large parking area in a 1980 clearcut.

The trail starts out downhill for 300 yards until it reaches an old-growth fir forest. Along this path are wild huckleberries so large they nearly rival commercial blueberries. If you've come before huckleberry season, admire the white woodland wildflowers instead: 3-petaled trillium, 4- or 6-petaled bunchberry, and 6-petaled queen's cup.

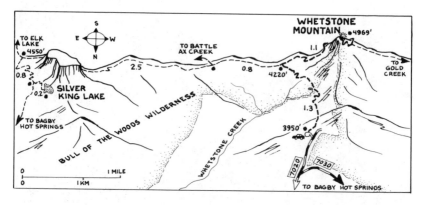

The trail passes between a pond and a rockslide (inhabited by cheeping pikas) at the 0.9-mile mark, and then switchbacks up to a broad, forested ridgetop crowded with rhododendrons. Watch carefully here for an inconspicuous sign and a faint trail joining from the right. Turn right onto this somewhat brushy path and follow it up the ridge. When the path forks at a scrawled signboard after 0.8 mile, go right and switchback up to the summit's bald rock knob.

From the foundation pier of the long-gone lookout tower you can see the entire route of your hike—including your flea-sized car in the clearcut, below the snowy tips of Mt. Adams and Mt. Rainier. Sharp eyes can spot the lookout tower atop Bull of the Woods (Hike #94), the tallest wooded peak to the east. Mt. Jefferson rises beside square-topped Battle Ax, while the Three Sisters brood beside square-topped Coffin Mountain to the south. Beyond a stripe of Willamette Valley to the west is the hump of Mary's Peak.

Other Hiking Options

Silver King Lake provides a more challenging goal. From the trail junction at the foot of Whetstone Mountain follow the ridgecrest path 3.3 miles east. At a small meadow in a saddle, fork left onto the Bagby Trail and switchback downhill 0.8 mile. At the foot of a rockslide, watch for a small sign on a tree to the left marking the 0.2-mile side path up to a campsite beside the forest-rimmed lake. The 11.2-mile round-trip has a cumulative elevation gain of 2100 feet.

Mt. Jefferson from Whetstone Mountain.   *Opposite: Stonecrop leaves at the summit.*

93 Bagby Hot Springs

Easy
3 miles round-trip
200 feet elevation gain
Open all year
Use: hikers, horses
Map: Bull of the Woods Wilderness (USFS)

Hollowed-out cedar logs form the bathtubs at this rustic, free hot springs. Even if you don't plan to soak, the trail here is a delight, leading through a towering old-growth forest along a fork of the Collawash River. Just don't expect solitude. On weekends and all through summer the trail is heavily used and there's a long waiting line at the bath house.

From Interstate 205 near Oregon City, take exit 12 and follow signs east 18 miles to Estacada. Go straight through town, continuing 26 miles on Highway 224 to the bridge at Ripplebrook. Then, following signs for Bagby Hot Springs, keep straight on paved Road 46 for 3.6 miles, turn right onto paved Road 63 for 3.5 miles, and turn right onto paved Road 70 for 6 miles to the trailhead parking lot on the left. Leave no valuables in your car, as this area has a history of theft.

The trail crosses a footbridge over Nohorn Creek and launches into a magnificent ancient forest of big Douglas firs and red cedars. In April and May look here for yellow clusters of Oregon grape blossoms and a variety of white blossoms: vanilla leaf, 3-petaled trillium, and bunchberry. In autumn, vine maple leaves become red pinwheels.

At the 1-mile mark pass an overlook of a 10-foot slide falls in the Hot Springs Fork. In another 0.2 mile cross the green-pooled river on a long bridge and climb to a signboard at the hot springs. The log cabin behind the signboard is the original Forest Service guard station. To the left is the bath house, with long

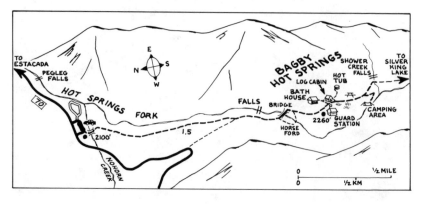

Trail to Bagby Hot Springs.   *Opposite: A cedar tub fills with hot water.*

benches outside for the waiting line. The old bath house burned in 1979 when nighttime bathers carelessly used candles for light. A non-profit group rebuilt the structure to include 5 private rooms and an annex with 4 additional 8-foot tubs.

To fill a tub, lower a wooden lever that diverts scalding water from a trough behind the wall. To adjust the temperature, use one of the plastic buckets to dip cold water from a vat outside. Remember the area's rules: no unleashed dogs, no music, no baths longer than 1 hour, and no soap—it pollutes the creek and harms the tubs. Swimsuits are rare.

If you keep right at the log cabin, you'll follow the Bagby Trail through a meadowed picnic area. After 0.2 mile, a side trail to the right descends to 8 riverside campsites. Shortly thereafter the Bagby Trail passes Shower Creek Falls—a thin, 50-foot cascade that some people use for a quick cold shower after their hot bath.

Other Hiking Options
If you continue up the Bagby Trail through this old-growth valley, you'll enter the Bull of the Woods Wilderness, leave the river, and cross 8 small side creeks. After hiking 6 miles from the hot springs (and gaining 1800 feet), you can take a spur trail to the right, climbing 0.2 mile to a campsite at forest-rimmed Silver King Lake.

Mt. Jefferson from Bull of the Woods.   *Below: The Bull of the Woods lookout.*

94   Pansy Lake

Easy (to Pansy Lake)
2.4 miles round-trip
500 feet elevation gain
Open mid-May to mid-November
Use: hikers, horses
Map: Bull of the Woods Wilderness (USFS)

Moderate (to Bull of the Woods)
7.1-mile loop
2000 feet elevation gain
Open July through October

The romp to this popular mountain lake is easy enough for children, but there's adventure here for hardier hikers as well. A scenic loop continues up to a historic lookout tower in the heart of the Bull of the Woods Wilderness.

This area is part of a 16- to 25-million-year-old volcanic mountain range predating the more famous High Cascade peaks. Erosion has carved up this older range, exposing quartz veins with ore that attracted prospectors in the late 1800s. One of these early visitors was Robert Bagby, who blazed a trail from Bagby Hot Springs (Hike #93) to a cabin he built by this lake. Because of the color of the copper ore he found here, he named his claim the Pansy Blossom Mine—and the lake became known as Pansy Lake. Some say the name "Bull of the Woods" refers to a big elk bagged by Bagby, but others note the phrase was common in Oregon's ox-logging days as a title for a tough crew boss.

From Interstate 205 near Oregon City, take exit 12 and follow signs east 18 miles to Estacada. Go straight through town, continuing 26 miles on Highway

224 to the bridge at Ripplebrook. Keep straight on paved Road 46 for 3.6 miles and then turn right onto Road 63. Follow this paved road straight for 5.6 miles. At a sign for the Pansy Basin Trail turn right onto Road 6340 for 7.8 miles. Then fork right onto Road 6341 for 3.5 miles. Park at an unmarked pullout on a right-hand curve amidst old-growth forest.

The trail starts at the register box on the left side of the road in a magnificent stand of 5-foot-thick Douglas firs and hemlocks. After climbing gradually for 0.8 mile, cross a charming creek and reach the first of three confusing trail junctions. Go left at this first junction (the path straight ahead promptly dives down through Pansy Basin's mini-meadow, following a rough, abandoned route to Pansy Lake). Continue uphill 140 yards, switchbacking to a second, possibly unmarked fork in the trail. This time go straight (the left-hand fork is the return route of the Bull of the Woods loop). Now continue 400 yards to the third confusing junction, almost within sight of Pansy Lake. A right-hand turn here leads around the lakeshore to a camping area.

If after enjoying the lakeshore you'd like to continue on the loop up to the lookout tower, return to the junction beside Pansy Lake and take the other fork, following a pointer toward Twin Lakes. This path climbs above Pansy Lake at a steady grade for 0.8 mile to trail junction at a wooded pass. Turn left and traverse 1.9 miles up a hillside with occasional views of Mt. Jefferson. At a marked junction just before a ridgecrest, turn left and switchback up 0.7 mile to the summit. The 1942-vintage lookout tower is rarely staffed, but the view is panoramic, encompassing every summit from the Three Sisters to Rainier. Below to the east is Big Slide Lake (see Hike #95).

To complete the loop, continue past the lookout on a path descending the ridge to the north. After 1.1 miles *watch carefully for a small signboard on the left* marking a side trail. Turn here, taking this switchbacking path downhill to the left. After 0.8 mile a short spur to the left leads to pretty, brush-rimmed Dickey Lake. Then continue half a mile down to the Pansy Lake Trail and turn right to return to your car.

Other Hiking Options

An easier route to the lookout tower starts near Dickey Peaks. Drive almost to the Pansy Basin Trailhead, but instead keep on Road 6340 to its end, following signs for the Bull of the Woods Trailhead. This 3.4-mile path gains only 900 feet.

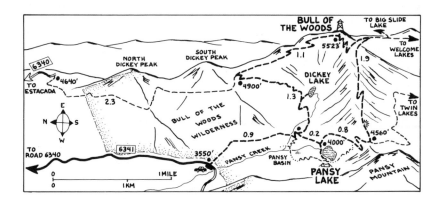

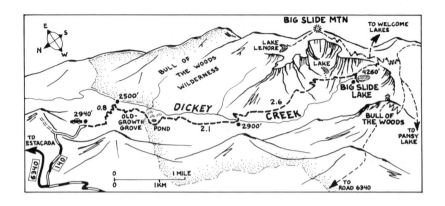

95 Dickey Creek

Moderate (to Dickey Creek crossing)
5.8 miles round-trip
900 feet elevation gain
Open May to early November
Use: hikers, horses
Map: Bull of the Woods Wilderness (USFS)

Difficult (to Big Slide Lake)
11 miles round-trip
2300 feet elevation gain
Open mid-June through October

Of the three major valleys cutting into the Bull of the Woods Wilderness from the north, Dickey Creek's is by far the least crowded. For all that, the old-growth forest here is as grand as anything in Bagby Hot Springs' hectic valley (Hike #93) and the mountain lakes are prettier than popular Pansy Lake (Hike #94). Why then the isolation? The Dickey Creek Trail begins with a 500-foot downhill scramble—elevation that must later be regained. Accept it as the price of admission to a secret wilderness retreat.

From Interstate 205 near Oregon City, take exit 12 and follow signs east 18 miles to Estacada. Go straight through town, continuing 26 miles on Highway 224 to the bridge at Ripplebrook. Keep straight on paved Road 46 for 3.6 miles and then turn right onto Road 63, following this road straight for 5.6 miles. At a sign for the Dickey Creek Trail turn right onto paved Road 6340. After 2.8 miles turn left onto gravel Road 140 for 1 mile. Then turn right at a T-shaped junction and continue half a mile to the trailhead at road's end.

The trail begins along an abandoned road overgrown with alder. After 0.3 mile, however, the roadbed ends and a rough trail plummets half a mile down into glorious green old-growth woods of 7-foot-thick Douglas firs. Scraggly, flat-needled yew trees and a plush shag carpet of moss add to the grand gloom.

After a few delinquent ups and downs the trail repents, goes straight, and skirts a meadow with a lilypad pond. Although Dickey Creek is audible most of the way, there's no access to the water until the trail finally reaches a small creekside campsite at the 2.9-mile mark. Here, arching cedar boughs overhang the bouldery stream.

There's no shame in turning back at this lovely lunch spot. But if you've set your sights on Big Slide Lake, hop across the bridgeless creek at this campsite. On the far shore the trail angles up to the left, switches back, and starts a long, hot climb along the valley wall. Rhododendrons overhang the path with pink blooms in early summer. After 2.2 miles the trail crosses the enormous rockslide that gave Big Slide Mountain its name. Listen here for the *meep!* of pikas, animals that look like round-eared rabbits. Pikas store tons of dried grass in their rockpile burrows so they can survive the winter without hibernating.

Shortly after the trail leaves the rockslide, a steep side trail to the right leads down to campsites beside Big Slide Lake. Here you can wade to a small island, swim from an underwater rock ledge, or simply watch the plentiful salamanders and small trout laze about in the shallows. Note the Bull of the Woods lookout tower on the ridge above.

Adventurers who love secret places can visit a trailless lake on the return trip. Hike back across the rockslide on the trail. A few hundred yards after reentering the woods, the trail crosses a (sometimes dry) creekbed. Just beyond this ravine bushwhack 200 yards up through a steep forest to a brush-lined lake below Big Slide Mountain's cliffs.

Other Hiking Options

Backpackers (or very hardy day hikers) can continue past Big Slide Lake to either of two colossal viewpoints. If you keep left at all trail junctions for 2 miles you'll end up atop 5526-foot Big Slide Mountain, overlooking beautiful Lake Lenore. If you keep right at all junctions you'll reach the lookout tower on 5523-foot Bull of the Woods in 2.2 miles.

Big Slide Mountain from Big Slide Lake.   Opposite: Newt in the lake.

96 Hawk Mountain

Easy (from Cachebox Meadow)
4.2 miles round-trip
800 feet elevation gain
Open late June through October
Use: hikers, horses, bicycles
Map: Breitenbush (Green Trails)

Moderate (from Graham Pass)
10.4 miles round-trip
1380 feet elevation gain

When fire lookout towers dotted the summits of hundreds of Cascade peaks in the 1940s, only a few staffers had the luxury of sleeping in a separate ground-level building. Even fewer of these rustic cabins remain today. The remote Rho Ridge Trail leads to Hawk Mountain's rare lookout cabin and a stunning, close-up view of Mt. Jefferson. The ridge was named for the rhododendrons that bloom here in June. The lichen-draped mountain hemlocks along the trail also shelter a good supply of beargrass and huckleberry bushes.

From Interstate 205 near Oregon City, take exit 12 and follow signs east 18 miles to Estacada. Go straight through town, continuing 26 miles on Highway 224 to the bridge at Ripplebrook. Keep straight on paved Road 46 for 3.6 miles and then turn right onto Road 63, following this road straight for 8.8 miles. At a sign for Graham Pass turn left onto paved Road 6350 for 1.2 miles, then fork to the right for 4.5 miles (trading pavement for gravel along the way), and finally fork to the left on what is still Road 6350. After another 1 mile you'll reach a pass with a 4-way junction.

Although there is no sign, this is Graham Pass, and to your right is the entrance to a large gravel parking lot for the Rho Ridge Trail. This is the trail's best parking area, preferred by equestrians, bicyclists, and some hikers. But if you're looking for a shorter route to the cabin viewpoint on Hawk Mountain, drive onward to a less obvious trailhead instead. From the intersection at Graham Pass, continue straight on gravel Road 6350 for 7.3 miles to another 4-way junction, turn right on Road 6355 for 0.3 mile to an ancient clearcut called Cachebox Meadow, and park on the shoulder where gravel Road 130 joins from the left. On the right you'll find a post marking the Rho Ridge Trail.

(If you're driving here from Salem or Bend, turn off Highway 22 at Detroit and follow Breitenbush Road 46 for 17.7 paved miles. A mile beyond a pass with a Mt. Hood National Forest boundary sign, turn left onto unmarked Road 6350. Follow this gravel road 4.8 mile (taking the largest, straightest route at junctions), until you reach a 4-way intersection. The Cachebox Meadow trailhead is 0.3 mile to the left on Road 6355, while the Graham Pass trailhead is 7.3 miles straight ahead on Road 6350.)

The relatively short trail from Cachebox Meadow switchbacks up a beargrass slope where the regrowing fir trees are still too small to block a stunning view of Mt. Jefferson. After 0.7 mile the path enters old-growth mountain hemlock woods. At the 1.7-mile mark, just after you spot Round Meadow's opening on

Mt. Jefferson from Hawk Mountain.   Opposite: Marsh marigolds.

the left, you'll reach an unmarked but obvious T-shaped junction.

Turn right and climb 0.4 mile to Hawk Mountain's summit and the foundations of the long-gone lookout tower. The cabin is just beyond, in a meadow of white yarrow, red paintbrush, and matted juniper. The 7 windows are shuttered, but the door is unlocked. Inside are a cot, a rickety stove, ratty cupboards, and a register. All artifacts are federally protected, right down to the rusty fire extinguisher and coat hangers. The view east includes, from left to right, Olallie Butte, Park Ridge (Hike #100), Mt. Jefferson, Three-Fingered Jack, the Three Sisters, and Mt. Washington.

If you're starting instead at the larger Graham Pass parking lot, the Rho Ridge Trail climbs a slope with views of Mt. Hood, crosses one dirt road, and then ends after 0.9 mile at abandoned Road 033. Following yellow diamond-shaped trail markers, turn right down this track 0.2 mile and turn right on abandoned gravel Road 270 for 1 mile. A few hundred yards after passing Road 290, look for a post on the right where the actual trail resumes. After another 2.7 miles the path follows a sometimes-dry creek up to Round Meadow, where marsh marigolds bloom in late June. This long, very narrow meadow was not named for its shape, but rather because it is the headwaters for Round Lake, a few miles below. When the trail curves left away from the meadow, turn left at an obvious but unsigned fork and climb 0.4 mile to Hawk Mountain's summit.

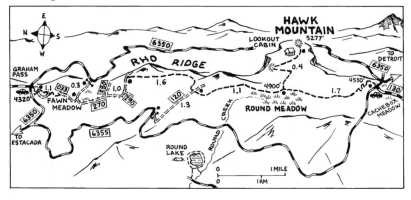

213

97   Red Lake

Easy (to Red Lake)
3.2 miles round-trip
1000 feet elevation gain
Open mid-June to early November
Use: hikers, horses, bicycles
Map: Olallie Butte (USGS)

Moderate (to Potato Butte)
7.2 miles round-trip
1700 feet elevation gain

Hundreds of lakes dot the forested Olallie Lake plateau north of Mt. Jefferson, but Red Lake is one of the few to offer a glimpse of the big snowy mountain itself. And once you've climbed to Red Lake, it's not much further to visit three other lakes on your way up Potato Butte, an old volcano with a far better view across the plateau to Mt. Jeff. Mosquitoes can be a problem the first half of July.

From Interstate 205 near Oregon City, take exit 12 and follow signs east 18 miles to Estacada. Go straight through town, continuing 26 miles on Highway 224 to the bridge at Ripplebrook. Keep straight on Road 46 for another 26.7 paved miles, following signs for Detroit. Beyond the Olallie Lake turnoff 4.9 miles, at a (possibly missing) sign for the Red Lake Trail, turn left on gravel Road 380 for 0.9 mile. The trail begins on the left, opposite a sign marking the end of road maintenance.

If you're driving here from Salem or Bend, turn off Highway 22 in Detroit and follow paved Breitenbush Road 46 for 18.2 miles to the feebly signed Red Lake Trail turnoff on the right.

The trail briefly crosses a clearcut before climbing steeply through an old-growth forest of western hemlock and Douglas fir trees, some of them 5 feet in diameter. After 0.4 mile the path enters a powerline clearing and joins a dirt road. Turn left on the road for 50 feet and then turn right on a spur road for 200 feet to find the continuation of the trail.

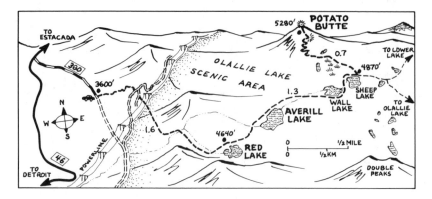

Mt. Jefferson from Potato Butte.   Opposite: Potato Butte from Wall Lake.

The path reenters the woods and climbs steadily for a mile to a plateau where huckleberries grow among lodgepole pines. At a big and obvious stump, turn right on a side path to a small beach beside shallow Red Lake. Dragonflies zoom and rough-skinned newts laze in the shallows. Campsites abound.

Having climbed all the way to Red Lake, it's hard not to continue another 1.3 level miles past larger Averill Lake and Wall Lake to Sheep Lake. And once you've reached the far end of Sheep Lake, why not turn left at the "Potato Butte" pointer for a climb to a really good viewpoint? The 0.7-mile trail heads left when it reaches a small meadow and then switchbacks steeply up a slippery cinder slope to the broad summit with its view of Mt. Hood and Olallie Butte. To see Mt. Jefferson, however, you'll have to hike back down the trail 300 yards and bushwhack left 50 feet to a slope of boulders. Atop these rocks is the view you really wanted, including most of the lakes you passed on the hike.

Other Hiking Options

Backpackers or hardy day hikers can explore the Red Lake Trail further east. It's 1.7 miles from Sheep Lake to Top Lake and the route described in Hike #99.

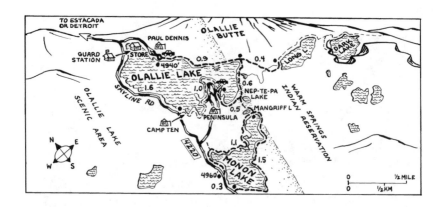

98   Monon Lake

Easy
6.8-mile loop
100 feet elevation gain
Open July to mid-October
Map: Olallie Butte (USGS)

An easy trail loops around the many-bayed shore of Monon Lake, the second largest lake in the Olallie Lake Scenic Area's high, forested plateau. Along the way you'll gain a view of nearby Mt. Jefferson, visit three other lakes, and pass bedrock worn smooth by Ice Age glaciers. Although a 2001 fire left much of the lakeshore lined with blackened snags and closed the trail until the fall of 2002, the slow natural recovery is underway, with huckleberries and wildflowers thriving. Mosquitoes can be a problem in July.

From Interstate 205 near Oregon City, take exit 12 and follow signs east 18 miles to Estacada. Go straight through town, continuing 26 miles on Highway 224 to the bridge at Ripplebrook. Keep straight on paved Road 46 for another 21.8 miles to a large junction with a sign for Olallie Lake, and turn left onto paved Road 4690. (Travelers from the south can reach this junction by taking Breitenbush Road 46 from Highway 22 at Detroit for 23.5 paved miles.) Drive Road 4690 for 8.1 miles to a stop sign, turn right onto gravel Road 4220 for 7 miles, and turn left at the Peninsula Campground entrance. Follow signs for the boat ramp, and park there.

From the boat ramp the trail heads to the right around Olallie Lake, with 7215-foot Olallie Butte as a backdrop. Among the burned snags along the shore expect blooming heather in July and lots of ripe huckleberries in August. Mile-long Olallie Lake is so pure it's a drinking water source, and as a result, this is the only lake in the area where swimming is banned. Motorboats aren't allowed either, but canoes are common and rowboats can be rented at the rustic store on the other side of the lake.

After 0.3 mile turn right at a junction with the Olallie Lake Trail. Hike past two small lakes and then turn right at the shore of Monon Lake, where there's a fine view of the top half of Mt. Jefferson. The rounded bedrock of the lakeshore here still bears the scratches of the glacial ice that sculpted this lake basin over 6000 years ago.

In 1.1 miles the Monon lakeshore path joins the gravel road. Follow the road's shoulder several hundred yards to find the continuation of the trail veering back into the woods. Complete the loop along the more remote east shore of Monon Lake — a good place to find a quiet lunch spot or backpacking campsite.

Other Hiking Options

For a slightly longer hike with better mountain views, start at Paul Dennis Campground instead. To find this trailhead, follow signs to the Olallie Lake Resort and continue straight to the end of the campground loop, where the trail starts at a post. The first 0.9 mile around Olallie Lake is a delight, with picture-postcard reflections of Mt. Jefferson. Keep right to join the Monon Lake loop.

Monon Lake before the 2001 forest fire.   Opposite: Mt. Jefferson from Olallie Lake.

Top Lake

Easy (to Top Lake)
3.1-mile loop
500 feet elevation gain
Open July to mid-October
Use: hikers, horses
Map: Olallie Butte (USGS)

Moderate (to Double Peaks)
5.3-mile loop
1100 feet elevation gain

Half a dozen woodsy lakes and a viewpoint of Mt. Jefferson make this loop on the Pacific Crest Trail fun even for children—if you wait until after the July mosquito season. Hikers with extra energy can add a short but very steep side trip up Double Peaks for an even better panorama of the lake-dotted Olallie Lake Scenic Area.

If you're driving here from the Portland area, take Interstate 205 near Oregon City to exit 12 and follow signs east 18 miles to Estacada. Go straight through town, continuing 26 miles on Highway 224 to the bridge at Ripplebrook. Keep straight on paved Road 46 for another 21.8 miles to a large junction with a sign for Olallie Lake, and turn left onto paved Road 4690. Drive this road 8.1 miles to a stop sign and turn right onto gravel Road 4220 for 5.1 miles to the junction for the Olallie Lake Resort. Keep right for 0.3 mile to a message board on the right and a small sign for the Red Lake Trail. Park at a pullout on the road's opposite shoulder.

If you're driving here from Salem or Bend, turn off Highway 22 in Detroit, follow Breitenbush Road 46 for 23.5 paved miles, turn right onto Road 4690 for 8.1 miles, and turn right on Road 4220 for 5.4 miles.

The Red Lake Trail ambles through a high-elevation forest of mountain hemlock and lodgepole pine where masses of blue huckleberries ripen in late August. After passing three ponds, keep right at a possibly unmarked trail

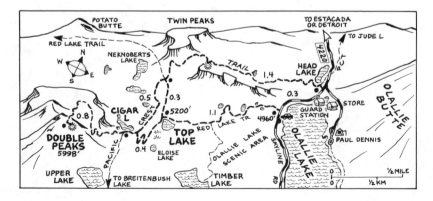

Double Peaks from Top Lake.   Opposite: Mt. Jefferson from Double Peaks.

junction (the left-hand fork deadends in 0.7 mile at Timber Lake). Soon the path reaches Top Lake, with a pebbly beach and a view ahead to Double Peaks. This is a nice spot to wade, pick berries, or simply watch dragonflies zoom about.

At the far end of Top Lake you'll reach a T-shaped junction. To take the easy loop back, simply turn right and keep right at every junction you find. You'll join the Pacific Crest, pass a rockslide, and descend along a cliff-edged ridge with a view of Mt. Jefferson. Stop here to notice how the clifftop rock has been rounded and scratched by the Ice Age glaciers that buried this whole landscape with moving ice just 6000 years ago. Then continue down the trail to Head Lake, turn right, and walk along the road 0.3 mile to your car.

To take the longer loop to Double Peaks, turn left at the Top Lake junction. This trail switchbacks up to the Pacific Crest Trail, where you turn left for 100 feet to a sign announcing Cigar Lake, a rock-lined, dumbbell-shaped lake. Walk 200 feet past the Cigar Lake sign and leave the PCT, turning right onto a faint side path toward Double Peaks. This path soon forks, but keep left until it starts scrambling steeply up a slope. The path levels off for a few hundred yards along a clifftop rim to the right before a final, very steep ascent between rockslides to Double Peak's ridgecrest. To the right is the first summit, with a view to Mt. Hood and the jumbled peaks of the Bull of the Woods Wilderness. To the left is the taller summit, with an aerial view of the route of your hike.

When you hike back down to Cigar Lake, follow the Pacific Crest Trail to the left for 1.9 miles to continue the loop.

Other Hiking Options

Backpackers or hardy day hikers can explore the Red Lake Trail further west across this forested plateau. It's 1.7 miles from Top Lake to Sheep Lake and the route described in Hike #97. Another option is to hike the PCT south to Breitenbush Lake. It's 2.3 miles from Cigar Lake to the Ruddy Hill junction described in Hike #207.

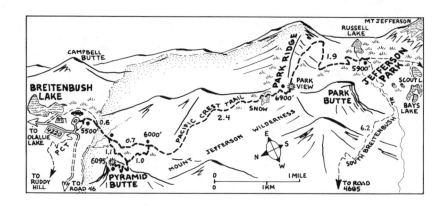

100   Jefferson Park Ridge

Easy (to Pyramid Butte)
4-mile loop
800 feet elevation gain
Open mid-July to mid-October
Use: hikers, horses
Map: Mt. Jefferson Wilderness (USFS)

Moderate (to Park Ridge)
7.4 miles round-trip
1400 feet elevation gain

Difficult (to Jefferson Park)
11.2 miles round-trip
2400 feet elevation gain

Mt. Jefferson fills half the sky from the green alpine meadows and sparkling lakes of Jefferson Park. A heavily-used portion of the Pacific Crest Trail climbs across Park Ridge to this patch of paradise. For a less difficult hike, consider setting your goal as the spectacular viewpoint atop Park Ridge itself. An even easier alternative is a short loop on a meadow-lined section of the old Skyline Trail past Pyramid Butte. Be forewarned, however, that the trailhead can be reached only by high-clearance vehicles, and that Jefferson Park is often crowded on summer weekends.

From Interstate 205 near Oregon City, take exit 12 and follow signs east 18 miles to Estacada. Go straight through town, continuing 26 miles on Highway 224 to the bridge at Ripplebrook. Keep straight on paved Road 46 for another 21.8 miles to a large junction with a sign for Olallie Lake, and turn left onto paved Road 4690. Drive this road 8.1 miles to a stop sign and turn right onto gravel Road 4220 for 10.5 miles. The final 2 miles of this road are *extremely* rough, impassable for most passenger cars. Just beyond Breitenbush Lake turn left to the Pacific Crest Trailhead's cinder turnaround.

If you're driving here from Salem or Bend, turn off Highway 22 in Detroit, follow Breitenbush Road 46 for 23.5 paved miles, turn right onto Road 4690 for 8.1 miles, and turn right on Road 4220 for 10.5 miles.

Start at the first message board on your right as you enter the PCT parking area. After 50 yards turn left and follow the PCT through subalpine woods with lots of lovely openings. Heather and blue lupine bloom here in mid-summer and masses of huckleberries ripen shortly afterwards.

After 0.6 mile the path crosses a footbridge and forks. To the left is the newer, more direct PCT route to Park Ridge and Jefferson Park. If you have the time, or if you're interested in a shorter loop, turn right on the old, unmarked Skyline Trail. This older path meanders past a gushing spring and several meadows to a junction at the base of Pyramid Butte. Here you can either turn right for the steep, switchbacking half-mile climb to a cliff-edge viewpoint atop Pyramid Butte, or you can head left to climb back to the PCT.

If you're continuing up the PCT to Park Ridge you'll gradually climb past timberline. Alpine heather, white partridge foot, purple aster, and red paintbrush give way to a rocky landscape with snowfields. Follow cairns carefully to keep on the trail. Finally reach Park Ridge's windy crest and a breathtaking view ahead to Jefferson Park.

Beyond this point the PCT descends 1.9 miles to the meadows beside swimmable Russell Lake, first and largest of the park's pools. If you're backpacking, tent at designated sites in the woods, away from the fragile meadows. Camping is banned on the peninsulas of Scout and Bays Lakes. Campfires are strongly discouraged and are banned altogether within 100 feet of water or trails.

Other Hiking Options

Two other routes reach Jefferson Park. The less crowded South Breitenbush Trail climbs 2800 feet in 6.2 miles. To find the trailhead, drive paved Road 46 south of Ripplebrook for 33.1 miles (or drive north from Detroit 11.5 miles), and take gravel Road 4685 east for 5 miles. The heavily used Whitewater Trail to Jefferson Park climbs 1800 feet in 5.1 miles. To find it, drive Highway 22 east of Detroit 10.3 miles and turn left on gravel Whitewater Road 2243 to its end.

Mt. Jefferson from Russell Lake.   Opposite: Western pasque flowers.

All-Accessible Trails in Northwest Oregon

People with limited physical abilities need not miss the fun of exploring new trails. Here are 31 paths within a two-hour drive of Portland accessible to everyone. Most of the trails are paved and several include interpretive signs about natural features or history. Some are open to bicycles. Unless otherwise noted, the paths are open year round. For more information, contact the trail's managing agency. For trails in the Portland area, call the Portland Park Bureau's Disabled Citizens Recreation program at (503) 823-4328 (voice or TDD).

PORTLAND AREA (map on page 13)

A. Greenway Park. Follow a paved path along Fanno Creek in Beaverton 2.5 miles from Bel-Aire Street to North Dakota Street. A side path near Hall Blvd leads to visitable Fanno Farm House, built 1859. Take Hwy 217 to Hall Blvd near Washington Square and go west 0.4 mile. Start at Albertson's parking lot.

B. Trillium Trail. These two interpretive nature paths loop 0.3 mile through the woods of Tryon Creek State Park. Start as for Hike #9 but stay on the paved path.

C. George Rogers Park. This paved 0.8-mile path along the Willamette River crosses Oswego Creek. Take Highway 43 (alias Macadam Avenue, alias State Street) to Lake Oswego and turn down on Ladd. Then turn right on Furnace to a historic iron smelter and the footbridge to the trail.

D. OMSI Willamette Riverbank. A paved bike path, the Eastbank Esplanade, extends 1.8 mile north from OMSI along the river (and sometimes *on* the river, using floats) to the Steel Bridge. An additional 3.2-mile section of the riverbank path, set to open in 2001, heads south from OMSI through Oaks Park to Umatilla Street, two blocks south of the Sellwood Bridge. See Hike #8.

E. Powell Butte. The Mountain View Trail climbs 0.6 mile to a broad, grassy summit with views, where the paved path ends. See Hike #10.

F. Springwater Corridor. This paved 11.6-mile bike path from Hogan Road to Tideman-Johnson Park follows a former railroad along Johnson Creek past farms, subdivisions, and Powell Butte. A good place to start is Gresham's Main City Community Park. See Hike #10.

G. The Grotto. Gardens, viewpoints, and Catholic statuary line a peaceful 0.9-mile path. An elevator accesses an upper loop, but has a $2 fee. Drive or take Tri-Met #12 out NE Sandy one block past 82nd.

H. Burnt Bridge Creek. Vancouver's Greenway bike path extends 1.6 miles through creekside meadows. Drive north on Interstate 5 to Vancouver's 39th Street exit, turn left for 1.5 miles, turn right on Fruit Valley Road for 1.7 miles, and park on the right.

I. Champoeg Park. Hike #13 has three all-accessible options: take the bike path from the Visitor Center 0.6 mile through a meadow to a pavilion, or take a gravel 0.4-mile interpretive nature loop from the campground, or start at the campground and take a bike path 1.5 miles east along the Willamette River.

J. Willamette Mission Park. Park as for Hike #14. Either take a 1.2-mile bike path east through a filbert grove to the Willamette River ferry landing, or go west on a challenging 3-mile paved bike loop through riverside woods.

Coldwater Lake's boardwalk in Mt. St. Helens Volcanic National Monument.

SOUTHWEST WASHINGTON (map on page 43)

K. Coldwater Ridge. From the large Mt. St. Helens visitor center on Coldwater Ridge, the 0.3-mile paved Winds of Change loop tours a blast-killed forest with mountain views. See Hike #17. Open Apr-Oct.

L. Coldwater Lake. The paved 0.2-mile Birth of a Lake Trail ends with a dramatic boardwalk pier into a lake created by Mt. St. Helens' 1980 eruption. Drive Highway 504 past the Coldwater Ridge Visitor Center 2 miles and turn left. See Hike #17. Expect a $3 per person fee. Open Apr-Oct.

M. Johnston Ridge. For close-up views of Mt. St. Helens' crater, take the paved but steep and challenging 0.4-mile Eruption Trail loop from the popular Johnston Ridge Visitor Center. See Hike #18. Open June-Oct.

N. Trail of Two Forests. This 0.3-mile interpretive loop tours a lava cast forest in a 1900-year-old basalt flow. Drive as to Hike #19 but park 0.6 mile before Ape Cave.

O. Lava Canyon. This spectacular path leads to waterfalls in a mudflow-scoured canyon (see Hike #22). The path is paved for first 0.5 mile, with boardwalks and interpretive signs. Open May-Nov.

P. Meta Lake. In Mt. St. Helen's recovering blast zone, take a paved 0.4-mile path from a scorched miner's car to a lake. Open June-Oct.

Q. Lewis River Viewpoints. Three graveled paths lead to waterfall views. Park as for Hike #25 for the 0.2-mile trail to massive Lower Lewis River Falls. Then drive 5.5 miles west on Rd 90 to Big Creek Trailhead for a 0.7-mile path from a 110-foot falls to a river overlook. Then drive 3.8 miles farther west on Road 90 to the turnoff for the 0.2-mile Curly Creek Falls trail.

R. St. Cloud Trail. A half-mile loop through homestead orchards on Washington's side of the Columbia River offers views of Multnomah Falls. Drive 23 miles east of Vancouver (or 14 miles west of Bonneville Dam) on Washington Hwy 14.

S. Sams-Walker Trail. A 1.1-mile loop tours forest, wetlands, and an orchard alongside the Columbia River. Drive 27 miles east of Vancouver (or 10 miles west of Bonneville Dam) on Highway 14, and turn south on Skamania Landing Road for 0.2 mile.

T. Fort Cascades. Near Bonneville Dam, this 1.2-mile loop visits the site of an 1856 Army fort and passes a petroglyph. Drive 3.2 mile west of Bridge of the Gods on Washington Highway 14.

COLUMBIA GORGE (map on page 93)

U. Latourell Falls. Park as for Hike #35, but take a 0.3-mile path *downhill* to Lower Latourell Falls and on to a picnic area, where steps block the route.

V. Wahkeena Falls. Another glorious Columbia Gorge waterfall. Park at the Wahkeena Falls Trailhead for Hike #38, where a 0.2-mile trail climbs to a stone footbridge beneath Wahkeena Falls.

W. Tooth Rock. Follow the historic Columbia River Hwy (now reopened as a paved trail) a mile to a cliff-edge viewpoint on a viaduct. See Hike #46.　　⊛

X. Columbia River Highway. Follow a 2.5-mile segment of the historic Columbia River Highway (now reopened as a paved trail) along I-84 from Cascade Locks to Eagle Creek. The trail starts at the on-ramp of exits 41 and 44.　　⊛

Y. Mosier Twin Tunnels. Follow a 4.7-mile segment of the historic Columbia River Highway (now reopened as a paved trail) to a viewpoint at two restored tunnels. See Hike #55.　　⊛

Z. The Dalles Riverfront. Park at the Columbia Gorge Discovery Center, an elegant museum off Interstate 84 at The Dalles exit 84. From here a paved bike path sets off past ponds along the Columbia River. Eventually the path will continue 3.8 miles to The Dalles' downtown.　　⊛

MOUNT HOOD - WEST (map on page 131)

AA. Wildwood Area. Two paved interpretive loop trails, each 3/4 mile long, tour streambank and wetlands along the Salmon River. See Hike #58.

BB. Lost Creek Nature Trail. A barrier-free campground and picnic area features a 0.5-mile paved and boardwalk loop to two all-accessible fishing piers at a creek with snags from 1790 Mt. Hood eruption. Drive as to Burnt Lake (Hike #64) but stop at Lost Creek Campground. Open May-Nov.

CC. Lost Lake Old Growth Trail. This dramatic 1-mile interpretive trail among massive red cedars is half gravel, half boardwalk with decked pullouts. Drive to Lost Lake (see Hike #63), but keep left at the lake to the east picnic area parking lot. Open June-Oct.

DD. Trillium Lake. Picture postcard views of Mt Hood highlight a 1.7-mile gravel loop around the lake. The route passes all-accessible picnic tables, camping sites, and fishing piers. Drive 3 mi east of Government Camp on Highway 26, follow signs 1.6 mile to Trillium Lake Campground, and park at a picnic area. Open June-Oct.

EE. Little Crater and Timothy Lakes. A paved 0.2-mile path leads to Little Crater Lake (see Hike #75), but a fence blocks access to the Pacific Crest Trail and the 10.8-mi loop around Timothy Lake. This larger route is level and all-accessible except for a roughish 0.2 mile from Oak Fork Campground to the PCT. Open May-Nov.

107 More Hikes in Northwest Oregon

Adventurous hikers can discover plenty of additional trails within a two-hour drive of the Portland area. The list below covers the most interesting, from urban promenades to rugged wilderness paths. Directions are brief, so be extra careful to bring appropriate maps. Estimated mileages are one-way. Most paths are open only in summer and fall, but symbols beside the entries note which hikes are open all year, and which are suitable for kids, horses, bicycles, or backpackers. For more information, check with the trail's administrative agency.

The appropriate ranger district or other offices are abbreviated as follows: (B)–Barlow, (C)–Columbia Gorge National Scenic Area, (D)–Washington Department of Natural Resources, (E)–Estacada, (HR)–Hood River, (MA)–Mt Adams, (MS)–Mt St Helens National Monument, (O)–Oregon State Parks, (P)–Portland Parks and Recreation, (S)–Sauvie Island Wildlife Area, (W)–Wind River, (Z)–Zigzag. Agency phone numbers are on page 11.

Easy / Moderate / Difficult

PORTLAND AREA (map on page 13)

101. Virginia Lake. Meadowed 2.2-mile loop around marshy lake on Sauvie Island. Expect birds, some cattle. Drive as to Hike #2 but go straight on Sauvie Is Rd 0.5 mile past Reeder Rd turnoff. (O)

102. Holman Park. Convenient 2.6-mi loop in woods S of Forest Park. Turn off Cornell Rd onto 53rd Dr for 0.6 mi. Hike down Birch Tr, turn R onto Wildwood Tr 1.6 mi, turn R to return on Holman Ln. (P)

103. Macleay Trail. Woodsy 5.5-mile loop along Balch Creek joins Wildwood Tr, crosses Cornell Rd, climbs to Pittock Mansion, and returns via Upper Macleay Tr. Gains 800 ft. Drive as to Hike #5 but park beneath Thurman St bridge. (P)

104. Audubon Bird Sanctuary. 3 miles of paths loop through woods at 101-acre Portland Audubon Soc nature ctr, 5151 NW Cornell Rd.

105. Terwilliger Bike Path. Paved 3.5-mi promenade parallels Terwilliger Blvd from Duniway Park (a block from the trailhead for Hike #7) to Barbur Blvd. (P)

106. Willamette Park. Paved riverside path starts in grassy park, continues 1.5 mi N to River Forum office bldg. Drive SW Macadam to Carolina St, turn W to Willamette Park. (P)

107. Leach Botanical Gardens. Spring blooms line a network of gravel paths in historic 9-acre Portland garden at 6704 SE 122nd. (P)

108. Reed College. Loop 1 mi around narrow, swampy lake on scenic campus. Drive SE 38th St to Steele St, turn W to Reed's North Parking Area, hike down to lake. 1-mi side trip follows lake's outlet cr to SE 28th Ave and famous 7-acre Crystal Sprs Rhododendron Garden. (P)

109. Elk Rock Island. Explore Willamette R peninsula on a 1-mi loop with cottonwoods and herons. Drive McLoughlin Blvd S, take River Rd exit 4 blocks, turn R on Sparrow St to corner of 19th Ave. (P) ⚹

110. Mary Young Park. State park on Willamette R has 2.3-mi sawdust path around perimeter amid maples and woodland wildflowers. Drive 2.5 mi S of Lake Oswego on Hwy 43 (alias Macadam Ave). (O) ⚹

111. Camassia Natural Area. Tall blue camas blooms Apr-May on trail network among ponds in 27-acre preserve behind high schl on West A St in West Linn. No pets or flower picking. (Nature Conservancy) ⚹

112. McIver Park. Start at a fish hatchery and end along the Clackamas River on this 4.2-mi wooded loop, muddy in winter due to horse use. From Estacada take Hwy 211 S toward Molalla 1 mi, follow signs to park and then to hatchery. Trail goes around hatchery to right. (O) ⚹ 🏕

113. Sandy River Delta. Undeveloped parkland, this 2-sq-mi Columbia R flood plain of mdws, cottonwoods, sloughs is open to cross-country rambling. Start on N side of I-84 at Lewis & Clark Park exit 18. (O) ⚹

SOUTHWEST WASHINGTON (map on page 43)

114. Ridgefield Wildlife Refuge. The 1.9-mi Oaks to Wetlands Wildlife Trail follows RR tracks to marshes with geese, ducks, and sandhill cranes. Drive N of Vancouver on I-5 to exit 15, turn L on Hwy 501 for 3 mi to Ridgefield, and head N on Main St a mile to the refuge's Carty Unit. (US Fish & Wildlife, 360-887-4106) ⚹

115. Tarbell Trail. Woodsy 5-mi path to 90-ft waterfall gains 700 ft, loses 500. Hike another 2.1 mi to join Hike #15. From Vancouver go N on Hwy 503 for 13.8 mi, turn R on Rock Cr Rd 8.8 mi, go R on Rd 12 for 1.9 mi, turn R on Dole Valley Rd 2.5 mi, go L 2.1 mi to Tarbell CG. (D) 🏕

116. Silver Star Mountain via Star Way. Steep, faint 3.8-mi path gains 2700 ft up N ridge of mtn (see Hike #15). From Vancouver go N on Hwy 503 for 13.8 mi, turn R on Rock Cr Rd 8.8 mi, go R on Rd 12 for 7 mi, turn R on Rd 41 for 4 mi, veer R on Rd 4107 for 0.8 mi. (MS) 🏕

117. Silver Star via Bluff Mountain. Open ridge E of mtn (see Hike #15) has views, flowers. 5.3-mi tr loses 500 ft, gains 1700. From Vancouver go N on Hwy 503 for 13.8 mi, turn R on Rock Cr Rd 8.8 mi, go R on Rd 12 for 7 mi, turn R on Rd 41 for 9.4 mi to pass, turn R and drive (or walk) along crest 2 very rough miles to trailhead. (MS) 🏕

118. Siouxon Peak. Easier route to Hike #16 viewpt gains 1300 ft in 2.2 mi. Drive as to #32 but go 17 mi on Hwy 30, veer L on Rd 64 for 10.2 mi, turn R on Rd 6403 for 3.5 mi to a saddle, hike up old rd to R. (MS) 🚲🏕

119. Goat Marsh Lake. 1-mi stroll to lilypad lake reflecting Mt St Helens. Drive as to Hike #20, but only go 0.6 mi on Rd 8123. (MS) 🛶

120. Castle Ridge. Descend ridge 2 mi to Loowit Tr on remote W flank of Mt St Helens in unrestricted part of blast zone. Map req'd for access via Weyerhaeuser rd system off Hwy 504. (MS) Λ

121. Loowit Trail. Backpack around Mt St Helens on this 29.5-mi loop, accessible via Hikes #18, 20, 22-24, 26, 119, 122,-123. Camping and off-trail hiking banned in 8.4-mi portion of blast zone. (MS) ⛺

Mt. Jefferson from Olallie Butte (Hike #207).

Easy
Moderate
Difficult

122. Butte Camp Trail. Mt St Helens climb route gains 5200 ft. It's 1.7 mi to campsite, then 1 mi to timberline and 2.3 mi cross-country to summit. Drive as to Hike #22 but go 3.1 mi on Rd 81. (MS)

123. Blue Lake Loop. 12.5-mi loop to Mt St Helens timberline follows Toutle, Sheep Canyon (see Hike #20), Loowit, Butte Camp Trails, gains 1700 ft. Drive as to #20 but only go 1.7 mi on Rd 8123. (MS)

124. Strawberry Mountain. Gain 1400 ft in 2.5 mi to viewpt of Mt St Helens, blast zone. Drive as to Spirit L (Hike #27), but only go 4.7 mi on Rd 99 to Bear Mdw, hike R on Boundary Tr 0.5 mi, turn R. (MS)

125. Goat Mountain. Follow blast zone rim 5.5 mi to Deadmans L. Gain 1500 ft, lose 800. Drive to #27 but turn R on Rd 26 for 5 mi. (MS)

126. Ghost Lake. From Norway Pass Trailhead (see Hike #27) hike E for 1.5 easy mi on Boundary Tr along blast zone edge to lk. (MS)

127. Badger Peak. Hike pumice-dusted Boundary Tr 4 mi E to Badger L, climb 0.9 to panoramic lookout site. Gain 1900 ft total. Drive as to Spirit L (#27) but only go 21.2 mi on Rd 25, park at Elk Pass. (MS)

128. Craggy Peak. Views await on 4.9-mi path to this Dark Divide peak. Gain 1700 ft. Drive as to Hike #27, but go 5.4 mi on Rd 25, veer R on Rd 93 for 18.7 mi, turn L on Rd 9327 for 0.3 mi. (MS)

129. Boundary Trail. Backpack 56 mi from Mt St Helens to Mt Adams, following Trail Number One along Dark Divide. Route connects with Hikes #18, 27, 126-128, 131-133, ends at Council Lake. (MS)

130. Lower Lewis River Trail. Quiet 9.5-mi part of river trail passes 1921 Bolt Camp Shelter, old-growth woods. Plan shuttle on Rd 90 between trailhds, 1.1 and 9.1 mi W of Lewis R Falls (#28) trailhead. (MS)

131. Quartz Creek. Steep up-and-down path through old-growth canyon leads 4.5 mi to creekside camp, continues 6 mi to Boundary Tr. Drive to Lewis R Falls (#28), continue 2.7 mi on Rd 90 to bridge. (MS)

132. Quartz Creek Ridge. Well-graded path climbs 1700 ft in 2.8 mi to a viewpoint, then continues 4 mi to Summit Prairie lookout site. Drive 5 mi past Lewis R Falls (#28) on Rd 90, turn left on Rd 9025, and then keep right for 5.5 mi. (MS)

133. Council Bluff. Hike old rd from Council L to view of Mt Adams, up 900 ft in 1.5 mi. Drive past #28 on Rd 90 for 17 mi, go L on Rd 23 for 3.2 mi, turn L on Rd 2334, keep R to CG. (Randle Ranger Dist)

134. Adams Glacier Meadows. Popular 3.1-mi Killen Cr Tr climbs 1500 ft to vast alpine mdws on N side of Mt Adams. Drive past #28 on Rd 90 17 mi, go L on Rd 23 for 4.7 mi, turn R 5.8 mi on Rd 2329. (MA)

135. Lookingglass Lake. Hike up Short Horn Tr 2.8 mi, go L on Round-the-Mtn Tr 2.2 mi, go L for 0.8 mi past Madcat Mdw to lake reflecting Mt Adams. Route gains 1500 ft, loses 600. Drive 6 mi N of Trout Lake on Rd 80, veer R on Rd 8040 for 5.7 mi to Morrison Cr CG. (MA)

136. Gotchen Creek. Stupendous 5.7-mi tr gains 2500 ft beside Aiken Lava Bed to wildflower-packed Bird Cr Mdws at Mt Adams timberline. From town of Trout Lake, drive 5 mi N on Rd 80, turn R on Rd 8020 for 4 mi, go L on Rd 150 for 1 mi to free Snipes Mtn Trailhead. (MA)

137. Horseshoe Meadow. Follow Pacific Cr Tr up 1400 ft in 4.3 mi to Mt Adams timberline. Take Rd 23 N of Trout Lake 14 mi. (MA)

138. Bird Creek Meadows. Despite bad road and $5 parking fee, the 5-mi loop through alpine wildflowers on Yakima Ind Res portion of Mt Adams draws August crowds. Follow signs from Trout Lake. (MA)

139. Round-the-Mountain Trail. Backpack 3/4 of the way around Mt Adams (rivers, Indian Res block final 1/4.) on 27-mi route from Bird Cr Mdws (see Hike#138) past Hikes #134-5 to Devils Gardens. (MA)

140. Sleeping Beauty Mountain. Landmark lookout site tops 1.4-mi tr gaining 1400 ft. From Trout Lake go W 1 mi, turn R on Rd 88 for 4.8 mi, veer R on Rd 8810 for 6.4 mi, go 0.5 mi R on Rd 040. (MA)

141. Steamboat Mountain. Gain 800 ft in 1.2 mi to cliff-rimmed lookout site. Drive as to Cultus L (#29) but at end of Rd 30 turn *left* on Rd 24 for 3.5 mi, veer L 1 mi on Rd 8854, go L 1.4 mi on Rd 021 to its end. (MA)

142. Sawtooth Mountain. Hike Pacific Cr Tr S through Indian Heaven huckleberry fields, return via craggy pk with view. 5.2-mi loop gains 1200 ft. Drive as to Cultus L (#29) but only go 0.5 mi on Rd 24. (MA)

143. Placid Lake. A popular 0.8-mi stroll leads to this large lake in the Indian Heaven Wilderness; if you like, continue 0.8 mi to the meadows at Chenamus Lake. Drive north of Carson 32.5 mi on Rd 30 and turn right at a Placid Lake sign for 1.2 mi. (MA)

144. Indian Racetrack via Falls Creek Trail. Rough 2.3-mi tr gains 700 ft to Indian Heaven lakelet, mdw where tribes raced horses until 1928. For view, continue 0.8 mi up to rd, lookout tower on Red Mtn. Drive as to Junction L (#30) but go 5 mi on Rd 65 past jct with Rd 60. (MA)

145. Indian Racetrack via PCT. Hike Pacific Cr Tr 3 mi N, turn L 0.5 mi to Indian Racetrack mdw, lakelet. For 7.5-mi loop, turn L to Red Mtn lookout, then descend rugged Rd 6048 to Rd 60 and car. Drive as to Junction L (#30) but only go 2 mi on Rd 60. (MA)

146. Nestor Peak Lookout. Gain 2000 ft in 4.1 mi to tower with view of Mt Hood, Gorge. Cross Hood R toll br, go L 1.5 mi on Hwy 14, go R 2.2 mi along river, go L 2 mi on Hwy 141, turn L 3 mi to Buck Cr Trhd No. 1. Hike Rd N1000 and N1300 for 1.9 mi to end, go L on tr. (D)

147. Little Huckleberry Mountain. Berry-lined trail gains 1800 ft in 2.7 mi to a panoramic viewpoint. Cross the Bridge of the Gods, go right 15 mi on Hwy 14, turn left for 7.5 mi through Willard, go left on Rd 66 for 12.8 mi. (MA)

148. Bunker Hill. This trail to a wooded knob overlooking the Wind River arboretum gains 1400 ft in 1.7 mi. Drive 8.5 mi north of Carson on Rd 30, turn left 1.5 mi to the ranger station, then turn right on Rd 43 for 0.6 mi, and finally turn right to the Pacific Crest Trail. (W)

149. Dry Creek Trail. Follow path along large cr through old-growth woods 4 mi. For 13-mi loop, continue up Big Hollow Tr to Observation Pk, gaining 3000 ft. Park as for Trapper Cr (#33). (W)

150. Soda Peaks Lake. Gain 700 ft to craggy Soda Pks, descend 400 ft to lake on 2.2-mi path. Drive 8.5 mi N of Carson on Rd 30, turn L at Stabler 0.5 mi, turn R on Rd 54 for 13 mi to end of pavement. (W)

151. Three Corner Rock. Follow the Pacific Cr Tr to a former lookout site with views of 5 snowpeaks and glimpses of the Columbia Gorge. Drive N across the Bridge of the Gods, turn R on Hwy 14 for 1.5 mi, turn L on Rock Cr Dr for 0.3 mi, turn L on Foster Cr Rd for 0.9 mi, turn L on Red Bluff Rd 0.3 mi, and veer R on gravel Rd CG2000 for 9.5 mi to its crest at Rock Cr Pass. Then go straight on Rd CG2090 for 0.3 mi to a pass with a pullout. Hike to the R on the PCT for 1.5 mi and turn R for 0.7 mi to the summit. (D)

152. Stebbins Creek. Woodsy 9.2-mi trail follows ridges up to Three Corner Rock (see also Hike #151), gaining 3100 ft and crossing Stebbins Cr twice. Drive Hwy 14 E of Vancouver 17 mi to Washougal, turn L on Washougal River Rd for 22 paved miles, and fork to the R on gravel Rd 2000 for 3.2 mi. (D)

153. Wind Mountain. Rough 1-mile trail gains 1120 ft to one of the Col Gorge's best views, on a knoll near Dog Mtn. Touch nothing, as the summit is sacred to local tribes. From Cascade Locks, cross Bridge of the Gods and turn R on Hwy 14 for 7.7 mi. Between mileposts 50 and 51, turn L on paved Wind Mtn Rd. After 1.1 mi, keep R. In another 0.4 mi turn R on paved Girl Scout Rd for 0.2 mi to a large gravel parking area in a pass. Park here and walk ahead, following a very rough road 200 yards to the steep, unmarked trail on the R. (C) 🏃

COLUMBIA GORGE (map on page 93)

154. Munra Point. Great grassy ridge-end viewpoint requires 1800-ft climb on unmaintained scramble trail. Park as for Wahclella Falls (Hike #45), take Gorge Tr 1.5 mi W, turn L 200 yds before Moffett Cr, climb 1.5 mi. (C) 🏃

155. Rudolph Spur. Rough 11-mi loop gains 3600 ft. Hike up Ruckel Cr Tr (#48), but as soon as tr reaches Benson Plateau turn L past blazes onto faint, unmaintained tr down Rudolph Spur's ridge. Turn L on PCT, go L on Gorge Tr to complete loop. Adventurers only. (C)

156. PCT to Benson Plateau. Hike to Herman Cr Bridge (see #50), continue 0.9 to Pacific Cr Tr, climb L to wildflowers, views at plateau rim. Gain 3600 ft in 5.6 mi. (C) 🐾

157. Wyeth Trail to North Lake. Steep 5.7-mi tr gains 3800 ft to woodsy lake. Continue, keeping R at all jcts, to complete 14.7-mi loop via Green Pt Mtn viewpoint. Take Exit 51 of I-84 to Wyeth CG. (C) 🐾🐾

158. Shellrock Mountain. Drive I-84 east 0.8 mi past milepost 52, park on shoulder, scramble up to old Col R Hwy, walk E to find tr up to 1872 wagon rd, walk E to find tr up to viewpt. Gain 1100 ft in 1.3 mi. (C) 🏃

159. Starvation Creek to Viento Park. Hikable/bikable 1.1-mi section of historic Columbia River Highway is under restoration, but open. Start at Starvation Cr Falls (Hike #52), but go east. (O) 🏃

160. Rainy Lake. Hike past campable lake, keep L at all jcts 1.4 mi to viewpoint atop Green Pt Mtn, gaining 700 ft. Drive as to Mt Defiance S (Hike #53), but continue 1.5 mi on Rd 2820. (C) 🐾🐾

161. Indian Mountain. Tr to stunning viewpt of Mt Hood gains 600 ft in 1 mi from Indian Sprs CG. Drive very rough Rd 1310 from Wahtum L (Hike #51) for 3 mi, or hike PCT 3.4 mi from Wahtum L. (C)

162. Lower Deschutes River. An 11.2-mi gravel bike path traces an old railroad grade alongside this desert river from a state campground. Hikers can take a prettier riverbank trail 1.4 mi to Moody Rapids and return on a 2.8-mi loop past Ferry Springs. Drive I-84 east of The Dalles to exit 97 and follow signs 2 mi to Deschutes Park. (O) 🚴🏃🐎

MOUNT HOOD - WEST (map on page 131)

163. Horseshoe Ridge. 3-mi climb to views in beargrass mdw gains 1900 ft, joins Zigzag Mtn Tr (see #71). For 11.7-mi loop, return via Cast L Tr (#164). Drive as to Ramona Falls (#65) but turn R off Rd 1825 on Rd 380 past Riley Horse CG for 2.2 mi. (Z) 🐾

164. Cast Lake. Ascend ridge 2300 ft in 3.5 mi, keep R for 0.9 mi to lake described in Hike #71. Drive as to Ramona Falls (#65) but turn R off Rd 1825 on Rd 380 past Riley Horse CG for 0.7 mi. (Z) ♿🐾

165. Yocum Ridge. Very difficult but extremely beautiful, this 8.7-mi route passes Ramona Falls as it climbs 3800 feet to spectacular alpine meadows beside Mt. Hood's Sandy Glacier. From Ramona Falls (see Hike #65), take the PCT toward Bald Mtn 0.6 mi, and turn R up Yocum Ridge 4.7 mi. (Z)

166. Buck Peak. Pacific Cr Tr follows wooded ridge 7.6 mi N from Lolo Pass to panoramic lookout site. No camping. (Columbia Ranger Dist)

167. Huckleberry Mountain Trail. Park just past the group camp at S end of Lost Lake (see Hike #69), climb 900 ft in 2 mi to Pacific Cr Tr, turn R for 3.5 mi to Buck Pk viewpoint. (HR)

168. Flag Mountain. 2.2-mi walk along wooded hill has Mt Hood views, gains 900 ft, ends at rd. Drive Hwy 26 to E edge of Rhododendron, turn S on Rd 20 (2620) for 0.8 mi, turn briefly L on Rd 200. (Z)

169. Paradise Park Trail. Quieter, longer route to famous alpine mdws than from Timberline Lodge (#74) gains 3000 ft in 6.3 mi. Drive 4.1 mi E of Rhododendron on Hwy 26, turn L on Rd 2639 for 1.2 mi. (Z)

170. Hidden Lake. Climb 2 mi to small, viewless lake with rhodies, continue 3 mi to PCT near Zigzag Canyon (see Hike #74). 2800 ft gain. For 13.2-mi loop, return via Paradise Park Tr (#169). Drive 4.1 mi E of Rhododendron on Hwy 26, turn L on Rd 2639 for 2 mi. (Z)

171. Alpine Ski Trail. Hike 3 mi from Gov't Camp to Timberline Lodge on wildflower-lined, road-like trail gaining 1900 ft. Walk to top of Summit Ski Area's chairlift and head right. (Z)

172. Timberline Trail. Classic 37.6-mi backpack route circles Mt Hood. from Timberline Lodge (#74). Tr connects with Hikes #65-68, 80, 79, 77. Allow 3-5 days. Unbridged crossings of Zigzag, Sandy, Muddy Fork, Eliot Branch, and White Rivers can be dangerous during snowmelt. Water is lower in mornings and after August. (Z, HR)

173. PCT to Timberline Lodge. Start at Barlow Pass on Hwy 35, gain 2000 ft in 5.3 mi amid flowers, views of White R Canyon. (Z)

174. Veda Lake. 1.2-mi tr to lovely 3-acre lake with huckleberries, Mt Hood view, gains 200 ft, loses 400. Drive as to upper trailhead for Devils Pk Hike #63, but only go 3.5 mi on Rd 2613 to Fir Cr CG. (Z)

175. Upper Salmon River. 5.9-mi loop dips 1200 feet to the Salmon River. Backpackers can continue downstream 11.5-mi to Salmon River Rd (Hike #61). Drive Hwy 26 E of Gov't Camp 3 mi, turn S past Trillium Lk on Rd 2656 for 1.7 mi, turn L to continue on Rd 2656 another 1.8 mi, and go straight onto Rd 309 for 2 mi to a pullout on the R. (Z)

176. Jackpot Meadows Trail. Park as for Hike #175, but descend 1 mi to the Salmon River bridge, and then climb 1.2 mi to Rd 240. The route loses 300 ft, gains 800. (Z, B)

MOUNT HOOD - EAST (map on page 171)

177. Frog Lake Buttes. Hike to Lower Twin L (see #76), but then follow signs 2.2 mi to Cascade crest panorama at Frog L Butte, also accessible by Rd 240. Follow signs for Frog L to complete 6.3-mi loop. (B)

178. Barlow Butte. 1.8-mi path to wooded knoll begins at PCT trailhead lot just off Hwy 35 at Barlow Pass. Walk S a few yards, veer L across rd, descend 0.4 mi to mdw, turn L, and climb to Mt Hood viewpoint just past butte's overgrown lookout site. Lose 200 ft, gain 1000. (B)

179. Umbrella Falls. 4.7-mi loop passes 2 falls, gains 600 ft. Take Hwy 35 to Hood R Mdws, drive loop to parking lot. Hike Elk Mdw Tr 0.4 mi, go L 2.2 mi to Umbrella Falls, return via Sahalie Falls. (HR) 🚴🐎

180. Boulder Lake via Bonney Meadows. Hike downhill (losing 700 ft) for 1.7 mi to cliff-rimmed lake in ancient forest. Drive Hwy 35 to Bennett Pass, turn S on miserably rocky Rd 3550 for 4.1 mi, turn R on even rougher Rd 4891 for 1.3 mi, turn L to Bonney Mdws CG. (B) 🏕🏔🚴🐎

181. Crane Prairie. Visit old growth, scenic mdws, cliff-backed lake on 7.8-mi loop. Park at Bonney Mdws CG as for Hike #180. Hike 1.7 mi to Boulder Lk, then turn left 1 mi (crossing a rd) to Crane Cr Tr, turn L for 1.5 mi to Crane Prairie, go L for 2.4 mi to Rd 4891, go L along rd 1.2 mi to Bonney Mdws CG and car. (B) 🏕🏔🚴🐎

182. Zigzag Trail. Switchback up 1200 ft in 1 mi, turn R on Dog River Tr to Mt Hood viewpt. Park at trailhead near milepost 73 on Hwy 35 (see Hike #78 map). (HR) 🚴🐎

183. Tilly Jane - Polallie Ridge Loop. Hike up 2.6-mi Tilly Jane Ski Tr with Mt Hood views, flowers to 1924 cookhouse at Tilly Jane CG (see Hike #78), turn L to return 2.9 mi via Polallie Ridge Tr. Gain 2000 ft. Drive as to #78, but only go 1.4 mi on Rd 3512 to tr sign on L. (HR) 🐎

184. Dog River Trail. Hike 2.1 mi up to a river bridge, then climb a ridge with Mt. Hood views 4.1 mi to paved Rd 44, gaining 2100 ft. Start on Highway 35 near milepost 78. (HR) 🚴🐎

185. Elk Cove Trail. Ridgecrest route to popular alpine mdws described in Hike #79 is slightly longer, gaining 2700 ft in 5.1 mi. Take Hwy 35 to Parkdale, turn W on Clear Lk Rd near RR track, turn R on Laurence Lk Dr. Halfway down the lakeshore, turn L on abandoned Rd 650 for 1.2 mi to the trail on the L (trail sign is 25 yds up the trail). (HR) 🥾🐎

186. Pinnacle Trail. Quiet 3.4-mi path to alpine mdws, Timberline Tr on N flank of Mt Hood gains 2200 ft. From Parkdale or Hwy 35, follow signs to Laurence L, turn L on Rd 2840, follow signs to Tr 630. (HR) 🐎

187. Surveyors Ridge Trail. Hikable, mostly level 11.7-mi horse/mtn bike path along roaded ridge overlooking Mt Hood includes Bald Butte (Hike #188). To find the southern trailhead, drive Hwy 35 to between mileposts 70 and 71, turn E on Rd 44 for 3.7 mi. (HR) 🚴🐎

188. Bald Butte. Old lookout site has May wildflowers and views across Hood River's orchards to Mt. Hood. The trail gains 2300 feet in 4.2 mi. From I-84 at Hood River, take exit 64, follow Hwy 35 south 14.8 mi, turn L on Smullen Rd 0.3 mi to a curve, and turn L on an unmarked gravel rd 200 yds. Take Oak Ridge Tr 2.5 mi, turn L on Surveyors Ridge Tr 0.9 mi, and continue straight on a dirt rd 0.7 mi to summit. (HR) 🚴🐎

189. Knebal Spring. 8.5-mile loop climbs wooded ridges, gaining 1800 ft, to a viewpt near Bottle Prairie, crossing some rds and clearcuts. Drive Hwy 35 around Mt. Hood to milepost 70, turn E on paved Rd 44 for 5.3 mi, turn L on paved Rd 1720 for 3 mi to Knebal Spr CG. (HR) 🚴🐎

Mt. Hood from Bald Butte (Hike #189).

190. Fifteenmile Creek. A 10.2-mile loop descends from Fifteenmile Campgd into a forested canyon (losing 1600 ft), and crosses Fifteenmile Creek. The return trail crosses several logging roads. Drive Hwy 35 around Mt. Hood to milepost 70, turn E on paved Rd 44 for 9 mi, turn R on Rd 4420 for 2 mi, and fork L on Rd 2730 for 2 mi. (B)

191. Tygh Creek Trail. Start by creek, climb 1600 ft in 2 mi to wildflowers, views on Pen Point, a knoll in Badger Cr Wilderness. Drive as to Ball Point (Hike #84), but go 1.7 extra mi on Rd 27. (B)

192. Douglas Cabin Trail. 4-mi tr gains 1200 ft to staffed Flag Pt lookout, view of Badger Cr Wilderness. 9.5-mi loop possible. Drive as to Hike #83, but continue on Rd 2710 an extra 3.8 mi, go L for 3.5 mi. Access rd is gated closed Oct 1 to May 1. (B)

193. Mill Creek Falls. For adventurers only, 2.3-mi path leads up box canyon to stupendous 150-ft falls near The Dalles. Expect poison oak, ticks, rattlesnakes, 8 bridgeless cr crossings. Call The Dalles Watershed at 298-1242 for req'd entry permit, access instructions.

194. Tygh Valley Falls. Descend 0.3 mi to a colossal 3-part waterfall in the desert. Drive Hwy 197 between The Dalles and Maupin to milepost 34 in Tygh Valley, turn E on Hwy 216 for 4 mi to picnic area. (O)

CLACKAMAS FOOTHILLS (map on page 191)

195. Eagle Creek. Often confused with the other Eagle Cr Trail (Hike #47), this little-known path near Estacada follows a creek 6.7 mi through old-growth woods of the Salmon-Huckleberry Wilderness. The unsigned roads to the trailhead have many confusing junctions. Drive Hwy 224 to milepost 19 (4 mi W of Estacada), take Wildcat Mtn Rd 2 mi, continue straight on Eagle Fern Park Rd 2.4 mi, veer R for 1.7 mi, go straight on George Rd 6.3 mi, turn R onto SE Harvey Rd 0.6 mi, turn L for 1.3 mi, fork to the R for 0.1 mi, fork to the R again for 0.6 mi and park. The trail begins as an overgrown rd down to the R. (Z)

196. Dry Ridge. Steep viewpoint tr from Roaring River CG (on Hwy 224 at milepost 42) switchbacks up 3500 ft in 5.9 mi to Mt Hood view at Grouse Point's beargrass meadow. Connects with Hikes #91, 197. (E)

233

197. Alder Flat. Convenient 0.9-mi path to Clackamas River passes a beaver pond, ends at lovely walk-in campground by the river with 6 picnic tables. Drive 25 mi south of Estacada on Hiwy 224 and park on the right, 500 feet before Ripplebrook Guard Station.

198. Shining Lake. Huckleberries, mtn views line 4.3-mi route to brush-rimmed lake. From Frazier Fk CG (see Rock Lks Hike #91), hike gated rd 3.5 mi, descend 600 ft on 0.8-mi trail to right. (E)

199. Cripple Creek Trail. Abandoned, unmaintained, steep path gains 2800 ft in 3.6 mi, crosses 3 logging roads, to Cripple Creek. Continue 1.7 easy mi to Cache Meadow shelter (see Rock Lakes Hike #91). Drive 22 mi S of Estacada on Hwy 224 to unsigned trailhead on the left, just after a bridge near Indian Henry Campground. (E)

200. Anvil Lake. Level 1.4-mi tr through Blackwolf Mdws to small lake. Drive Hwy 224 through Ripplebrook, turn L on Rd 57 for 7.4 mi, turn L on Rd 58 for 6.2 mi, turn R on Rd 160 for 0.5 mi. (E)

201. Fish Creek Mountain. Now abandoned, this trail climbs 2.2 mi (gaining 1400 ft) to a viewpoint peak, and a spur drops 0.7 mi to High Lake. All roads to the trailhead have been closed. The old route followed Rd 54 into the Fish Creek valley, but to restore fish habitat, this watershed is now off-limits to motor vehicles. Mountain bikers or determined hikers could still follow closed roads 14 mi to the old trailhead. (E)

202. Welcome Lakes. 5-mi route gains 2000 ft to small lks in in Bull-of-the-Woods Wilderness. Drive as to Dickey Cr Hike #95 but go straight on Rd 63, follow signs to Elk Lake Tr. (E)

203. Round Lake. Hike gated rd 0.5 mi through old growth to campground, continue on tr 0.5 mi around lake (see map for Hike #96). Drive Hwy 224 south of Estacada 26 mi, go str on Rd 46 for 27.4 mi, turn R on Rd 6350 for 4.8 mi, turn L on Rd 6355 for 0.2 mi, turn L on Rd 150 for 0.8 mi, turn R on Rd 220 for 2 mi, Turn L on Rd 6370 for 3.5 mi. (E)

204. Fish and Si Lakes. Level 1.2-mi path passes Si L to Fish L in dramatic, forested bowl. Tr continues 1.6 mi across Olallie L Scenic Area to Lower Lake CG. Drive as to Hike #98, but only go 3.4 mi on Rd 4690, turn R on Rd 4691 for 1.5 mi, go R on Rd 120 for 1.2 mi. (E)

205. Russ and Jude Lakes. Stroll 0.8 mi from Olallie Mdws CG past Brook and Jude Lks to Russ L, view of Olallie Butte. Warm Springs tribal permits req'd for fishing. No camping on Ind Reservation lands. Drive as to Hike #203, but only go 1.4 mi on Rd 4220, veer L to CG. (E)

206. Olallie Butte. Tr gains 2600 ft in 3.8 mi to views atop NW Oregon's 3rd tallest pk, but final 2.3 mi are on Warm Springs Ind Res, so hiking this part is not encouraged. Drive as to Hike #98, but only go 2.7 mi on Rd 4220, park under 3rd set of powerlines. Tr starts on L of rd. (E)

207. Ruddy Hill. Climb from Horseshoe Lake to a lookout site with a front-row view of Mt. Jefferson, gaining 650 ft in 1.6 mi. Drive as to Hike #99, but continue past Olallie Lk on Rd 4220 for 3 mi to Horseshoe Lk. Hike 1 mi up to the Pacific Crest Tr, turn R for 300 yds, and turn L on an unmaintained path 0.5 mi to the top. (E)

Index

About the Author

William L. Sullivan is the author of nine books and numerous articles about Oregon, including a monthly "Oregon Trails" column for the Eugene *Register-Guard*. A fifth-generation Oregonian, Sullivan began hiking at the age of five and has been exploring new trails ever since. After receiving an English degree from Cornell Univeristy and studying at Germany's Heidelberg University, he completed an M.A. at the Unviersity of Oregon.

In 1985 Sullivan set out to investigate Oregon's wilderness on a 1,361-mile solo backpacking trek from the state's westernmost shore at Cape Blanco to Oregon's easternmost point in Hells Canyon. His journal of that two-month adventure, published as *Listening for Coyote*, was a finalist for the Oregon Book Award in creative nonfiction. Since then he has authored *Hiking Oregon's History*, *A Deeper Wild*, *Exploring Oregon's Wild Areas*, and a series of 100 Hikes guidebooks for the state. Information about Sullivan's speaking schedule, his books, and his favorite adventures is available online at *www.oregonhiking.com*.

He and his wife Janell live in Eugene, but spend summers in the log cabin they built by hand on a roadless tract in Oregon's Coast Range.